T[HE CROWD]
A STUDY OF THE POPULAR MIND
By Gustave Le Bon

&

EXTRAORDINARY
POPULAR DELUSIONS
AND THE
MADNESS OF CROWDS
By Charles Mackay

TWIN CLASSICS OF CROWD

PSYCHOLOGY

TM

TRADERS PRESS
P.O. BOX 6206
GREENVILLE, S.C. 29606

*Books and Gifts
for Investors and Traders*

EXTRAORDINARY POPULAR DELUSIONS
AND THE
MADNESS OF CROWDS

By Charles Mackay
Originally published in 1841 under the title:
Memoirs of
Extraordinary Popular Delusions.

THE CROWD:

A STUDY OF THE POPULAR MIND

By Gustave Le Bon
was published in 1897.

Foreword Copyright ©*1994 by* **TRADERS PRESS, INC.**
ISBN 0-934380-23-6

TRADERS PRESS ™
P.O.BOX 6206
GREENVILLE, S.C. 29606

Books and Gifts
for Investors and Traders

THE CROWD
♦
EXTRAORDINARY POPULAR DELUSIONS

FOREWORD

When customers of **TRADERS PRESS** seek guidance from me in selecting the best books and what they should be reading to further their education as a trader, they inevitably ask "what's new?" Often, when I recommend an older title as being the best available on a particular subject, such as the venerable ***TECHNICAL ANALYSIS OF STOCK TRENDS*** by Edwards and Magee on charting, I encounter surprise and disbelief that a book written in 1948 can still be relevant today. Only after careful explanation that I personally used the principles in this book to trade soybeans last month and will again use them to trade Swiss Francs next year and again ten years from now do they cease asking, "But isn't there a newer and more up-to-date book?"

Often, the best books are NOT the newest, many of which simply rephrase and repeat old ideas, but the oldest. Thus it is with Mackay's ***EXTRAORDINARY POPULAR DELUSIONS***, and Le Bon's ***THE CROWD***: two of the oldest works on the psychology of crowd behavior are among the best.

Written in 1841 by Charles Mackay, a Scottish barrister, ***EXTRAORDINARY POPULAR DELUSIONS AND THE MADNESS OF CROWDS*** is a compelling work which recounts several mass manias of centuries past, including the Tulip Mania in Holland in 1634, and the South Seas stock swindle and investment bubble in England in 1720. These and other manias are highly effective illustrations of the extremes of greed and fear, the two greatest enemies of the investor and trader. At least one modern financial writer, Alexander Elder in his superb ***TRADING FOR A LIVING***, states his belief that this book lays down the foundations of the contrary opinion theory.

EXTRAORDINARY POPULAR DELUSIONS, in its original form, was a monumental tome of over seven hundred pages. Only the first hundred of these pages are concerned with events which are relevant to speculation and investment, and this is the section of the book which is reprinted here, in this abridged edition. In his foreword to a 1980 edition of this book, Andrew Tobias opines "If you read no more of this book than the first hundred pages -on money mania-it will be worth many times its purchase."

After learning that famed fellow South Carolinian Bernard Baruch also wrote a foreword to a 1932 edition of this book, during the month of the exact low of the Great Crash of 1929, this writer feels honored to be included in such august company.

Written in 1885 (and published in 1897) by Gustave Le Bon, a French philosopher and politician, ***THE CROWD; A STUDY OF THE POPULAR MIND*** is one of the best books available on mass psychology. It explains how speculators and investors who fail to analyze and think for themselves when they become involved in a group or crowd can lose their ability to objectively evaluate their investment actions and decisions.

This book and the principles it teaches and illustrates are still as relevant and meaningful today as a hundred years ago when it was written. Such recent events as the silver market bubble and collapse of 1979-1980 are perfect examples of these principles at work. Alexander Elder expresses this in his articulate style: "A trader who reads (this book) today can see his reflection in a century-old mirror."

Read, enjoy, and learn from these two old classics. Bear in mind as you do so that you are really reading about your own two greatest enemies as a trader: FEAR and GREED. They both reside within you and can undermine all your best efforts to succeed in the great game of trading, but the self-knowledge you can gain from these books can help you overcome these roadblocks to success.

TRADERS PRESS is a publisher and distributor of books and gifts of interest to traders and investors. To receive a free copy of our current 56-page catalog, write to us today at: *P.O. Box 6206, Greenville,S.C. 29606.*

Edward Dobson

Edward D. Dobson

Greenville, South Carolina
June, 1994

THE CROWD:

A STUDY OF THE POPULAR MIND

By Gustave Le Bon

TRADERS PRESS ™
P.O.BOX 6206
GREENVILLE, S.C. 29606

Books and Gifts
for Investors and Traders

CONTENTS

EXTRAORDINARY POPULAR DELUSIONS

PREFACE

The following work is devoted to an account of the characteristics of crowds.

The whole of the common characteristics with which heredity endows the individuals of a race constitute the genius of the race. When, however, a certain number of these individuals are gathered together in a crowd for purposes of action, observation proves that, from the mere fact of their being assembled, there result certain new psychological characteristics, which are added to the racial characteristics and differ from them at times to a very considerable degree.

Organized crowds have always played an important part in the life of peoples, but this part has never been of such moment as at present. The substitution of the unconscious action of crowds for the conscious activity of individuals is one of the principal characteristics of the present age.

I have endeavored to examine the difficult problem presented by crowds in a purely scientific manner—that is, by making an effort to proceed with method, and without being influenced by opinions, theories, and doctrines. This, I believe, is the only mode of arriving at the discovery of some few particles of truth, especially when dealing, as is the case here, with a question that is the subject of impassioned controversy. A man of science bent on verifying a phenomenon is not called upon to concern himself with the interests his verifications may hurt. In a recent publication an eminent thinker, M. Goblet d'Alviela, made the remark that, belonging to none of the contemporary schools, I am occasionally found in opposition of sundry of the conclusions of all of them. I hope this new work will merit a similar observation. To belong to a school is necessarily to espouse its prejudices and preconceived opinions.

Still I should explain to the reader why he will find me draw conclusions from my investigations which it might be thought at first sight they do not bear; why, for instance, after noting the extreme mental inferiority of crowds, picked assemblies included, I yet affirm it would be dangerous to meddle with their organization, notwithstanding this inferiority.

The reason is, that the most attentive observation of the facts of history has invariably demonstrated to me that social organisms being every bit as complicated as those of all beings, it is in no wise in our power to force them to undergo on a sudden farreaching transformations. Nature has recourse at times to radical measures, but never after our fashion, which explains how it is that nothing is more fatal to a people than the mania for great reforms, however excellent these reforms may appear theoretically. They would only be useful were it possible to change instantaneously the genius of nations. This power, however, is only possessed by time. Men are ruled by ideas, sentiments, and customs—matters which are of the essence of ourselves. Institutions and laws are the outward manifestation of our character, the expression of its needs. Being its outcome, institutions and laws cannot change this character.

The study of social phenomena cannot be separated from that of the peoples among whom they have come into existence. From the philosophic point of view these phenomena may have an absolute value; in practice they have only a relative value.

It is necessary, in consequence, when studying a social phenomenon, to consider it successively under two very different aspects. It will then be seen that the teachings of pure reason are very often contrary to those of practical reason. There are scarcely any data, even physical, to which this distinction is not applicable. From the point of view of absolute truth a cube or a circle are invariable geometrical figures, rigorously defined by certain formulas. From the point of view of the impression they make on our eye these geometrical figures may assume very varied shapes. By perspective the cube may be transformed into a pyramid or a square, the circle into an ellipse or a straight line. Moreover, the consideration of these fictitious shapes is far more important than that of the real shapes, for it is they and they alone that we see and that can be reproduced by photography or in pictures. In certain cases there is more truth in the unreal than in the real. To present objects with their exact geometrical forms would be to distort nature and render it unrecognizable. If we imagine a world whose inhabitants could only copy or photograph objects, but were unable to touch them, it would be very difficult for such persons to attain to an exact idea of their form. Moreover, the knowledge of this form, accessible only to a small number of learned men, would present but a very minor interest.

The philosopher who studies social phenomena should bear in mind that side by side with their theoretical value they possess a practical value, and that this latter, so far as the evolution of civilization is concerned, is alone of importance. The recognition of this fact should render him very circumspect with regard to the conclusions that logic would seem at first to enforce upon him.

There are other motives that dictate to him a like reserve. The complexity of social facts is such, that it is impossible to grasp them as a whole and to foresee the effects of their reciprocal influence. It seems, too, that behind the visible facts are hidden at times thousands of invisible causes. Visible social phenomena appear to be the result of an immense, unconscious working, that as a rule is beyond the reach of our analysis. Perceptible phenomena may be compared to the waves, which are the expression on the surface of the ocean of deep-lying disturbances of which we know nothing. So far as the majority of their acts are considered, crowds display a singularly inferior mentality; yet there are other acts in which they appear to be guided by those mysterious forces which the ancients denominated destiny, nature or providence, which we call the voices of the dead, and whose power it is impossible to overlook, although we ignore their essence. It would seem, at times, as if there were latent forces in the inner being of nations which serve to guide them. What, for instance, can be more complicated, more logical, more marvelous than a language? Yet whence can this admirably organized production have arisen, except it be the outcome of the unconscious genius of crowds? The most learned academics, the most esteemed gramarians can do no more than note down the laws that govern languages; they would be utterly incapable of creating them. Even with respect to the ideas of great men are we certain that they are exclusively the offspring of their brains? No doubt such ideas are always created by solitary minds, but is it not the genius of crowds that has furnished the thousands of grains of dust forming the soil in which they have sprung up?

Crowds, doubtless, are always unconscious, but this very unconsciousness is perhaps one of the secrets of their strength. In the natural world beings exclusively governed by instinct accomplish acts whose marvellous complexity astounds us. Reason is an attribute of humanity of too recent date and still too imperfect to reveal to us the laws of the unconscious, and still more to take its place. The part played by the unconscious in all our acts is immense, and that played by reason very small. The unconscious acts like a force still unknown.

If we wish, then, to remain within the narrow but safe limits within which science can attain to knowledge, and not to wander in the domain of vague conjecture and vain hypothesis, all we must do is simply to take note of such phenomena as are accessible to us, and confine ourselves to their consideration. Every conclusion drawn from our observation as a rule, premature, for behind the phenomena which we see clearly are other phenomena that we see indistinctly, and perhaps behind these latter, yet others which do not see at all.

INTRODUCTION

THE ERA OF CROWDS

The evolution of the present age—The great changes in civilization are the consequence of changes in National thought—Modern belief in the power of crowds—It transforms the traditional policy of the European states —How the rise of the popular classes comes about, and the manner in which they exercise their power—The necessary consequences of the power of the crowd—Crowds unable to play a part other than destructive—The dissolution of worn-out civilizations is the work of the crowd—General ignorance of the psychology of crowds—Importance of the study of crowds for legislators and statesmen.

THE great upheavals which precede changes of civilization, such as the fall of the Roman Empire and the foundation of the Arabian Empire, seem at first sight determined more especially by political transformations, foreign invasion, or the over-throw of dynasties. But a more attentive study of these events shows that behind their apparent causes the real cause is generally seen to be a profound modification in the ideas of the peoples. The true historical upheavals are not those which astonish us by their grandeur and violence. The only important changes whence the renewal of civilizations results, affect ideas, conceptions and beliefs. The memorable events of history are the visible effects of the invisible changes of human thought. The reason these great events are so rare is that there is nothing so stable in a race as the inherited groundwork of its thoughts.

The present epoch is one of these critical moments in which the thought of mankind is undergoing a process of transformation.

Two fundamental factors are at the base of this transformation. The first is the destruction of those religious, political, and social beliefs in which all the elements of our civilization are rooted. The second is the creation of entirely new conditions of existence and thought as the result of modern scientific and industrial discoveries.

The ideas of the past, although half destroyed, being still very powerful, and the ideas which are to replace them being still in process of formation, the modern age represents a period of transition and anarchy.

It is not easy to say as yet what will one day be evolved from this necessarily somewhat chaotic period. What will be the fundamental ideas on which the societies that are to succeed our own will be built up? We do not at present know. Still it is already clear that on whatever lines the societies of the future are organized, they will have to count with a new power, with the last surviving sovereign force of modern times, the power of crowds. On the ruins of so many ideas formerly considered beyond discussion, and today decayed or decaying, of so many sources of authority that successive revolutions have destroyed, this power, which alone has arisen in their stead, seems soon destined to absorb the others. While all our ancient beliefs are tottering and disappearing, while the old pillars of society are giving way one by one, the power of the crowd is the only force that nothing menaces, and of which the prestige is continually on the increase. The age we are about to enter will in truth be the ERA OF CROWDS.

Scarcely a century ago the traditional policy of European states and the rivalries of sovereigns were the principal factors that shaped events. The opinion of the masses scarcely counted, and most frequently indeed did not count at all. Today it is the traditions which used to obtain in politics, and the individual tendencies and rivalries of rulers which do not count; while, on the contrary, the voice of the masses has become preponderant. It is this voice that dictates their conduct to kings, whose endeavor is to take note of its utterances. The destinies of nations are elaborated at present in the heart of the masses, and no longer in the councils of princes.

The entry of the popular classes into political life —that is to say, in reality, their progressive transformation into governing classes—is one of the most striking characteristics of our epoch of transition. The introduction of universal suffrage, which exercised for a long time but little influence, is not, as might be thought, the distinguishing feature of this transference of political power. The progressive growth of the power of the masses took place at first by the propagation of certain ideas, which have slowly implanted themselves in men's minds, and afterwards by the gradual association of individuals bent on bringing about the realization of theoretical conceptions. It is by association that crowds have come to procure ideas with respect to their interests which are very clearly defined if not particularly just, and have arrived at a consciousness of their strength. The masses are founding syndicates before which the authorities capitulate one after the other; they are also founding labor unions, which in spite of all economic laws tend to regulate the conditions of labor and wages. They return to assemblies in which the Government is vested, representatives utterly lacking initiative and independence, and reduced most often to nothing else than the spokesmen of the committees that have chosen them.

Today the claims of the masses are becoming more and more sharply defined, and amount to nothing less than a determination to utterly destroy society as it now exists, with a view to making it hark back to that primitive communism which was the normal condition of all human groups before the dawn of civilization. Limitations of the hours of labor, the nationalisation of mines, railways, factories, and the soil, the equal distribution of all products, the elimination of all the upper classes for the benefit of the popular classes, etc., such are these claims.

Little adapted to reasoning, crowds, on the contrary, are quick to act. As the result of their present organization their strength has become immense. The dogmas whose birth we are witnessing will soon have the force of the old dogmas; that is to say, the tyrannical and sovereign force of being above discus-sion. The divine right of the masses is about to replace the divine right of kings.

The writers who enjoy the favor of our middle classes, those who best represent their rather narrow ideas, their somewhat prescribed views, their rather superficial scepticism, and their at times somewhat excessive egoism, display profound alarm at this new power which they see growing; and to combat the disorder in men's minds they are addressing despairing appeals to those moral forces of the Church for which they formerly professed so much disdain. They talk to us of the bankruptcy of science, go back in penitence to Rome, and remind us of the teachings of revealed truth. These new converts forget that it is too late. Had they been really touched by grace, a like operation could not have the same influence on minds less concerned with the preoccupations which beset these recent adherents to religion. The masses repudiate today the gods which their admonishers repudiated yesterday and helped to destroy. There is no power, Divine or human, that can oblige a stream to flow back to its source.

There has been no bankruptcy of science, and science has had no share in the present intellectual anarchy, nor in the making of the new power which is springing up in the midst of this anarchy. Science promised us truth, or at least a knowl-edge of such relations as our intelligence can seize: it never promised us peace or happiness. Sovereignly indifferent to our feelings, it is deaf to our lamentations. It is for us to endeavour to live with science, since nothing can bring back the illusions it has destroyed.

Universal symptoms, visible in all nations, show us the rapid growth of the power of crowds, and do not admit of our supposing that it is destined to cease growing at an early date.

Whatever fate it may reserve for us, we shall have to submit to it. All reasoning against it is a mere vain war of words. Certainly it is possible that the advent to power of the masses marks one of the last stages of Western civilization, a complete return to those periods of confused anarchy which seem always destined to precede the birth of every new society. But may this result be prevented?

Up to now these thoroughgoing destructions of a worn-out civilization have constituted the most obvious task of the masses. It is not indeed today merely that this can be traced. History tells us, that from the moment when the moral forces on which a civilization rested have lost their strength, its final dissolution is brought about by those unconscious and brutal crowds known, justifiably enough, as barbarians. Civilizations as yet have only been created and directed by a small intellectual aristocracy, never by crowds. Crowds are only powerful for destruction. Their rule is always tantamount to a barbarian phase. A civilization involves fixed rules, discipline, a passing from the instinctive to the rational state, forethought for the future, an elevated degree of culture—all of them conditions that crowds, left to themselves, have invariably shown themselves incapable of realizing. In consequence of the purely destructive nature of their power crowds act like those microbes which hasten the dissolution of enfeebled or dead bodies. When the structure of a civilization is rotten, it is always the masses that bring about its downfall. It is at such a juncture that their chief mission is plainly visible, and that for a while the philosophy of number seems the only philosophy of history.

Is the same fate in store for our civilizations. There is ground to fear that this is the case, but we are not as yet in a position to be certain of it.

However this may be, we are bound to resign ourselves to the reign of the masses, since want of foresight has in succession overthrown all the barriers that might have kept the crowd in check.

We have a very slight knowledge of these crowds which are beginning to be the object of so much discussion. Professional students of psychology, having lived far from them, have always ignored them, and when, as of late, they have turned their attention in this direction it has only been to consider the crimes crowds are capable of committing. Without a doubt criminal crowds exist, but virtuous and heroic crowds, and crowds of many other kinds, are also to be met with. The crimes of crowds only constitute a particular phase of their psychology. The mental constitution of crowds is not to be learned merely by a study of their crimes, any more than that of an individual by a mere description of his vices.

However, in point of fact, all the world's masters, all the founders of religions or empires, the apostles of all beliefs, eminent statesmen, and, in a more modest sphere, the mere chiefs of small groups of men have always been unconscious psychologists, possessed of an instinctive and often very sure knowledge of the character of crowds, and it is their accurate knowledge of this character that has enabled them to so easily establish their mastery. Napoleon had a marvellous insight into the psychology of the masses of the country over which he reigned, but he, at times, completely misunderstood the psychology of crowds belonging to other races;[1] and it is because he thus misunderstood it that he engaged in Spain, and notably in Russia, in conflicts in which a brief space of time to ruin it. A knowledge of the psychology of crowds is today the last resource of the statesman who wishes not to govern them-that is becoming a very difficult matter-but at any rate not to be too much governed by them.

It is only by obtaining some sort of insight into the psychology of crowds that it can be understood how slight is the action upon them of laws and institutions, how powerless they are to hold any opinions other than those which are imposed upon them, and that it is not with rules based on theories of pure equity that they are to be led, but by seeking what produces an impression on them and what seduces them. For instance,

1 His most subtle advisers, moreover, did not understand this psychology any better. Talleyrand wrote him that "Spain would receive his soldiers as liberators." It received them as beasts of prey. A psychologist acquainted with the hereditary instincts of the Spanish race would have easily foreseen this reception..

should a legislator, wishing to impose a new tax, choose that which would be theoretically the most just? By no means. In practice the most unjust may be the best for the masses. Should it at the same time be the least obvious, and apparently the least burdensome, it will be the most easily tolerated.

It is for this reason that an indirect tax, however exorbitant it be, will always be accepted by the crowd, because, being paid daily in fractions of a farthing on objects of consumption, it will not interfere with the habits of the crowd, and will pass unperceived. Replace it by a proportional tax on wages or income of any other kind, to be paid in a lump sum, and were this new imposition theoretically ten times less burdensome than the other, it would give rise to unanimous protest. This arises from the fact that a sum relatively high, which will appear immense, and will in consequence strike the imagination, has been substituted for the unperceived fractions of a farthing. The new tax would only appear light had it been saved farthing by farthing, but this economic proceeding involves an amount of foresight of which the masses are incapable.

The example which precedes is of the simplest. Its appositeness will be easily perceived. It did not escape the attention of such a psychologist as Napoleon, but our modern legislators, ignorant as they are of the characteristics of a crowd, are unable to appreciate it. Experience has not taught them as yet to a sufficient degree that men never shape their conduct upon the teaching of pure reason.

Many other practical applications might be made of the psychology of crowds. A knowledge of this science throws the most vivid light on a great number of historical and economic phenomena totally incomprehensible without it. I shall have occasion to show that the reason why the most remarkable of modern historians, Taine, has at times so imperfectly understood the events of the great French Revolution is, that it never occurred to him to study the genius of crowds. He took as his guide in the study of this complicated period the descriptive method resorted to by naturalists; but the moral forces are almost absent in the case of the phenomena which naturalists have to study. Yet it is precisely these forces that constitute the true mainsprings of history.

In consequence, merely looked at from its practical side, the study of the psychology of crowds deserved to be attempted. Were its interest that resulting from pure curiosity only, it would still merit attention. It is as interesting to decipher the motives of the actions of men as to determine the characteristics of a mineral or a plant. Our study of the genius of crowds can merely be a brief synthesis, a simple summary of our investigations. Nothing more must be demanded of it than a few suggestive views. Others will work the ground more thoroughly. Today we only touch the surface of a still almost virgin soil.

BOOK I

MIND OF CROWDS

CHAPTER I

GENERAL CHARACTERISTICS OF CROWDS—PSYCHOLOGICAL LAW OF THEIR MENTAL UNITY

What constitutes a crowd from the psychological point of view—A numerically strong agglomeration of individuals does not suffice to form a crowd   Special characteristics of psychological crowds—The turning in a fixed direction of the ideas and sentiments of individuals composing such a crowd, and the disappearance of their personality — The crowd is always dominated by considerations of which it is unconscious—The disappearance of brain activity and the predominance of medullar activity—The lowering of the intelligence and the complete transformation of the sentiments—The transformed sentiments may be better or worse than those of the individuals of which the crowd is composed—A crowd is as easily heroic as criminal.

IN its ordinary sense the word "crowd " means a gathering of individuals of whatever nationality, profession, or sex, and whatever be the chances that have brought them together. From the psychological point of view the expression "crowd" assumes quite a different signification. Under certain given circumstances, and only under those circumstances, an agglomeration of men presents new characteristics very different from those of the individuals composing it. The sentiments and ideas of all the persons in the gathering take one and the same direction, and their conscious personality vanishes. A collective mind is formed, doubtless transitory, but presenting very clearly defined characteristics. The gathering has thus become what, in the absence of a better expression, I will call an organized crowd, or, if the term is considered preferable, a psychological crowd. It forms a single being, and is subjected to the *law of the mental unity of crowds.*

It is evident that it is not by the mere fact of a number of individuals finding themselves accidentally side by side that they acquire the character of an organized crowd. A thousand individuals accidentally gathered in a public place without any determined object in no way constitute a crowd from the psychological point of view. To acquire the special characteristics of such a crowd, the influence is necessary of certain predisposing causes of which we shall have to determine the nature.

The disappearance of conscious personality and the turning of feelings and thoughts in a definite direction, which are the primary characteristics of a crowd about to become organized, do not always involve the simultaneous presence of a number of individuals on one spot. Thousands of isolated individuals may acquire at certain moments, and under the influence of certain violent emotions—such, for example, as a great national event—the characteristics of a psychological crowd. It will be sufficient in that case that a mere chance should bring them together for their acts to at once assume the characteristics peculiar to the acts of a crowd. At certain moments half a dozen men might constitute a psychological crowd, which may not happen in the case of hundreds of men gathered together by accident. On the other hand, an entire nation, though there may be no visible agglomeration, may become a crowd under the action of certain influences.

A psychological crowd once constituted, it acquires certain provisional but determinable general characteristics. To these general characteristics there are adjoined particular characteristics which vary according, to the elements of which the crowd is composed, and may modify its mental constitution. Psychological crowds, then, are susceptible of classification; and when we come to occupy ourselves with this matter, we shall see that a heterogeneous crowd—that is, a crowd composed of dissimilar elements—presents certain characteristics in common with homogeneous crowds—that is, with crowds composed of elements more or less akin (sects, castes, and classes)—and side by side with these common characteristics particularities which permit of the two kinds of crowds being differentiated.

But before occupying ourselves with the different categories of crowds, we must first of all examine the characteristics common to them all. We shall set to work like the naturalist, who begins by describing the general characteristics common to all the members of a family before concerning himself with the particular characteristics which allow the differentiation of the genera and species that the family includes.

It is not easy to describe the mind of crowds with exactness, because its organization varies not only according to race and composition, but also according to the nature and intensity of the exciting causes to which crowds are subjected. The same difficulty, however, presents itself in the psychological study of an individual. It is only in novels that individuals are found to traverse their whole life with an unvarying character. It is only the uniformity of the environment that creates the apparent uniformity of characters. I have shown elsewhere that all mental constitutions contain possibilities of character which may be manifested in consequence of a sudden change of environment. This explains how it was that among the most savage members of the French Convention were to be found inoffensive citizens who, under ordinary circumstances, would have been peaceable notaries or virtuous magistrates. The storm past, they resumed their normal character of quiet, law-abiding citizens. Napoleon found amongst them his most docile servants.

It being impossible to study here all the successive degrees of organization of crowds, we shall concern ourselves more especially with such crowds as have attained to the phase of complete organization. In this way we shall see what crowds may become, but not what they invariably are. It is only in this advanced phase of organization that certain new and special characteristics are superposed on the unvarying and dominant character of the race; then takes place that turning already alluded to of all the feelings and thoughts of the collectivity in an identical direction. It is only under such circumstances, too, that what I have called above the psychological law of the mental unity of crowds comes into play.

Among the psychological characteristics of crowds there are some that they may present in common with isolated individuals, and others, on the contrary, which are absolutely peculiar to them and are only to be met with in collectivities. It is these special characteristics that we shall study, first of all, in order to show their importance.

The most striking peculiarity presented by a psychological crowd is the following: Whoever be the individuals that compose it, however like or unlike be their mode of life, their occupations, their character, or their intelligence, the fact that they have been transformed into a crowd puts them in possession of a sort of collective mind which makes them feel, think, and act in a manner quite different from that in which each individual of them would feel, think, and act were he in a state of isolation. There are certain ideas and feelings which do not come into being, or do not transform themselves into acts except in the case of individuals forming a crowd. The psychological crowd is a provisional being formed of heterogeneous elements, which for a moment are combined, exactly as the cells which constitute a living body form by their reunion a new being which displays characteristics very different from those possessed by each of the cells singly.

Contrary to an opinion which one is astonished to find coming from the pen of so acute a philosopher as Herbert Spencer, in the aggregate which constitutes a crowd there is in no sort a summing-up of or an average struck between its elements. What really takes place is a combination followed by the creation of new characteristics, just as in chemistry certain elements, when brought into contact—bases and acids, for example—combine to form a new body possessing properties quite different from those of the bodies that have served to form it.

It is easy to prove how much the individual forming part of a crowd differs from the isolated individual, but it is less easy to discover the causes of this difference.

To obtain at any rate a glimpse of them it is necessary in the first place to call to mind the truth established by modern psychology, that unconscious phenomena play an altogether preponderating part not only in organic life, but also in the operations of the intelligence. The conscious life of the mind is of small importance in comparison with its unconscious life. The most subtle analyst, the most acute observer, is scarcely successful in discovering more than a very small number of the unconscious motives that determine his conduct. Our conscious acts are the outcome of an unconscious substratum created in the mind in the main by hereditary influences. This substratum consists of the innumerable common characteristics handed down from generation to generation, which constitute the genius of a race. Behind the avowed causes of our acts there undoubtedly lie secret causes that we do not avow, but behind these secret causes there are many others more secret still which we ourselves ignore. The greater part of our daily actions are the result of hidden motives which escape our observation.

It is more especially with respect to those unconscious elements which constitute the genius of a race that all the individuals belonging to it resemble each other, while it is principally in respect to the conscious elements of their character—the fruit of education, and yet more of exceptional hereditary conditions—that they differ from each other. Men the most unlike in the matter of their intelligence possess instincts, passions, and feelings that are very similar. In the case of everything that belongs to the realm of sentiment—religion, politics, morality, the affections and antipathies, etc.—the most eminent men seldom surpass the standard of the most ordinary individuals. From the intellectual point of view an abyss may exist between a great mathematician and his boot maker, but from the point of view of character the difference is most often slight or non-existent.

It is precisely these general qualities of character, governed by forces of which we are unconscious, and possessed by the majority of the normal individuals of a race in much the same degree—it is precisely these qualities, I say, that in crowds become common property. In the collective mind the intellectual aptitudes of the individuals, and in consequence their individuality, are weakened. The heterogeneous is swamped by the homogeneous, and the unconscious qualities obtain the upper hand.

This very fact that crowds possess in common ordinary qualities explains why they can never accomplish acts demanding a high degree of intelligence. The decisions affecting matters of general interest come to by an assembly of men of distinction, but specialists in different walks of life, are not sensibly superior to the decisions that would be adopted by a gathering of imbeciles. The truth is, they can only bring to bear in common on the work in hand those mediocre qualities which are the birthright of every average individual. In crowds it is stupidity and not mother-wit that is accumulated. It is not all the world, as is so often repeated, that has more wit than Voltaire, but assuredly Voltaire that has more wit than all the world, if by "all the world" crowds are to be understood.

If the individuals of a crowd confined themselves to putting in common the ordinary qualities of which each of them has his share, there would merely result the striking of an average, and not, as we have said is actually the case, the creation of new characteristics. How is it that these new characteristics are created? This is what we are now to investigate.

Different causes determine the appearance of these characteristics peculiar to crowds, and not possessed by isolated individuals. The first is that the individual forming part of a crowd acquires, solely from numerical considerations, a sentiment of invincible power which allows him to yield to instincts which, had he been alone, he would perforce have kept under restraint. He will be the less disposed to check himself from the consideration that, a crowd being anonymous, and in consequence irresponsible, the sentiment of responsibility which always controls individuals disappears entirely.

The second cause, which is contagion, also intervenes to determine the manifestation in crowds of their special characteristics, and at the same time the trend they are to take. Contagion is a phenomenon of which it is easy to establish the presence, but that it is not easy to explain. It must be classed among those phenomena of a hypnotic order, which we shall shortly study. In a crowd every sentiment and act is contagious, and contagious to such a degree that an individual readily sacrifices his personal interest to the collective interest. This is an aptitude very contrary to his nature, and of which a man is scarcely capable, except when he makes part of a crowd.

A third cause, and by far the most important, determines in the individuals of a crowd special characteristics which are quite contrary at times to those presented by the isolated individual. I allude to that suggestibility of which, moreover, the contagion mentioned above is neither more nor less than an effect.

To understand this phenomenon it is necessary to bear in mind certain recent physiological discoveries. We know today that by various processes an individual may be brought into such a condition that, having entirely lost his conscious personality, he obeys all the suggestions of the operator who has deprived him of it, and commits acts in utter contradiction with his character and habits. The most careful observations seem to prove that an individual immerged for some length of time in a crowd in action soon finds himself —either in consequence of the magnetic influence given out by the crowd, or from some other cause of which we are ignorant—in a special state, which much resembles the state of fascination in which the hypnotized individual finds himself in the hands of the hypnotizer. The activity of the brain being paralyzed in the case of the hypnotised subject, the latter becomes the slave of all the unconscious activities of his spinal cord, which the hypnotiser directs at will. The conscious personality has entirely vanished; will and discernment are lost. All feelings and thoughts are bent in the direction determined by the hypnotizer.

Such also is approximately the state of the individual forming part of a psychological crowd. He is no longer conscious of his acts. In his case, as in the case of the hypnotized subject, at the same time that certain faculties are destroyed, others may be brought to a high degree of exaltation. Under the influence of a suggestion, he will undertake the accomplishment of certain acts with irresistible impetuosity. This impetuosity is the more irresistible in the case of crowds than in that of the hypnotized subject, from the fact that, the suggestion being the same for all the individuals of the crowd, it gains in strength by reciprocity. The individualities in the crowd who might possess a personality sufficiently strong to resist the suggestion are too few in number to struggle against the current. At the utmost, they may be able to attempt a diversion by means of different suggestions. It is in this way, for instance, that a happy expression, an image opportunely evoked, have occasionally deterred crowds from the most blood-thirsty acts.

We see, then, that the disappearance of the conscious personality, the predominance of the unconscious personality, the turning by means of suggestion and contagion of feelings and ideas in an identical direction, the tendency to immediately transform the suggested ideas into acts; these, we see, are the principal characteristics of the individual forming part of a crowd. He is no longer himself, but has become an automaton who has ceased to be guided by his will.

Moreover, by the mere fact that he forms part of an organized crowd, a man descends several rungs in the ladder of civilization. Isolated, he may be a cultivated individual; in a crowd, he is a barbarian—that is, a creature acting by instinct. He possesses the spontaneity, the violence, the ferocity, and also the enthusiasm and heroism of primitive beings, whom he further tends to resemble by the facility with which he allows himself to be impressed by words and images —which would be entirely without action on each of the isolated individuals composing the crowd—and to be induced to commit acts contrary to his most obvious interests and his best-known habits. An individual in a crowd is a grain of sand amid other grains of sand, which the wind stirs up at will.

It is for these reasons that juries are seen to deliver verdicts

of which each individual juror would disapprove, that parliamentary assemblies adopt laws and measures of which each
of their members would disapprove in his own person. Taken
separately, the men of the Convention were enlightened
citizens of peaceful habits. United in a crowd, they did not
hesitate to give their adhesion to the most savage proposals,
to guillotine individuals most clearly innocent, and, contrary to
their interests, to renounce their inviolability and to decimate
themselves.

It is not only by his acts that the individual in a crowd differs
essentially from himself. Even before he has entirely lost his
independence, his ideas and feelings have undergone a
transformation, and the transformation is so profound as to
change the miser into a spendthrift, the sceptic into a believer,
the honest man into a criminal, and the coward into a hero.
The renunciation of all its privileges which the nobility voted
in a moment of enthusiasm during the celebrated night of
August 4, 1789, would certainly never have been consented
to by any of its members taken singly.

The conclusion to be drawn from what precedes is, that the
crowd is always intellectually inferior to the isolated individual,
but that, from the point of view of feelings and of the acts these
feelings provoke, the crowd may, according to circumstances,
be better or worse than the individual. All depends on the
nature of the suggestion to which the crowd is exposed. This
is the point that has been completely misunderstood by writers
who have only studied crowds from the criminal point of view.
Doubtless a crowd is often criminal, but also it is often heroic.
It is crowds rather than isolated individuals that may be
induced to run the risk of death to secure the triumph of a
creed or an idea, that may be fired with enthusiasm for glory
and honor, that are led on—almost without bread and without
arms, as in the age of the Crusades —to deliver the tomb of
Christ from the infidel, or, as in '93, to defend the fatherland.
Such heroism is without doubt somewhat unconscious, but it
is of such heroism that history is made. Were peoples only to
be credited with the great actions performed in cold blood, the

annals of the world would register but few of them.

CHAPTER II

THE SENTIMENTS AND MORALITY OF CROWDS

1. *Impulsiveness, mobility, and irritability of crowds.* The crowd is at the mercy of all exterior exciting causes, and reflects their incessant variations—The impulses which the crowd obeys are so imperious as to annihilate the feeling of personal interest——Premeditation is absent from crowds—Racial influence. 2. Crowds are credulous and readily influenced by suggestion. The obedience of crowds to suggestions—The images evoked in the mind of crowds are accepted by them as realities—Why these images are identical for all the individuals composing a crowd—The equality of the educated and the ignorant man in a crowd—Various examples of the illusions to which the individuals in a crowd are subject—The impossibility of according belief to the testimony of crowds—The unanimity of numerous witnesses is one of the worst proofs that can be invoked to establish a fact—The slight Value of works of history. 3. *The exaggeration and ingenuousness of the sentiments of crowds.* Crowds do not admit doubt or uncertainty, and always go to extremes—Their sentiments always excessive. 4.*The intolerance, dictatorialness, and conservatism of crowds.* The reasons of these sentiments—The servility of crowds in the face of a strong authority—The momentary revolutionary instincts of crowds do not prevent them from being extremely conserservative—Crowds instinctively hostile to changes and progress.

HAVING indicated in a general way the principal characteristics of crowds, it remains to study these characteristics in detail.

It will be remarked that among the special characteristics of crowds there are several—such as impulsiveness, irritability, incapacity to reason, the absence of judgement and of the critical spirit, the exaggeration of the sentiments, and others besides—which are almost always observed in beings belonging to inferior forms of evolution—in women, savages, and children, for instance. However, I merely indicate this analogy in passing; its demonstration is outside the scope of this work. It would, moreover, be useless for persons acquainted with the psychology of primitive beings, and would scarcely carry conviction to those in ignorance of this matter.

I now proceed to the successive consideration of the different characteristics that may be observed in the majority of crowds.

1. *IMPULSIVENESS, MOBILITY, AND IRRITABILITY OF CROWDS*

When studying the fundamental characteristics of a crowd we stated that it is guided almost exclusively by unconscious motives. Its acts are far more under the influence of the spinal cord than of the brain. In this respect a crowd is closely akin to quite primitive beings. The acts performed may be perfect so far as their execution is concerned, but as they are not directed by the brain, the individual conducts himself according as the exciting causes to which he is submitted may happen to decide. A crowd is at the mercy of all external exciting causes, and reflects their incessant variations. It is the slave of the impulses which it receives. The isolated individual may be submitted to the same eliciting causes as the man in a crowd, but as his brain shows him the inadvisability of yielding to them, he refrains from yielding. This truth may be psysiologically expressed by saying that the isolated individual saying that the isolated individual possesses the capacity of dominating his reflex actions, while a crowd is devoid of this capacity.

The varying impulses which crowds obey may be, according to their exciting causes, generous or cruel, heroic or cowardly, but they will always be so imperious that the interest of the individual, even the interest of self-preservation, will not dominate them. The exciting causes that may act on crowds being so varied, and crowds always obeying them, crowds are in consequence extremely mobile. This explains how it is that we see them pass in a moment from the most bloodthirsty ferocity to the most extreme generosity and heroism. A crowd may easily enact the part of an executioner, but not less easily that of a martyr. It is crowds that have furnished the torrents of blood requisite for the triumph of every belief. It is not necessary to go back to the heroic ages to see what crowds are capable of in this latter direction. They are never sparing of their life in an insurrection, and not long since a general,[1] becoming suddenly popular, might easily have found a hundred thousand men ready to sacrifice their lives for his cause had he demanded it.

Any display of premeditation by crowds is in consequence out of the question. They may be animated in succession by the most contrary sentiments, but they will always be under the influence of the exciting causes of the moment. They are like the leaves which a tempest whirls up and scatters in every direction and then allows to fall. When studying later on certain revolutionary crowds we shall give some examples of the variability of their sentiments.

This mobility of crowds renders them very difficult to govern, especially when a measure of public authority has fallen into their hands. Did not the necessities of everyday life constitute a sort of invisible regulator of existence, it would scarcely be possible for democracies to last. Still, though the wishes of crowds are frenzied they are not durable. Crowds are as incapable of willing as of thinking for any length of time.

A crowd is not merely impulsive and mobile. Like a savage, it is not prepared to admit that anything can come between its desire and the realization of its desire. It is the less capable of understanding such an intervention, in consequence of the feeling of irresistible power given it by its numerical strength. The notion of impossibility disappears for the individual in a crowd. An isolated individual knows well enough that alone he

1 General Boulanger.

cannot set fire to a palace or loot a shop, and should he be tempted to do so, he will easily resist the temptation. Making part of a crowd, he is conscious of the power given him by number, and it is sufficien. to suggest to him ideas of murder or pillage for him to yield immediately to temptation. An unexpected obstacle will be destroyed with frenzied rage. Did the human organism allow of the perpetuity of furious passion, it might be said that the normal condition of a crowd baulked in its wishes is just such a state of furious passion.

The fundamental characteristics of the race, which constitute the unvarying source from which all our sentiments spring, always exert an influence on the irritability of crowds, their impulsiveness and their mobility, as on all the popular sentiments we shall have to study. All crowds are doubtless always irritable and impulsive, but with great variations degree. For instance, the difference between a Latin and an Anglo-Saxon crowd is striking. The most recent facts in French history throw a vivid light on this point. The mere publication, twenty-five years ago, of a telegram, relating an insult supposed to have been offered an ambassador, was sufficient to determine an explosion of fury, whence followed immediately a terrible war. Some years later the telegraphic announcement of an insignificant reverse at Langson provoked a fresh explosion which brought about the instantaneous overthrow of the government. At the same moment a much more serious reverse undergone by the English expedition to Khartoum produced only a slight emotion in England, and no ministry was overturned. Crowds are everywhere distinguished by feminine characteristics, but Latin crowds are the most feminine of all. Whoever trusts in them may rapidly attain a lofty destiny, but to do so is to be perpetually skirting the brink of a Tarpeian rock, with the certainty of one day being precipitated from it.

2. THE SUGGESTIBILITY AND CREDULITY OF CROWDS

When defining crowds, we said that one of their general

characteristics was an excessive suggestibility, and we have shown to what an extent suggestions are contagious in every human agglomeration; a fact which explains the rapid turning of the sentiments of a crowd in a definite direction. However indifferent it may be supposed, a crowd, as a rule, is in a state of expectant attention, which renders suggestion easy. The first suggestion formulated which arises implants itself immediately by a process of contagion in the brains of all assembled, and the identical bent of the sentiments of the crowd is immediately an accomplished fact.

As is the case with all persons under the influence of suggestion, the idea which has entered the brain tends to transform itself into an act. Whether the act is that of setting fire to a palace, or involves self-sacrifice, a crowd lends itself to it with equal facility. All will depend on the nature of the exciting cause, and no longer, as in the case of the isolated individual, on the relations existing between the act suggested and the sum total of the reasons which may be urged against its realization.

In consequence, a crowd perpetually hovering on the borderland of unconsciousness, readily yielding to all suggestions, having all the violence of feeling peculiar to beings who cannot appeal to the influence of reason, deprived of all critical faculty, cannot be otherwise than excessively credulous.[1] The improbable does not exist for a crowd, and it is necessary to bear this circumstance well in mind to understand the facility with which are created and propagated the most improbable legends and stories.

The creation of the legends which so easily obtain circulation in crowds is not solely the consequence of their extreme credulity. It is also the result of the prodigious perversions that events undergo in the imagination of a throng. The simplest event that comes under the observation of a crowd is soon totally transformed. A crowd thinks in images, and the image

1 Persons who went through the siege of Paris saw numerous examples of this credulity of crowds. A candle alight in an upper story was immediately looked upon as a signal given the besiegers, although it was evident, after a moment of reflection, that it was utterly impossible to catch sight of the light of the candle at a distance of several miles

itself immediately calls up a series of other images, having no logical connection with the first. We can easily conceive this state by thinking of the fantastic succession of ideas to which we are sometimes led by calling up in our minds any fact. Our reason shows us the incoherence there is in these images, but a crowd is almost blind to this truth, and confuses with the real event what the deforming action of its imagination has superimposed thereon. A crowd scarcely distinguishes between the subjective and the objective. It accepts as real the images evoked in its mind, though they most often have only a very distant relation with the observed fact.

The ways in which a crowd perverts any event of which it is a witness ought, it would seem, to be innumerable and unlike each other, since the individuals composing the gathering are of very different temperaments. But this is not the case. As the result of contagion the perversions are of the same kind, and take the same shape in the case of all the assembled individuals.

The first perversion of the truth effected by one of the individuals of the gathering is the starting-point of the contagious suggestion. Before St. George appeared on the walls of Jerusalem to all the Crusaders he was certainly perceived in the first instance by one of those present. By dint of suggestion and contagion the miracle signalized by a single person was immediately accepted by all.

Such is always the mechanism of the collective hallucinations so frequent in history—hallucinations which seem to have all the recognized characteristics of authenticity, since they are phenomena observed by thousands of persons.

To combat what precedes, the mental quality of the individuals composing a crowd must not be brought into consideration. This quality is without importance. From the moment that they form part of a crowd the learned man and the ignoramus are equally incapable of observation.

This thesis may seem paradoxical. To demonstrate it beyond doubt it would be necessary to investigate a great number of historical facts, and several volumes would be insufficient for the purpose.

Still, as I do not wish to leave the reader under the impression of unproved assertions, I shall give him some examples taken at hazard from the immense number of those that might be quoted.

The following fact is one of the most typical, because chosen from among collective hallucinations of which a crowd is the victim, in which are to be found individuals of every kind, from the most ignorant to the most highly educated. It is related incidentally by Julian Felix, a naval lieutenant, in his book on " Sea Currents," and has been previously cited by the *Revue Scientifique.*

The frigate, the Belle Poule, was cruising in the open sea for the purpose of finding the cruiser Le Berceau, from which she had been separated by a violent storm. It was broad daylight and in full sunshine. Suddenly the watch signal led a disabled vessel; the crew looked in the direction signal led, and every one, officers and sailors, clearly perceived a raft covered with men towed by boats which were displaying signals of distress. Yet this was nothing more than a collective hallucination. Admiral Desfosses lowered a boat to go to the rescue of the wrecked sailors. On nearing the object sighted, the sailors and officers on board the boat saw " masses of men in motion, stretching out their hands, and heard the dull and confused noise of a great number of voices." When the object was reached those in the boat found themselves simply and solely in the presence of a few branches of trees covered with leaves that had been swept out from the neighboring coast. Before evidence so palpable the hallucination vanished. The mechanism of a collective hallucination of the kind we have explained is clearly seen at work in this example. On the one hand we have a crowd in a state of expectant attention, on the other a suggestion made by the watch signaling a disabled vessel at sea, a suggestion which, by a process of contagion, was accepted by all those present, both officers and sailors.

It is not necessary that a crowd should be numerous for the faculty of seeing what is taking place before its eyes to be destroyed and for the real facts to be replaced by hallucinations unrelated to them. As soon as a few individuals are gathered together they constitute a crowd, and, though they should be distinguished men of learning, they assume all the characteristics of crowds with regard to matters outside their speciality. The faculty of observation and the critical spirit possessed by each of them individually at once disappears. An ingenious psychologist, Mr. Davy, supplies us with a very curious example in point, recently cited in the *Annales des Sciences Psychiques*, and deserving of relation here. Mr. Davey, having convoked a gathering of distinguished observers, among them one of the most prominent of English scientific men, Mr. Wallace, executed in their presence, and after having allowed them to examine the objects and to place seals where they wished, all the regulation spiritualistic phenomena, the materialization of spirits, writing on slates, etc. Having subsequently obtained from these distinguished observers written reports admitting that the phenomena observed could only have been obtained by supernatural means, he revealed to them that they were the result of very simple tricks. " The most astonishing feature of Monsieur Davey's investigation," writes the author of this account, "is not the marvelousness of the tricks themselves, but the extreme weakness of the reports made with respect to them by the non-initiated witnesses. It is clear, then," he says, " that witnesses even in number may give circumstantial relations which are completely erroneous, but whose result is *that, if their descriptions are accepted as exact,* the phenomena they describe are inexplicable by trickery. The methods invented by Mr. Davey were so simple that one is astonished that he should have had the boldness to employ them; but he had such a power over the mind of the crowd that he could persuade it that it saw what it did not see." Here, as always, we have the power of the hypnotizer over the hypnotized. Moreover, when this power is seen in action on minds of a superior order and previously invited to be suspicious, it is understandable how easy it is to deceive ordinary crowds.

Analogous examples are innumerable. As I write these lines

the papers are full of the story of two little girls found drowned in the Seine. These children, to begin with, were recognized in the most unmistakable manner by half a dozen witnesses. All the affirmations were in such entire concordance that no doubt remained in the mind of the juge d'instruction. He had the certificate of death drawn up, but just as the burial of the children was to have been proceeded with, a mere chance brought about the discovery that the supposed victims were alive, and had, moreover, but a remote resemblance to the drowned girls. As in several of the examples previously cited, the affirmation of the first witness, himself a victim of illusion had sufficed to influence the other witnesses.

In parallel cases the starting-point of the suggestion is always the illusion produced in an individual by more or less vague reminiscences, contagion following as the result of the affirmation of this initial illusion. If the first observer be very impressionable, it will often be sufficient that the corpse he believes he recognizes should present—apart from all real resemblance—some peculiarity, a scar, or some detail of toilet which may evoke the idea of another person. The idea evoked may then become the nucleus of a sort of crystallization which invades the understanding and paralysis all critical faculty. What the observer then sees is no longer the object itself, but the image evoked in his mind. In this way are to be explained erroneous recognitions of the dead bodies of children by their own mother, as occurred in the following case, already old, but which has been recently recalled by the newspapers. In it are to be traced precisely the two kinds of suggestions of which I have just pointed out the mechanism.

" The child was recognized by another child, who was mistaken." The series of unwarranted recognitions then began.

"An extraordinary thing occurred. The day after a school-boy had recognized the corpse a woman exclaimed, 'Good Heavens, it is my child ! '

" She was taken up to the corpse; she examined the

clothing, and noted a scar on the forehead. ' It is certainly,' she said, ' my son who disappeared last July. He has been stolen from me and murdered.'

"The woman was concierge in the Rue du Four; her name was Chavandret. Her brother-in-law was summoned, and when questioned he said, 'That is the little Filibert.' Several persons living in the street recognized the child found at La Villette as Filibert Chavandret, among them being the boy's schoolmaster,who based his opinion on a medal worn by the lad.

"Nevertheless, the neighbors, the brother-in-law, the school-master, and the mother were mistaken. Six weeks later the identity of the child was established. The boy, belonging to Bordeaux, had been murdered there and brought by a carrying company to Paris." [1]

It will be remarked that these recognitions are most often made by women and children—that is to say, by precisely the most impressionable persons. They show us at the same time what is the worth in law courts of such witnesses. As far as children, more especially, are concerned, their statements ought never to be invoked. Magistrates are in the habit of repeating that children do not lie. Did they possess a psycho-logical culture a little less rudimentary than is the case they would know that, on the contrary, children invariably lie; the lie is doubtless innocent, but it is none the less a lie. It would be better to decide the fate of an accused person by the toss of a coin than, as has been so often done, by the evidence of a child.

To return to the faculty of observation possessed by crowds, our conclusion is that their collective observations are as erroneous as possible, and that most often they merely represent the illusion of an individual who, by a process of contagion, has suggestioned his fellows. Facts proving that the most utter mistrust of the evidence of crowds is advisable might be multiplied to any extent. Thousands of men were present twenty-five years ago at the celebrated cavalry charge during,

1 *L'Eclair*, April 21, 1895.

the battle of Sedan, and yet it is impossible, in the face of the most contradictory ocular testimony, to decide by whom it was commanded. The English general, Lord Wolseley, has proved in a recent book that up to now the gravest errors of fact have been committed with regard to the most important incidents of the battle of Waterloo—facts that hundreds of witnesses had nevertheless attested.[2]

Such facts show us what is the value of the testimony of crowds. Treatises on logic include the unanimity of numerous witnesses in the category of the strongest proofs that can be invoked in support of the exactness of a fact. Yet what we know of the psychology of crowds shows that treatises on logic need on this point to be rewritten. The events with regard to which there exists the most doubt are certainly those which have been observed by the greatest number of persons. To say that a fact has been simultaneously verified by thousands of witnesses is to say, as a rule, that the real fact is very different from the accepted account of it.

It clearly results from what precedes that works of history must be considered as works of pure imagination. They are fanciful accounts of ill-observed facts, accompanied by explanations the result of reflection. To write such books is the most absolute waste of time. Had not the past left us its literary, artisitic, and monumental works, we should know absolutely nothing in reality with regard to bygone times. Are we in possession of a single word of truth concerning the lives of the great men who have played preponderating parts in humanity--men such as Hercules, Buddha, or Mahomet? In all probability we are not. In point of fact, moreover, their real

2 Do we know in the case of one single battle exactly how it took place? I am very doubtful on the point. We know who were the conquerors and the conquered, but this is probably all. What M. D'Harcourt has said with respect to the battle of Salferino, which he witnessed, and in which he was personally engaged, may be applied to all battles—" The generals (informed, of course, by the evidence of hundreds of witnesses) forward their official reports; the orderly officers modify these documents and draw up a definite narrative; the chief of the staff raises objections and rewrites the whole on a fresh basis. It is carried to the Marshal, who exclaims, 'You are entirely in error,' and he substitutes a fresh edition. Scarcely anything remains of the original report." M. D'Harcourt relates this fact as proof of the impossibility of establishing the truth in connection with the most striking,the best observed events.

lives are slight importance to us. Our interest is to know what our great men were as they are presented by popular legend. It is legendary heroes, and not for a moment real heroes, who have impressed the minds of crowds.

Unfortunately, legends--even although they have been definitely put on record by books--have in themselves no stability. The imagination of the crowd continually transforms them as the result of the lapse of time and especially in consequence of racial causes. There is great gulf fixed between the sanguinary Jehovah of the Old Testament and the God of Love of Sainte Therese, and the Buddha worshipped in China has no traits in common with that venerated in India.

It is not even necessary that heroes should be separated from us by centuries for their legend to be transformed by the imagination of the crowd. The transformation occasionally takes place within a few years. In our own day we have seen the legend of one of the greatest heroes of history modified several times in less than fifty years. Under the Bourbons Napoleon became a sort of idyllic and liberal philanthropist, a friend of the humble who, according to the poets, was destined to be long remembered in the cottage. Thirty years afterwards this easy-going hero had become a sanguinary despot, who, after having usurped power and destroyed liberty, caused the slaughter of three million men solely to satisfy his ambition. At present we are witnessing a fresh transformation of the legend. When it has undergone the influence of some dozens of centuries the learned men of the future, face to face with these contradictory accounts, will perhaps doubt the very existence of the hero, as some of them now doubt that of Buddha, and will see in him nothing more than a solar myth or a development of the legend of Hercules. They will doubtless console themselves easily for this uncertainty, for, better initiated than we are today characteristics and psychology of crowds, they will know that history is scarcely capable of preserving the memory of anything except myths.

3. *THE EXAGGERATION AND INGENUOUSNESS OF THE SENTIMENTS OF CROWDS.*

Whether the feelings exhibited by a crowd be good or bad, they present the double character of being very simple and very exaggerated. On this point, as on do many others, an individual in a crowd resembles primitive beings. Inaccessible to fine distinctions, he sees things as a whole, and is blind to their intermediate phases. The exaggeration of the sentiments of a crowd is heightened by the fact that any feeling when once it is exhibited communicating itself very quickly by a process of suggestion and contagion, the evident approbation of which it is the object considerably increases its force.

The simplicity and exaggeration of the sentiments of crowds have for result that a throng knows neither doubt nor uncertainty. Like women, it goes at once to extremes. A suspicion transforms itself as soon as announced into incontrovertible evidence. A commencement of antipathy or disapprobation, which in the case of an isolated individual would not gain strength, becomes at once furious hatred in the case of an individual in a crowd.

The violence of the feelings of crowds is also increased, especially in heterogeneous crowds, by the absence of all sense of responsibility. The certainty of impunity, a certainty the stronger as the crowd is more numerous, and the notion of a considerable momentary force due to number, make possible in the case of crowds sentiments and acts impossible for the isolated individual. In crowds the foolish, ignorant, and envious persons are freed from the sense of their insignificance and powerlessness, and are possessed instead by the notion of brutal and temporary but immense strength.

Unfortunately, this tendency of crowds to exaggeration is often brought to bear upon bad sentiments. These sentiments are atavistic residuum of the instincts of the primitive man, which the fear of punishment obliges the isolated and responsible individual to curb. Thus it is that crowds are so easily led into the worst excesses.

Still this does not mean that crowds, skillfully influenced, are not capable of heroism and devotion and of evincing the loftiest virtues; they are even more capable of showing these qualities than the isolated individual. We shall soon have occasion to revert to this point when we come to study the morality of crowds.

Given to exaggeration in its feelings, a crowd is only impressed by excessive sentiments. An orator wishing to move a crowd must make an abusive use of violent affirmations. To exaggerate, to affirm, to resort to repetitions, and never to attempt to prove anything by reasoning are methods of argument well known to speakers at public meetings.

Moreover, a crowd exacts a like exaggeration in the sentiments of its heroes. Their apparent qualities and virtues must always be amplified. It has been justly remarked that on the stage a crowd demands from the hero of the piece a degree of courage, morality, and virtue that is never to be found in real life.

Quite rightly importance has been laid on the special standpoint from which matters are viewed in the theatre. Such a standpoint exists no doubt, but its rules for the most part have nothing to do with common sense and logic. The art of appealing to crowds is no doubt of an inferior order, but it demands quite special aptitudes. It is often impossible on reading plays to explain their success. Managers of theatres when accepting pieces are themselves, as a rule, very uncertain of their success,[1] because to judge the matter it would be necessary that they should be able to transform themselves into

1 It is understandable for this reason why it sometimes happens that pieces refused by all theatrical managers obtain a prodigious success when by a stroke of chance they are put on the stage. The recent success of Francois Coppee's play "Pour la Couronne," is well known, and yet, in spite of the name of its author, it was refused during ten years by managers of the principal Parisian theatres. "Charley's Aunt," refused at every theatre, and finally staged at the expense of a stockbroker, has had two hundred representations in France, and more than a thousand in London. Without the explanation given above of the impossibility for theatrical managers to mentally substitute themselves for a crowd, such mistakes in judgment on the part of competent individuals, who are most interested not to commit such grave blunders, would be inexplicable. This is a subject that I cannot deal with here, but it might worthily tempt the pen of a writer acquainted with theatrical matters, and at the same time a subtle psychologist—of such a writer, for instance, as M. Francisque Sarcey.

a crowd.

Here, once more, were we able to embark on more extensive explanations, we should show the preponderating influence of racial considerations. A play which provokes the enthusiasm of the crowd in one country has sometimes no success in another, or has only a partial and conventional success, because it does not put in operation influences capable of working on an altered public.

I need not add that the tendency to exaggeration in crowds is only present in the case of sentiments and not at all in the matter of intelligence. I have already shown that, by the mere fact that an individual forms part of a crowd, his intellectual standard is immediately and considerably lowered. A learned magistrate, M. Tarde, has also verified this fact in his researches on the crimes of crowds. It is only, then, with respect to sentiment that crowds can rise to a very high or, on the contrary, descend to a very low level.

4. THE INTOLERANCE, DICTATORIALNESS, AND CONSERVATISM OF CROWDS

Crowds are only cognizant of simple and extreme sentiments; the opinions, ideas, and beliefs suggested to them are accepted or rejected as a whole, and considered as absolute truths or as not less absolute errors. This is always the case with beliefs induced by a process of suggestion instead of engendered by reasoning. Every one is aware of the intolerance that accompanies religious beliefs, and of the despotic empire they exercise on men's minds.

Being in doubt as to what constitutes truth or error, and having, on the other hand, a clear notion of its strength, a crowd is as disposed to give authoritative effect to its inspirations as it is intolerant. An individual may accept contradiction and discussion; a crowd will never do so. At public meetings the slightest contradiction on the part of an orator is immediately received with howls of fury and violent invective, soon followed by blows, and expulsion should the orator stick to his point. Without the restraining presence of the representatives of authority the contradictor, indeed, would often be done to death.

Dictatorialness and intolerance are common to all categories of crowds, but they are met with in a varying degree of intensity. Here, once more, reappears that fundamental notion of race which dominates all the feelings and all the thoughts of men. It is more especially in Latin crowds that authoritativeness and intolerance are found developed in the highest measure. In fact, their development is such in crowds of Latin origin that they have entirely destroyed that sentiment of the independence of the individual so powerful in the Anglo-Saxon. Latin crowds are only concerned with the collective independence of the sect to which they belong, and the characteristic feature of their conception of independence is the need they experience of bringing those who are in disagreement with themselves into immediate and violent subjection to their beliefs. Among the Latin races the Jacobins of every epoch, from those of the Inquisition downwards, have never been able to attain to a different conception of liberty.

Authoritativeness and intolerance are sentiments of which crowds have a very clear notion, which they easily conceive and which they entertain as readily as they put them in practice when once they are imposed upon them. Crowds exhibit a docile respect for force, and are but slightly impressed by kindness, which for them is scarcely other than a form of weakness. Their sympathies have never been bestowed on easy-going masters, but on tyrants who vigorously oppressed them. It is to these latter that they always erect the loftiest statues. It is true that they willingly trample on the despot whom they have stripped of his power, but it is because, having lost his strength, he has resumed his place among the feeble, who are to be despised because they are not to be feared. The type of hero dear to crowds will always have the semblance of a Caesar. His insignia attracts them, his authority overawes them, and his sword instils them with fear.

A crowd is always ready to revolt against a feeble, and to bow down servilely before a strong authority. Should the strength of an authority be intermittent, the crowd, always obedient to its extreme sentiments, passes alternately from anarchy to servitude, and from servitude to anarchy.

However, to believe in the predominance among crowds of revolutionary instincts would be to entirely misconstrue their psychology. It is merely their tendency to violence that deceives us on this point. Their rebellious and destructive outbursts are always very transitory. Crowds are too much governed by unconscious considerations, and too much subject in consequence to secular hereditary influences not to be extremely conservative. Abandoned to themselves, they soon weary of disorder, and instinctively turn to servitude. It was the proudest and most untractable of the Jacobins who acclaimed Bonaparte with greatest energy when he suppressed all liberty and made his hand of iron severely felt.

It is difficult to understand history, and popular revolutions in particular, if one does not take sufficiently into account the profoundly conservative instincts of crowds. They may be desirous, it is true, of changing the names of their institutions, and to obtain these changes they accomplish at times even violent revolutions, but the essence of these institutions is too much the expression of the hereditary needs of the race for them not invariably to abide by it. Their incessant mobility only exerts its influence on quite superficial matters. In fact, they possess conservative instincts as indestructible as those of all primitive beings. Their fetish-like respect for all traditions is absolute; their unconscious horror of all novelty capable of changing the essential conditions of their existence is very deeply rooted. Had democracies possessed the power they wield today at the time of the invention of mechanical looms or of the introduction of steam-power and of railways, the realization of these inventions would have been impossible, or would have been achieved at the cost of revolutions and repeated massacres. It is fortunate for the progress of civilization that the power of crowds only began to exist when the great discoveries of science and industry had already been effected.

5. THE MORALITY OF CROWDS

Taking the word "morality" to mean constant respect for certain social conventions, and the permanent repression of selfish impulses, it is quite evident that crowds are too impulsive and too mobile to be moral. If, however, we include in the term morality the transitory display of certain qualities such as abnegation, self-sacrifice, disinterestedness, devotion, and the need of equity, we may say, on the contrary, that crowds may exhibit at times a very lofty morality.

The few psychologists who have studied crowds have only considered them from the point of view of their criminal acts, and noticing how frequent these acts are, they have come to the conclusion that the moral standard of crowds is very low.

Doubtless this is often the case; but why? Simply because our savage, destructive instincts are the inheritance left dormant in all of us from the primitive ages. In the life of the isolated individual it would be dangerous for him to gratify these instincts, while his absorption in an irresponsible crowd, in which in consequence he is assured of impunity, gives him entire liberty to follow them. Being unable, in the ordinary course of events, to excercise these destructive instincts on our fellow-men, we confine ourselves to exercising them on animals. The passion, so widespread, for the chase and the acts of ferocity of crowds proceed from one and the same source. A crowd which slowly slaughters a defenseless victim displays a very cowardly ferocity; but for the philosopher this ferocity is very closely related to that of the huntsmen who gather in dozens for the pleasure of taking part in the pursuit and killing of a luckless stag by their hounds.

A crowd may be guilty of murder, incendiarism, and every kind of crime, but it is also capable of very lofty acts of devotion, sacrifice, and disinterestedness, of acts much loftier indeed than those of which the isolated individual is capable. Appeals to sentiments of glory, honor, and patriotism are particularly likely to influence the individual forming part of a crowd, and often to the extent of obtaining from him the sacrifice of his life. History is rich in examples analogous to those furnished by the Crusaders and the volunteers of 1793. Collectivities alone are capable of great disinterestedness and great devotion. How numerous are the crowds that have heroically faced death for beliefs, ideas, and phrases that they scarcely understood! The crowds that go on strike do so far more in obedience to an order than to obtain an increase of the slender salary with which they make shift. Personal interest is very rarely a powerful motive force with crowds, while it is almost the exclusive motive of the conduct of the isolated individual. It is assuredly not self-interest that has guided crowds in so many wars, incomprehensible as a rule to their intelligence—wars in which they have allowed themselves to be massacred as easily as the larks hypnotized by the mirror of the hunter.

Even in the case of absolute scoundrels it often happens that the mere fact of their being in a crowd endows them for the moment with very strict principles of morality. Taine calls attention to the fact that the perpetrators of the September massacres deposited on the table of the committees the pocketbooks and jewels they had found on their victims, and with which they could easily have been able to make away. The howling, swarming, ragged crowd which invaded the Tuileries during the revolution of 1848 did not lay hands on any of the objects that excited its astonishment, and one of which would have meant bread for many days.

This moralization of the individual by the crowd is not certainly a constant rule, but it is a rule frequently observed. It is even observed in circumstances much less grave than those I have just cited. I have remarked that in the theatre a crowd exacts from the hero of the piece exaggerated virtues, and it is a commonplace observation that an assembly, even though composed of inferior elements, shows itself as a rule very prudish. The debauchee, the *souteneur,* the rough often break out into murmurs at a slightly risky scene or expression, though they be very harmless in comparison with their customary conversation.

If, then, crowds often abandon themselves to low instincts, they also set the example at times of acts of lofty morality. If disinterestedness, resignation, and absolute devotion to a real or chimerical ideal are moral virtues, it may be said that crowds often possess these virtues to a degree rarely attained by the wisest philosophers. Doubtless they practice them unconsciously, but that is of small import. We should not complain too much that crowds are more especially guided by unconscious considerations and are not given to reasoning. Had they, in certain cases, reasoned and consulted their immediate interests, it is possible that no civilization would have grown up on our planet and humanity would have had no history.

CHAPTER III

THE IDEAS, REASONING POWER, AND IMAGINATION OF CROWDS

1. *The ideas of crowds*. Fundamental and accessory ideas — How contradictory ideas may exist simultaneously—The transformation that must be undergone by lofty ideas before they are accessible to crowds—The social influence of ideas is independent of the degree of truth they may contain. 2. The reasoning power of crowds. Crowds are not to be influenced by reasoning—The reasoning of crowds is always of a very inferior order—There is only the appearance of analogy or succession in the ideas they associate. 3. The imagination of crowds. Strength of the imagination of crowds-Crowds think in images, and these images succeed each other without any connecting link—Crowds are especially impressed by the marvellous —Legends and the marvellous are the real pillars of civilization—The popular imagination has always been the basis of the power of statesmen—The manner in which facts capable of striking   the imagination of crowds present themselves for obser- vation.

1. THE IDEAS OF CROWDS

WHEN studying in a preceding work the part played by ideas in the evolution of nations, we showed that every civilization is the outcome of a small number of fundamental ideas that are very rarely renewed. We showed how these ideas are implanted in the minds of crowds, with what difficulty the process is effected, and the power possessed by the ideas in question when once it has been accomplished. Finally we saw that great historical perturbations are the result, as a rule, of changes in these fundamental ideas.

Having treated this subject at sufficient length, I shall not return to it now, but shall confine myself to saying a few words on the subject of such ideas as are accessible to crowds, and of the forms under which they conceive them.

They may be divided into two classes. In one we shall place accidental and passing ideas created by the influences of the moment; infatuation for an individual or a doctrine, for instance. In the other will be classed the fundamental ideas, to which the environment, the laws of heredity and public opinion give a very great stability; such ideas are the religious beliefs of the past and the social and democratic ideas of today.

These fundamental ideas resemble the volume of the water of a stream slowly pursuing its course; the transitory ideas are like the small waves, forever changing, which agitate its surface, and are more visible than the progress of the stream itself although without real importance.

At the present day the great fundamental ideas which were the mainstay of our fathers are tottering more and more. They have lost all solidity, and at the same time the institutions resting upon them are severely shaken. Every day there are formed a great many of those transitory minor ideas of which I have just been speaking; but very few of them to all appearance seem endowed with vitality and destined to acquire a preponderating influence.

Whatever be the ideas suggested to crowds they can only excercise effective influence on condition that they assume a very absolute, uncompromising, and simple shape. They present themselves then in the guise of images, and are only accessible to the masses under this form. These imagelike ideas are not connected by any logical bond of analogy or succession, and may take each other's place like the slides of a magic-lantern which the operator withdraws from the groove in which they were placed one above the other. This explains how it is that the most contradictory ideas may be seen to be simultaneously current in crowds. According to the chances of the moment, a crowd will come under the influence of one of the various ideas stored up in its understanding, and is capable, in consequence, of committing the most dissimilar acts. Its complete lack of the critical spirit does not allow of its perceiving these contradictions.

This phenomenon is not peculiar to crowds. It is to be observed in many isolated individuals, not only among primitive beings, but in the case of all those—the fervent sectaries of a religious faith, for instance—who by one side or another of their intelligence are akin to primitive beings. I have observed its presence to a curious extent in the case of educated Hindoos brought up at our European universities and having taken their degree. A number of Western ideas had been superposed on their unchangeable and fundamental hereditary or social ideas. According to the chances of the moment, the one or the other set of ideas showed themselves each with their special accompaniment of acts or utterances, the same individual presenting in this way the most flagrant contradictions. These contradictions are more apparent than real, for it is only hereditary ideas that have sufficient influence over the isolated individual to become motives of conduct. It is only when, as the result of the intermingling of different races, a man is placed between different hereditary tendencies that his acts from one moment to another may be really entirely contradictory. It would be useless to insist here on these phenomena, although their psychological importance is capital. I am of opinion that at least ten years of travel and observation would be necessary to arrive at a comprehension of them.

Ideas being only accessible to crowds after having assumed a very simple shape must often undergo the most thoroughgoing transformations to become popular. It is especially when we are dealing with somewhat lofty philosophic or

scientific ideas that we see how far-reaching are the modifications they require in order to lower them to the level of the
intelligence of crowds. These modifications are dependent on
the nature of the crowds, or of the race to which the crowds
belong, but their tendency is always belittling and in the
direction of simplification. This explains the fact that, from the
social point of view, there is in reality scarcely any such thing
as a hierarchy of ideas—that is to say, as ideas of greater or less
elevation. However great or true an idea may have been to
begin with, it is deprived of almost all that which constituted its
elevation and its greatness by the mere fact that it has come
within the intellectual range of crowds and exerts an influence
upon them.

Moreover, from the social point of view the hierarchical
value of an idea, its intrinsic worth, is without importance. The
necessary point to consider is the effects it produces. The
Christian ideas of the Middle Ages, the democratic ideas of the
last century, or the social ideas of today are assuredly not very
elevated. Philosophically considered, they can only be regarded as somewhat sorry errors, and yet their power has been
and will be immense, and they will count for a long time to
come among the most essential factors that determine the
conduct of States.

Even when an idea has undergone the transformations
which render it accessible to crowds, it only exerts influence
when, by various processes which we shall examine elsewhere,
it has entered the domain of the unconscious, when indeed it
has become a sentiment, for which much time is required.

For it must not be supposed that merely because the justness
of an idea has been proved it can be productive of effective
action even on cultivated minds. This fact may be quickly
appreciated by noting how slight is the influence of the clearest
demonstration on the majority of men. Evidence, if it be very
plain, may be accepted by an educated person, but the convert
will be quickly brought back by his unconscious self to his
original conceptions. See him again after the lapse of a few
days and he will put forward afresh his old arguments in exactly

the same terms. He is in reality under the influence of anterior ideas, that have become sentiments, and it is such ideas alone that influence the more recondite motives of our acts and utterances. It cannot be otherwise in the case of crowds.

When by various processes an idea has ended by penetrating into the minds of crowds, it possesses an irresistible power, and brings about a series of effects, opposition to which is bootless. The philosophical ideas which resulted in the French Revolution took nearly a century to implant themselves in the mind of the crowd. Their irresistible force, when once they had taken root, is known. The striving of an entire nation towards the conquest of social equality, and the realization of abstract rights and ideal liberties, caused the tottering of all thrones and profoundly disturbed the Western world. During twenty years the nations were engaged in internecine conflict, and Europe witnessed hecatombs that would have terrified Ghengis Khan and Tamerlane. The world had never seen on such a scale what may result from the promulgation of an idea.

A long time is necessary for ideas to establish themselves in the minds of crowds, but just as long a time is needed for them to be eradicated. For this reason crowds, as far as ideas are concerned, are always several generations behind learned men and philosophers. All statesmen are well aware today of the admixture of error contained in the fundamental ideas I referred to a short while back, but as the influence of these ideas is still very powerful they are obliged to govern in accordance with principles in the truth of which they have ceased to believe.

2. THE REASONING POWER OF CROWDS.

It cannot absolutely be said that crowds do not reason and are not to be influenced by reasoning.

However, the arguments they employ and those which are capable of influencing them are, from a logical point of view, of such an inferior kind that it is only by way of analogy that they can be described as reasoning.

The inferior reasoning of crowds is based, just as is reasoning of a high order, on the association of ideas, but between the ideas associated by crowds there are only apparent bonds of analogy or succession. The mode of reasoning of crowds resembles that of the Esquimaux who, knowing from experience that ice, a transparent body, melts in the mouth, concludes that glass, also a transparent body, should also melt in the mouth; or that of the savage who imagines that by eating the heart of a courageous foe he acquires his bravery; or of the workman who, having been exploited by one employer of labor, immediately concludes that all employers exploit their men.

The characteristics of the reasoning of crowds are the association of dissimilar things possessing a merely apparent connection between each other, and the immediate generalization of particular cases. It is arguments of this kind that are always presented to crowds by those who know how to manage them. They are the only arguments by which crowds are to be influenced. A chain of logical argumentation is totally incomprehensible to crowds, and for this reason it is permissible to say that they do not reason or that they reason falsely and are not to be influenced by reasoning. Astonishment is felt at times on reading certain speeches at their weakness, and yet they had an enormous influence on the crowds which listened to them, but it is forgotten that they were intended to persuade collectivities and not to be read by philosophers. An orator in intimate communication with a crowd can evoke images by which it will be seduced. If he is successful his object has been attained, and twenty volumes of harangues—always the outcome of reflection—are not worth the few phrases which appealed to the brains it was required to convince.

It would be superfluous to add that the powerlessness of crowds to reason aright prevents them displaying any trace of the critical spirit, prevents them, that is, from being capable of discerning truth from error, or of forming a precise judgment on any matter. Judgements accepted by crowds are merely judgments forced upon them and never judgments adopted after discussion. In regard to this matter the individuals who do not rise above the level of a crowd are numerous. The ease with which certain opinions obtain general acceptance results more especially from the impossibility experienced by the majority of men of forming an opinion peculiar to themselves and based on reasoning of their own.

3. THE IMAGINATION OF CROWDS

Just as is the case with respect to persons in whom the reasoning power is absent, the figurative imagination of crowds is very powerful, very active and very susceptible of being keenly impressed. The images evoked in their mind by a personage, an event, an accident, are almost as lifelike as the reality. Crowds are to some extent in the position of the sleeper whose reason, suspended for the time being, allows the arousing in his mind of images of extreme intensity which would quickly be dissipated could they be submitted to the action of reflection. Crowds, being incapable both of reflection and of reasoning, are devoid of the notion of improbability; and it is to be noted that in a general way it is the most improbable things that are the most striking.

This is why it happens that it is always the marvelous and legendary side of events that more specially strike crowds. When a civilization is analyzed it is seen that, in reality, it is the marvelous and the legendary that are its true supports. Appearances have always played a much more important part than reality in history, where the unreal is always of greater moment than the real.

Crowds being only capable of thinking in images are only to be impressed by images. It is only images that terrify or attract them and become motives of action.

For this reason theatrical representations, in which the image is shown in its most clearly visible shape, always have an enormous influence on crowds. Bread and spectacular shows constituted for the phlabeians of ancient Rome the ideal happiness, and they asked for nothing more. Throughout the successive ages this ideal has scarcely varied. Nothing has a greater effect on the imagination of crowds of every category than theatrical representations. The entire audience experiences at the same time the same emotions, and if these emotions are not at once transformed into acts, it is because the most unconscious spectator cannot ignore that he is the victim of illusions, and that he has laughed or wept over imaginary adventures. Sometimes, however, the sentiments suggested by the images are so strong that they tend, like habitual suggestions, to transform themselves into acts. The story has often been told of the manager of a popular theatre who, in consequence of his only playing sombre dramas, was obliged to have the actor who took the part of the traitor protected on his leaving the theatre, to defend him against the violence of the spectators, indignant at the crimes, imaginary though they were, which the traitor had committed. We have here, in my opinion, one of the most remarkable indications of the mental state of crowds, and especially of the facility with which they are suggestioned. The unreal has almost as much influence on them as the real. They have an evident tendency not to distinguish between the two.

The power of conquerors and the strength of States is based on the popular imagination. It is more particularly by working upon this imagination that crowds are led. All great historical facts, the rise of Buddhism, of Christianity, of Islamism, the Reformation, the French Revolution, and, in our own time, the threatening invasion of Socialism are the direct or indirect consequences of strong impressions produced on the imagination of the crowd.

Moreover, all the great statesmen of every age and every country, including the most absolute despots, have regarded the popular imagination as the basis of their power, and they have never attempted to govern in opposition to it. "It was by becoming a Catholic," said Napoleon to the Council of State, " that I terminated the Vendeen war. By becoming a Mussulman that I obtained a footing in Egypt. By becoming an

Ultramontane that I won over the Italian priests, and had I to govern a nation of Jews I would rebuild Solomon's temple." Never perhaps since Alexander and Caesar has any great man better understood how the imagination of the crowd should be impressed. His constant preoccupation was to strike it. He bore it in mind in his victories, in his harangues, in his speeches, in all his acts. On his deathbed it was still in his thoughts.

How is the imagination of crowds to be impressed? We shall soon see. Let us confine ourselves for the moment to saying that the feat is never to be achieved by attempting to work upon the intelligence or reasoning faculty, that is to say, by way of demonstration. It was not by means of cunning rhetoric that Antony succeeded in making the populace rise against the murderers of Caesar; it was by reading his will to the multitude and pointing to his corpse.

Whatever strikes the imagination of crowds presents itself under the shape of a startling and very clear image, freed from all accessory explanation, or merely having as accompaniment a few marvellous or mysterious facts; examples in point are a great victory, a great miracle, a great crime, or a great hope. Things must be laid before the crowd as a whole, and their genesis must never be indicated. A hundred petty crimes or petty accidents will not strike the imagination of crowds in the least, whereas a single great crime or a single great accident will profoundly impress them, even though the results be infinitely less disastrous than those of the hundred small accidents put together. The epidemic of influenza, which caused the death but a few years ago of five thousand persons in Paris alone, made very little impression on the popular imagination. The reason was that this veritable hecatomb was not embodied in any visible image, but was only learnt from statistical information furnished weekly. An accident which should have caused the death of only five hundred instead of five thousand persons, but on the same day and in public, as the outcome of an accident appealing strongly to the eye, by the fall, for instance, of the Eiffel Tower, would have produced, on the contrary, an immense impression on the imagination of the crowd. The probable loss of a transatlantic steamer that was supposed, in the absence of news, to have gone down in mid-ocean profoundly impressed the imagination of the crowd for a whole week. Yet official statistics show that 850 sailing vessels and 203 steamers were lost in the year 1894 alone. The crowd. however, was never for a moment concerned by these successive losses, much more important though they were as far as regards the destruction of life and property, than the loss of the Atlantic liner in question could possibly have been.

It is not, then, the facts in themselves that strike the popular imagination, but the way in which they take place and are brought under notice. It is necessary that by their condensation, if I may thus express myself, they should produce a startling image which fills and besets the mind. To know the art of impressing the imagination of crowds is to know at the same time the art of governing them.

CHAPTER IV

A RELIGIOUS SHAPE ASSUMED BY ALL THE CONVICTIONS OF CROWDS

What is meant by the religious sentiment—It is independent of the worship of a divinity—Its characteristics—The strength of convictions assuming a religious shape—Various examples—Popular gods have never disappeared —New forms under which they are revived—Religious forms of atheism—Importance of these notions from the historical point of view—The Reformation, Saint Bartholomew, the Terror, and all analogous events are the result of the religious sentiments of crowds and not of the will of isolated individuals.

WE have shown that crowds do not reason, that they accept or reject ideas as a whole, that they tolerate neither discussion nor contradiction, and that the suggestions brought to bear on them invade the entire field of their understanding and tend at once to transform themselves into acts. We have shown that crowds suitably influenced are ready to sacrifice themselves for the ideal with which they have been inspired. We have also seen that they only entertain violent and extreme sentiments, that in their case sympathy quickly becomes adoration, and antipathy almost as soon as it is aroused is transformed into hatred. These general indications furnish us already with a presentiment of the nature of the convictions of crowds.

When these convictions are closely examined, whether at epochs marked by fervent religious faith, or by great political upheavals such as those of the last century, it is apparent that they always assume a peculiar form which I cannot better define than by giving it the name of a religious sentiment.

This sentiment has very simple characteristics, such as worship of a being supposed superior, fear of the power with which the being is credited, blind submission to its commands, inability to discuss its dogmas, the desire to spread them, and a tendency to consider as enemies all by whom they are not accepted. Whether such a sentiment apply to an invisible God, to a wooden or stone idol, to a hero or to a political conception, provided that it presents the preceding characteristics, its essence always remains religious. The supernatural and the miraculous are found to be present to the same extent. Crowds unconsciously accord a mysterious power to the political formula or the victorious leader that for the moment arouses their enthusiasm.

A person is not religious solely when he worships a divinity, but when he puts all the resources of his mind, the complete submission of his will, and the whole-souled ardour of fanaticism at the service of a cause or an individual who becomes the goal and guide of his thoughts and actions.

Intolerance and fanaticism are the necessary accompaniments of the religious sentiment. They are inevitably displayed by those who believe themselves in the possession of the secret of earthly or eternal happiness. These two characteristics are to be found in all men grouped together when they are inspired by a conviction of any kind. The Jacobins of the Reign of Terror were at bottom as religious as the Catholics of the Inquisition, and their cruel ardour proceeded from the same source.

The convictions of crowds assume those characteristics of blind submission, fierce intolerance, and the need of violent propaganda which are inherent in the religious sentiment, and it is for this reason that it may be said that all their beliefs have a religious form. The hero acclaimed by a crowd is a veritable god for that crowd. Napoleon was such a god for fifteen years, and a divinity never had more frequent worshippers or sent men to their death with greater ease. The Christian and Pagan Gods never exercised a more absolute empire over the minds that had fallen under their sway.

All founders of religious or political creeds have established them solely because they were successful in inspiring crowds with those fanatical sentiments which have as result that men find their happiness in worship and obedience and are ready to lay down their lives for their idol. This has been the case at all epochs. Fustel de Coulangea, in his excellent work on Roman Gaul, justly remarks that the Roman Empire was in no wise maintained by force, but by the religious admiration it inspired. "It would be without a parallel in the history of the world," he observes rightly, " that a form of government held in popular detestation should have lasted for five centuries.... It would be inexplicable that the thirty legions of the Empire should have constrained a hundred million men to obedience." The reason of their obedience was that the Emperor, who personified the greatness of Rome, was worshipped like a divinity by unanimous consent. There were altars in honor of the Emperor in the smallest townships of his realm. "From one end of the Empire to the other a new religion was seen to arise in those days which had for its divinities the emperors themselves. Some years before the Christian era the whole of Gaul, represented by sixty cities, built in common a temple near the town of Lyons in honor of Augustus. . . . Its priests, elected by the united Gallic cities, were the principal personages in their country. . . . It is impossible to attribute all this to fear and servility. Whole nations are not servile, and especially for three centuries. It was not the courtiers who worshipped the prince, it was Rome, and it was not Rome merely, but it was Gaul, it was Spain, it was Greece and Asia."

Today the majority of the great men who have swayed men's minds no longer have altars, but they have statues, or their portraits are in the hands of their admirers, and the cult of which they are the object is not notably different from that accorded to their predecessors. An understanding of the philosophy of history is only to be got by a thorough appreciation of this fundamental point of the psychology of crowds. The crowd demands a god before everything else.

It must not be supposed that these are the superstitions of

a bygone age which reason has definitely banished. Sentiment has never been vanquished in its eternal conflict with reason. Crowds will hear no more of the words divinity and religion, in whose name they were so long enslaved; but they have never possessed so many fetishes as in the last hundred years, and the old divinities have never had so many statues and altars raised in their honor. Those who in recent years have studied the popular movement known under the name of Boulangism have been able to see with what ease the religious instincts of crowds are ready to revive. There was not a country inn that did not possess the hero's portrait. He was credited with the power of remedying all injustices and all evils, and thousands of men would have given their lives for him. Great might have been his place in history had his character been at all on a level with his legendary reputation.

It is thus a very useless commonplace to assert that a religion is necessary for the masses, because all political, divine, and social creeds only take root among them on the condition of always assuming the religious shape—a shape which obviates the danger of discussion. Were it possible to induce the masses to adopt atheism, this belief would exhibit all the intolerant ardor of a religious sentiment, and in its exterior forms would soon become a cult. The evolution of the small Positivist sect furnishes us a curious proof in point. What happened to the Nihilist whose story is related by that profound thinker Dostoiewsky has quickly happened to the Positivists. Illumined one day by the light of reason he broke the images of divinities and saints that adorned the altar of a chapel, extinguished the candles, and, without losing a moment, replaced the destroyed objects by the works of atheistic philosophers such as Buchner and Moleschott, after which he piously relighted the candles. The object of his religious beliefs had been transformed, but can it be truthfully said that his religious sentiments had changed?

Certain historical events—and they are precisely the most important—I again repeat, are not to be understood unless one has attained to an appreciation of the religious form which the convictions of crowds always assume in the long run. There are social phenomena that need to be studied far more from the point of view of the psychologist than from that of the naturalist. The great historian Taine has only studied the Revolution as a naturalist, and on this account the real genesis of events has often escaped him. He has perfectly observed the facts, but from want of having studied the psychology of crowds he has not always been able to trace their causes. The facts having appalled him by their bloodthirsty, anarchic, and ferocious side, he has scarcely seen in the heroes of the great drama anything more than a horde of epileptic savages abandoning themselves without restraint to their instincts. The violence of the Revolution, its massacres, its need of propaganda, its declarations of war upon all things, are only to be properly explained by reflecting that the Revolution was merely the establishment of a new religious belief in the mind of the masses. The Reformation, the massacre of Saint Bartholomew, the French religious wars, the Inquisition, the Reign of Terror are phenomena of an identical kind, brought about by crowds animated by those religious sentiments which necessarily lead those imbued with them to pitilessly extirpate by fire and sword whoever is opposed to the establishment of the new faith. The methods of the Inquisition are those of all whose convictions are genuine and sturdy. Their convictions would not deserve these epithets did they resort to other methods.

Upheavals analogous to those I have just cited are only possible when it is the soul of the masses that brings them about. The most absolute despots could not cause them. When historians tell us that the massacre of Saint Bartholomew was the work of a king, they show themselves as ignorant of the psychology of crowds as of that of sovereigns. Manifestations of this order can only proceed from the soul of crowds. The most absolute power of the most despotic monarch can scarcely do more than hasten or retard the moment of their apparition. The massacre of Saint Bartholomew or the religious wars were no more the work of kings than the Reign of Terror was the work of Robespierre, Danton, or Saint Just. At the bottom of such events is always to be found the working of the soul of the masses and never the power of potentates.

BOOK II

THE OPINIONS AND BELIEFS OF CROWDS.

CHAPTER I.

REMOTE FACTORS OF THE OPINIONS AND BELIEFS OF CROWDS.

Preparatory factors of the beliefs of crowds—The origin of the beliefs of crowds is the consequence of a preliminary process of elaboration—Study of the different factors of these beliefs. 1. *Race.* The predominating influence it exercises—It represents the suggestions of ancestors. 2.*Traditions.* They are the synthesis of the soul of the race--Social importance of traditions—How, after having been necessary, they become harmful—Crowds are the most obstinate maintainers of traditional ideas. 3. *Time.* It prepares in succession the establishment of beliefs and then their destruction. It is by the aid of this factor that order may proceed from chaos. 4. *Political and Social Institutions.* Erroneous idea of their part—Their influence extremely weak—They are effects, not causes—Nations are incapable of choosing what appear to them the best institutions—Institutions are labels which shelter the most dissimilar things under the same title--How institutions may come to be created —Certain institutions theoretically bad, such as centralization obligatory for certain nations. 5. *Institutions and education.* Falsity of prevalent ideas as to the influence of instruction on crowds—Statistical indications —Demoralizing effect of Latin system of education—Part instruction might play—Examples furnished by various peoples.

HAVING studied the mental constitution of crowds and become acquainted with their modes of feeling, thinking, and reasoning, we shall now proceed to examine how their opinions and beliefs arise and become established.

The factors which determine these opinions and beliefs are of two kinds: remote factors and immediate factors.

The remote factors are those which render crowds capable of adopting certain convictions and absolutely refractory to the acceptance of others. These factors prepare the ground in which are suddenly seen to germinate certain new ideas whose force and consequences are a cause of astonishment, though they are only spontaneous in appearance. The outburst and putting in practice of certain ideas among crowds present at times a startling suddenness. This is only a superficial effect, behind which must be sought a preliminary and preparatory action of long duration.

The immediate factors are those which, coming on the top of this long, preparatory working, in whose absence they would remain without effect, serve as the source of active persuasion on crowds; that is, they are the factors which cause the idea to take shape and set it loose with all its consequences. The resolutions by which collectivities are suddenly carried away arise out of these immediate factors; it is due to them that a riot breaks out or a strike is decided upon, and to them that enormous majorities invest one man with power to overthrow a government.

The successive action of these two kinds of factors is to be traced in all great historical events. The French Revolution—to cite but one of the most striking of such events—had among its remote factors the writings of the philosophers, the exactions of the nobility, and the progress of scientific thought. The mind of the masses, thus prepared, was then easily roused by such immediate factors as the speeches of orators, and the resistance of the court party to insignificant reforms.

Among the remote factors there are some of a general nature, which are found to underlie all the beliefs and opinions of crowds. They are race, traditions, time, institutions, and education. We now proceed to study the influence of these different factors.

1. RACE

This factor, race, must be placed in the first rank, for in itself it far surpasses in importance all the others. We have sufficiently studied it in another work; it is therefore needless to deal with it again. We showed, in a previous volume, what an historical race is, and how, its character once formed, it possesses, as the result of the laws of heredity such power that its beliefs, institutions, and arts—in a word, all the elements of its civilization—are merely the outward expression of its genius. We showed that the power of the race is Buck that no element can pass from one people to another without undergoing the most profound transformations.[1]

Environment, circumstances, and events represent the social suggestions of the moment. They may have a considerable influence, but this influence is always momentary if it be contrary to the suggestions of the race; that is, to those which are inherited by a nation from the entire series of its ancestors.

We shall have occasion in several of the chapters of this work to touch again upon racial influence, and to show that this influence is so great that it dominates the characteristics peculiar to the genius of crowds. It follows from this fact that the crowds of different countries offer very considerable differences of beliefs and conduct and are not to be influenced in the same manner.

2. TRADITIONS.

Traditions represent the ideas, the needs, and the sentiments of the past. They are the synthesis of the race, and weigh upon us with immense force.

The biological sciences have been transformed since embry-

---

1 The novelty of this proposition being still considerable and history being quite unintelligible without it, I devoted four chapters to its demonstration in my last book ("The Psychological Laws of the Evolution of Peoples"). From it the reader will see that, in spite of fallacious appearances, neither language, religion, arts, or, in a word, any element of civilizations, can pass, ill tact, from one people to another.

ology has shown the immense influence of the past on the evolution of living beings; and the historical sciences will not undergo a less change when this conception has become more widespread. As yet it is not sufficiently general, and many statesmen are still no further advanced than the theorists of the last century, who believed that a society could break off with its past and be entirely recast on lines suggested solely by the light of reason.

A people is an organism created by the past, and, like every other organism, it can only be modified by slow hereditary accumulations.

It is tradition that guides men, and more especially so when they are in a crowd. The changes they can effect in their traditions with any ease, merely bear, as I have often repeated, upon names and outward forms.

This circumstance is not to be regretted. Neither a national genius nor civilization would be possible without traditions. In consequence man's two great concerns since he has existed have been to create a network of traditions which he afterwards endeavors to destroy when their beneficial effects have worn themselves out. Civilizations is impossible without traditions, and progress impossible without the destruction of those traditions. The difficulty, and it is an immense difficulty, is to find a proper equilibrium between stability and variability. Should a people allow its customs to become too firmly rooted, it can no longer change, and becomes, like China, incapable of improvement. Violent revolutions are in this case of no avail; for what happens is that either the broken fragments of the chain are pieced together again and the past resumes its empire without change, or the fragments remain apart and decadence soon succeeds anarchy.

The ideal for a people is in consequence to preserve the institutions of the past, merely changing them insensibly and little by little. This ideal is difficult to realize. The Romans in ancient and the English in modern times are almost alone in having realized it.

It is precisely crowds that cling the most tenaciously to

traditional ideas and oppose their being changed with the most obstinacy. This is notably the case with the category of crowds constituting castes. I have already insisted upon the conservative spirit of crowds, and shown that the most violent rebellions merely end in a changing of words and terms. At the end of the last century, in the presence of destroyed churches, of priests expelled the country or guillotined, it might have been thought that the old religious ideas had lost all their strength, and yet a few years had barely lapsed before the abolished system of public worship had to be re-established in deference to universal demands. Blotted out for a moment, the old traditions had resumed their sway.

No example could better display the power of tradition on the mind of crowds. The most redoubtable idols do not dwell in temples, nor the most despotic tyrants in palaces; both the one and the other can be broken in an instant. But the invisible masters that reign in our innermost selves are safe from every effort at revolt, and only yield to the slow wearing away of centuries.

3. TIME.

In social as in biological problems time is one of the most energetic factors. It is the sole real creator and the sole great destroyer. It is time that has made mountains with grains of sand and raised the obscure cell of geological eras to human dignity. The action of centuries is sufficient to transform any given phenomenon. It has been justly observed that an ant with enough time at its disposal could level Mont Blanc. A being possessed of the magical force of varying time at his will would have the power attributed by believers to God.

1 The report of the ex-Conventionist, Fourcroy, quoted by Taine, is very clear on this point. 'What is everywhere seen with respect to the keeping of Sunday and attendance at the churches proves that the majority of Frenchmen desire to return to their old usages and that it is no longer opportune to resist this natural tendency. . . . The great majority of men stand in need of religion, public worship, and priests It is an error of some modern philosophers, by which I myself have been led away, to believe in the possibility of instruction being so general as to destroy religious prejudices, which for a great number of unfortunate persons are a source of consolation. . . . The mass of the people, then, must be allowed its priests, its altars, and its public worship."

In this place, however, we have only to concern ourselves with the influence of time on the genesis of the opinions of crowds. Its action from this point of view is still immense. Dependent upon it are the great forces such as race, which cannot form themselves without it. It causes the birth, the growth, and the death of all beliefs. It is by the aid of time that they acquire their strength and also by its aid that they lose it.

It is time in particular that prepares the opinions and beliefs of crowds, or at least the soil on which they will germinate. This is why certain ideas are realizable at one epoch and not at another. It is time that accumulates that immense detritus of beliefs and thoughts on which the ideas of a given period spring up. They do not grow at hazard and by chance; the roots of each of them strike down into a long past. When they blossom it is time that has prepared their blooming; and to arrive at a notion of their genesis it is always back in the past that it is necessary to search. They are the daughters of the past and the mothers of the future, but throughout the slaves of time.

Time, in consequence, is our veritable master, and it suffices to leave it free to act to see all things transformed. At the present day we are very uneasy with regard to the threatening aspirations of the masses and the destructions and upheavals foreboded thereby. Time, without other aid, will see to the restoration of equilibrium. "No form of government," M. Lavisse very properly writes, " was founded in a day. Political and social organizations are works that demand centuries. The feudal system existed for centuries in a shapeless, chaotic state before it found its laws; absolute monarchy also existed for centuries before arriving at regular methods of government, and these periods of expectancy were extremely troubled."

4. POLITICAL AND SOCIAL INSTITUTIONS.

The idea that institutions can remedy the defects of societies, that national progress is the consequence of the improvement of institutions and governments, and that social changes can be effected by decrees—this idea, I say, is still generally accepted. It was the starting-point of the French Revolution, and the social theories of the present day are based upon it.

The most continuous experience has been unsuccessful in shaking this grave delusion. Philosophers and historians have endeavored in vain to prove its absurdity, but yet they have had no difficulty in demonstrating that institutions are the outcome of ideas, sentiments, and customs, and that ideas, sentiments, and customs are not to be recast by recasting legislative codes. A nation does not choose its institutions at will any more than it chooses the color of its hair or its eyes. Institutions and governments are the product of the race. They are not the creators of an epoch, but are created by it. Peoples are not governed in accordance with their caprices of the moment, but as their character determines that they shall be governed. Centuries are required to form a political system and centuries needed to change it. Institutions have no intrinsic virtue: in themselves they are neither good nor bad. Those which are good at a given moment for a given people may be harmful in the extreme for another nation.

Moreover, it is in no way in the power of a people to really change its institutions. Undoubtedly, at the cost of violent revolutions, it can change their name, but in their essence they remain unmodified. The names are mere futile labels with which an historian who goes to the bottom of things need scarcely concern himself. It is in this way, for instance, that England[1] the most democratic country in the world, lives, nevertheless, under a monarchical regime whereas the countries in which the most oppressive despotism is rampant are the Spanish-American Republics, in spite of their republican constitutions. The destinies of peoples are determined by their character and not by their government. I have endeavored to

1 The most advanced republicans, even of the United States, recognize this fact. The American magazine, The Forum, recently gave categorical expression to the opinion in terms which I reproduce here from the Review of reviews for December, 1894 —
"It should never be forgotten, even by the most ardent enemies of an aristocracy, that England is today the most democratic country of the universe, the country in which the rights of tile individual are most respected, and in which to individual possesses the most liberty."

establish this view in my previous volume by setting forth categorical examples.

To lose time in the manufacture of cut-and-dried constitutions is, in consequence, a puerile task, the useless lab our of an ignorant rhetorician. Necessity and time undertake the charge of elaborating constitutions when we are wise enough to allow these two factors to act. This is the plan the Anglo-Saxons have adopted, as their great historian, Macaulay, teaches us in a passage that the politicians of all Latin countries ought to learn by heart. After having shown all the good than can be accomplished by laws which appear from the point of view of pure reason a chaos of absurdities and contradictions, he compares the scores of constitutions that have been engulfed in the convulsions of the Latin peoples with that of England, and points out that the latter has only been very slowly changed part by part, under the influence of immediate necessities and never of speculative reasoning.

"To think nothing of symmetry and much of convenience; never to remove an anomaly merely because it is an anomaly; never to innovate except when some grievance is felt; never to innovate except so far as to get rid of the grievance; never to lay down any proposition of wider extent than the particular case for which it is necessary to provide; these are the rules which have, from the age of John to the rise of Victoria, generally guided the deliberations of our two hundred and fifty Parliaments."

It would be necessary to take one by one the laws and institutions of each people to show to what extent they are the expression of the needs of each race and are incapable, for that reason, of being violently transformed. It is possible, for instance, to indulge in philosophical dissertations on the advantages and disadvantages of centralization; but when we see a people composed of very different races devote a thousand years of efforts to attaining to this centralization; when we observe that a great revolution, having for object the destruction of all the institutions of the past has been forced to respect this centralization, and has even strengthened it; under these circumstances we should admit that it is the outcome of imperious needs, that it is a condition of the existence of the nation in question, and we should pity the poor mental range of politicians who talk of destroying it. Could they by chance succeed in this attempt[1] their success would at once be the signal for a frightful civil war, which, moreover, would immediately bring back a new system of centralization much more oppressive than the old.

The conclusion to be drawn from what precedes is, that it is not in institutions that the means is to be sought of profoundly influencing the genius of the masses. When we see certain countries, such as the United States, reach a high degree of prosperity under democratic institutions, while others, such as the Spanish-American Republics, are found existing in a pitiable state of anarchy under absolutely similar institutions, we should admit that these institutions are as foreign to the greatness of the one as to the decadence of the others. Peoples are governed by their character, and all institutions which are not intimately model led on that character merely represent a borrowed garment, a transitory disguise. No doubt sanguinary wars and violent revolutions have been undertaken, and will continue to be undertaken, to impose institutions to which is attributed, as to the relics of saints, the supernatural power of creating welfare. It may be said, then, in one sense, that institutions react on the mind of the crowd in as much as they engender such upheavals. But in reality it is not the institutions that react in this manner, since we know that, whether triumphant or vanquished, they possess in themselves no virtue. It is illusions and words that have influenced the mind of the crowd, and especially words—

1 If a comparison be made between the profound religious and political dissensions which separate the various parties in France, and are more especially the result of social questions, and the separatist tendencies which were manifested at the time of the Revolution, and began to again display themselves towards the close of the Franco-German war, it will be seen that the different races represented in France are still far from being completely blended. The vigorous centra ligation of the Revolution and the creation of artificial departments destined to bring about the fusion of the ancient provinces was certainly its most useful work. Were it possible to bring about the decentralization which is today preoccupying minds lacking in foresight, the achievement would promptly have for consequence the most sanguinary disorders. To overlook this fact is to leave out of account the entire history of France.

words which are as powerful as they are chimerical, and whose astonishing sway we shall shortly demonstrate.

5. INSTRUCTION AND EDUCATION.

Foremost among the dominant ideas of the present epoch is to be found the notion that instruction is capable of considerably changing men, and has for its unfailing consequence to improve and even to make them equal. By the mere fact of its being constantly repeated, this assertion has ended by becoming one of the most steadfast democratic dogmas. It would be as difficult now to attack it as it would have been formerly to have at backed the dogmas of the Church.

On this point, however, as on many others, democratic ideas are in profound disagreement with the results of psychology and experience. Many eminent philosophers, among them Herbert Spencer, have had no difficulty in showing that instruction neither renders a man more moral nor happier, that it changes neither his instincts nor his hereditary passions, and that at times—for this to happen it need only be badly directed —it is much more pernicious than useful. Statisticians have brought confirmation of these views by telling us that criminality increases with the generalization of instruction, or at any rate of a certain kind of instruction, and that the worst enemies of society, the anarchists, are recruited among the prize-winners of schools; while in a recent work a distinguished magistrate, M. Adolphe Guillot, made the observation that at present 3,000 educated criminals are met with for every 1,000 illiterate delinquents, and that in fifty years the criminal percentage of the population has passed from 227 to 552 for every 100,000 inhabitants, an increase of 133 percent. He has also noted in common with his colleagues that criminality is particularly on the increase among young persons, for whom, as is known, gratuitous and obligatory schooling has— in France—replaced apprenticeship.

It is not assuredly—and nobody has ever maintained this proposition—that well-directed instruction may not give very useful practical results, if not in the sense of raising the standard of morality, at least in that of developing professional capacity. Unfortunately the Latin peoples, especially in the last twenty-five years, have based their systems of instruction on very erroneous principles, and in spite of the observations of the most eminent minds, such as Breal, Fustel de Coulanges, Taine, and many others, they persist in their lamentable mistakes. I have myself shown, in a work published some time ago, that the French system of education transforms the majority of those who have undergone it into enemies of society, and recruits numerous disciples for the worst forms of socialism.

The primary danger of this system of education—very properly qualified as Latin—consists in the fact that it is based on the fundamental psychological error that the intelligence is developed by the learning by heart of textbooks. Adopting this view, the endeavor your has been made to enforce a knowledge of as many handbooks as possible. From the primary school till he leaves the university a young man does nothing but acquire books by heart without his judgement or personal initiative being ever called into play. Education consists for him in reciting by heart and obeying.

"Learning lessons, knowing by heart a grammar or a compendium, repeating well and imitating well—that," writes a former Minister of Public Instruction, M. Jules Simon, "is a ludicrous form of education whose every effort is an act of faith tacitly admitting the infallibility of the master, and whose only results are a belittling of ourselves and a rendering of us impotent."

Were this education merely useless, one might confine one's self to expressing compassion for the unhappy children who, instead of making needful studies at the primary school, are instructed in the genealogy of the sons of Clotaire, the conflicts between Neustria and Austrasia, or zoological classifications. But the system presents a far more serious danger. It gives those who have been submitted to it a violent dislike to the state of life in which they were born, and an intense desire to escape from it. The working man no longer wishes to remain a working man, or the peasant to continue a peasant, while the most humble members of the middle classes admit of no possible career for their sons except that of State-paid functionaries. Instead of preparing men for life French schools solely prepare them to occupy public functions, in which success can be attained without any necessity for self-direction or the exhibition of the least glimmer of personal initiative. At the bottom of the social ladder the system creates an army of proletarians discontented with their lot and always ready to revolt, while at the summit it brings into being a frivolous bourgeoisie, at once skeptical and credulous, having a superstitious confidence in the State, whom it regards as a sort of Providence, but without forgetting to display towards it a ceaseless hostility, always laying its own faults to the door of the Government, and incapable of the least enterprise without the intervention of the authorities.

The State, which manufactures by dint of textbooks all these persons possessing diplomas, can only utilize a small number of them, and is forced to leave the others without employment. It is obliged in consequence to resign itself to feeding the first-mentioned and to having the others as its enemies. From the top to the bottom of the social pyramid, from the humblest clerk to the professor and the prefect, the immense mass of persons boasting diplomas besiege the professions. While a business man has the greatest difficulty in finding an agent to represent him in the colonies, thousands of candidates solicit the most modest official posts. There are 20,000 schoolmasters and mistresses without employment in the department of the Seine alone, all of them persons who, disdaining the fields

1 This phenomenon, moreover, is not peculiar to the Latin peoples. It is also to be observed in China, which is also a country in the hands of a solid hierarchy of mandarins or functionaries, and where a function is obtained, as in France, by competitive examination, in educating purposes, as is the case in England itself, but simply to furnish the indigenous inhabitants with instruction, there has been formed a special class of educated persons, the Baboos, who, when they do not obtain employment, become the irreconcilable enemies of the English rule. In the case of all the Baboos, whether provided with employment or not, the first effect of their instruction has been to lower their standard of morality. This is a fact on which I have insisted at length in my book, " The Civilizations of India"—a fact, too, which has been observed by all authors who have visited the great peninsula.

or the workshops, look to the State for their livelihood. The number of the chosen being restricted, that of the discontented is perforce immense. The latter are ready for any revolution, whoever be its chiefs and whatever the goal they aim at. The acquisition of knowledge for which no use can be found is a sure method of driving a man to revolt.

It is evidently too late to retrace our steps. Experience alone, that supreme educator of peoples, will be at pains to show us our mistake. It alone will be powerful enough to prove the necessity of replacing our odiuos textbooks and our pitiable examinations by industrial instruction capale of inducing our young men to return to the fields, to the workshop, and to the colonial enterprise which they avoid today at all costs.

The professional instruction which all enlightened minds are now demanding was the instruction received in the past by our forefathers. It is still in vigor at the present day among the nations who rule the world by their force of will, their initiative, and their spirit of enterprise. In a series of remarkable pages, whose principal passages I reproduce further on, a great thinker, M. Taine, has clearly shown that our former system of education was approximately that in vogue today in England and America, and in a remarkable parallel between the Latin and Anglo-Saxon systems he has plainly pointed out the consequences of the two methods.

One might consent, perhaps, at a pinch, to continue to accept all the disadvantages of our classical education, although it produced nothing but discontented men, and men unfitted for their station in life, did the superficial acquisition of so much knowledge, the faultless repeating by heart of so many textbooks, raise the level of intelligence. But does it really raise this level? Alas no! The conditions of success in life are the possession of judgment, experience, initiative, and character qualities which are not bestowed by books. Books are dictionaries, which it is useful to consult, but of which it is perfectly useless to have lengthy portions in one's head. How is it possible for professional instruction to develop the intelligence in a measure quite beyond the reach of classical instructions This has been well shown by M. Taine. "Ideas," he says, "are only formed in their natural and normal surroundings; the promotion of the growth is effected by the innumerable impressions appealing to the senses which a young man receives daily in the workshop, the mine, the law court, the study, the builder's yard, the hospital; at the sight of tools, materials, and operations; in the presence of customers, workers, and lab our, of work well or ill done, costly or lucrative. In such a way are obtained those trifling perceptions of detail of the eyes, the ear, the hands, and even the sense of smell, which, picked up involuntarily, and silently elaborated, take shape within the learner, and suggest to him sooner or later this or that new combination, simplification, economy, improvement, or invention. The young Frenchman is deprived, and precisely at the age when they are most fruitful, of all these precious contacts, of all these indispensable elements of assimilation. For seven or eight years on end he is shut up in a school, and is cut off from that direct personal experience which would give him a keen and exact notion of men and things and of the various ways of handling them."

" . . . At least nine out of ten have wasted their time and pains during several years of their life—telling, important, even decisive years. Among such are to be counted, first of all, the half or two-thirds of those who present themselves for examination—I refer to those who are rejected; and then among those who are successful, who obtain a degree, a certificate, a diploma, there is still a half or two-thirds—I refer to the overworked. Too much has been demanded of them by exacting that on a given day, on a chair or before a board, they should, for two hours in succession, and with respect to a group of sciences, be living repertories of all human knowledge. In point of fact they were that, or nearly so, for two hours on that particular day, but a month later they are so no longer. They could not go through the examination again. Their too numerous and too burdensome acquisitions slip incessantly from their mind, and are not replaced. Their mental vigor has declined, their fertile capacity for growth has dried up, the fully-developed man appears, and he is often a used-up man. Settled down, married, resigned to turning in a circle, and indefinitely in the same circle, he shuts himself up in his confined function, which he fulfils adequately, but nothing more. Such is the average yield; assuredly the receipts do not balance the expenditure. In England or America, where, as in France previous to 1789, the contrary proceeding is adopted, the outcome obtained is equal or superior."

The illustrious psychologist subsequently shows us the difference between our system and that of the Anglo-Saxons. The latter do not possess our innumerable special schools. With them instruction is not based on book-learning, but on object lessons. The engineer, for example, is trained in a workshop, and never at a school, a method which allows of each individual reaching the level his intelligence permits of. He becomes a workman or a foreman if he can get no further, an engineer if his aptitudes take him as far. This manner of proceeding is much more democratic and of much greater benefit to society than that of making the whole career of an individual depend on an examination, lasting a few hours, and undergone at the age of nineteen or twenty.

"In the hospital, the mine, the factory, in the architect's or the lawyer's office, the student, who makes a start while very young, goes through his apprenticeship, stage by stage, much as does with us a law clerk in his office, or an artist in his studio. Previously, and before making a practical beginning, he has had an opportunity of following some general and summary course of instruction, so as to have a framework ready prepared in which to store the observations he is shortly to make. Furthermore he is able, as a rule, to avail himself of sundry technical courses which he can follow in his leisure hours, so as to coordinate step by step the daily experience he is gathering. Under such a system the practical capabilities increase and develop of themselves in exact proportion to the faculties of the student, and in the direction requisite for his future task and the special work for which from now onwards he desires to fit himself. By this means in England or the

United States a young man is quickly in a position to develop his capacity to the utmost. At twenty-five years of age, and much sooner if the material and the parts are there, he is not merely a useful performer, he is capable also of spontaneous enterprise; he is not only a part of a machine, but also a motor. In France, where the contrary system prevails—in France, which with each succeeding generation is falling more and more into line with China—the sum total of the wasted forces is enormous."

The great philosopher arrives at the following conclusion with respect to the growing incongruity between our Latin system of education and the requirements of practical life:—

"In the three stages of instruction, those of childhood, adolescence and youth, the theoretical and pedagogic preparation by books on the school benches has lengthened out and become overcharged in view of the examination, the degree, the diploma, and the certificate, and solely in this view, and by the worst methods, by the application of an unnatural and anti-social *régime,* by the excessive postponement of the practical apprenticeship, by our boarding-school system, by artificial training and mechanical cramming, by overwork, without thought for the time that is to follow, for the adult age and the functions of the man, without regard for the real world on which the young man will shortly be thrown, for the society in which we move and to which he must be adapted or be taught to resign himself in advance, for the struggle in which humanity is engaged, and in which to defend himself and to keep his footing he ought previously to have been equipped, armed, trained, and hardened. This indispensable equipment, this acquisition of more importance than any other, this sturdy common sense and nerve and will-power our schools do not procure the young Frenchman; on the contrary, far from qualifying him for his approaching and definite state, they disqualify him. In consequence, his entry into the world and his first steps in the field of action are most often merely a succession of painful falls, whose effect is that he long remains wounded and bruised, and sometimes disabled for life. The test is severe and dangerous. In the course of it the mental and moral equilibrium is affected, and runs the risk of not being re-established. Too sudden and complete disillusion has supervened. The deceptions have been too great, the disappointments too keen." [1]

Have we digressed in what precedes from the psychology of crowds? Assuredly not. If we desire to understand the ideas and beliefs that are germinating today in the masses, and will spring up tomorrow, it is necessary to know how the ground has been prepared. The instruction given the youth of a country allows of a knowledge of what that country will one day be. The education accorded the present generation justifies the most gloomy previsions. It is in part by instruction and education that the mind of the masses is improved or deteriorated. It was necessary in consequence to show how this mind has been fashioned by the system in vogue, and how the mass of the indifferent and the neutral has become progressively an army of the discontented ready to obey all the suggestions of utopians and rhetoricians. It is in the schoolroom that socialists and anarchists are found nowadays, and that the way is being paved for the approaching period of decadence for the Latin peoples.

---

1 Taine, "Le Regime moderne," vol. ii., 1894. These pages are almost the last that Taine wrote. They resume admirably the results of the great philosopher's long experience. Unfortunately they are in my opinion totally incomprehensible for such of our university professors who have not lived abroad. Education is the only means at our disposal of influencing to some extent the mind of a nation, and it is profoundly saddening to have to think that there is scarcely anyone in France who can arrive at understanding that our present system of teaching is a grave cause of rapid decadence which instead of elevating our youth, lowers and perverts it.

A useful comparison may be made between Taine's pages and the observations on American education recently made by M. Paul Bourget in his excellent book, " Outre-Mer." He, too, after having noted that our education merely produces narrow-minded bourgeois, lacking in initiative and will-power, or anarchists—"those two equally harmful types of the civilized man, who degenerates into impotent platitude or insane destructiveness"—he too, I say draws a comparison that cannot be the object of too much reduction between our French *lycees* (public schools), those factories of degeneration, and the American schools, which prepare a man admirably for life. The gulf existing between truly democratic nations and those who have democracy in their speeches, but in no wise in their thoughts, is clearly brought out in this comparison.

CHAPTER II.

THE IMMEDIATE FACTORS OF THE OPINIONS OF CROWDS.

1. *Images, words, and formulae.* The magical power of words and formulae—The power of words bound up with the images they evoke, and independent of their real sense –These images vary from age to age, and from race to race—The wear and tear of words—Examples of the considerable variations of sense of much-used words—The political utility of baptizing old things with new names when the words by which they were designated produced an unfavorable impression on the masses—Variations of the sense of words in consequence of race differences—The different meanings of the word "democracy" in Europe and America. 2. *Illusions.* Their importance –They are to be found at the root of all civilizations—The social necessity of illusions—Crowds always prefer them to truths. 3. *Experience.* Experience alone can fix in the mind of crowds truths become necessary and destroy illusions grown dangerous—Experience is only effective on the condition that it be frequently repeated –The cost of the experiences requisite to persuade crowds. 4. *Reason.* The nullity of its influence on crowds –Crowds only to be influenced by their unconscious sentiments—The rôle of logic in history—The secret causes of improbable events.

WE have just investigated the remote and preparatory factors which give the mind of crowds a special receptivity, and make possible therein the growth of certain sentiments and certain ideas. It now remains for us to study the factors capable of acting in a direct manner. We shall see in a forthcoming chapter how these factors should be put in force in order that they may produce their full effect.

In the first part of this work we studied the sentiments, ideas, and methods of reasoning of collective bodies, and from the knowledge thus acquired it would evidently be possible to deduce in a general way the means of making an impression on their mind. We already know what strikes the imagination of crowds, and are acquainted with the power and contagiousness of suggestions, of those especially that are presented under the form of images. However, as suggestions may proceed from very different sources, the factors capable of acting on the minds of crowds may differ considerably. It is necessary, then, to study them separately. This is not a useless study. Crowds are somewhat like the sphinx of ancient fable: it is necessary to arrive at a solution of the problems offered by their psychology or to resign ourselves to being devoured by them.

1. IMAGES, WORDS, AND FORMULAS.

When studying the imagination of crowds we saw that it is particularly open to the impressions produced by images. These images do not always lie ready to hand, but it is possible to evoke them by the judicious employment of words and formulas. Handled with art, they possess in sober truth the mysterious power formerly attributed to them by the adepts of magic. They cause the birth in the minds of crowds of the most formidable tempests, which in turn they are capable of stilling. A pyramid far loftier than that of old Cheops could be raised merely with the bones of men who have been victims of the power of words and formulas.

The power of words is bound up with the images they evoke, and is quite independent of their real significance. Words whose sense is the most ill-defined are sometimes those that possess the most influence. Such, for example, are the terms democracy, socialism, equality, liberty, etc., whose meaning is so vague that bulky volumes do not suffice to precisely fix it. Yet it is certain that a truly magical power is attached to those short syllables, as if they contained the solution of all problems. They synthesize the most diverse unconscious aspirations and the hope of their realization.

Reason and arguments are incapable of combatting certain words and formulas. They are uttered with solemnity in the presence of crowds, and as soon as they have been pronounced an expression of respect is visible on every countenance, and all heads are bowed. By many they are considered as natural forces, as supernatural powers. They evoke grandiose and vague images in men's minds, but this very vagueness that wraps them in obscurity augments their mysterious power. They are the mysterious divinities hidden behind the tabernacle, which the devout only approach in fear and trembling.

The images evoked by words being independent of their sense, they vary from age to age and from people to people, the formulas remaining identical. Certain transitory images are attached to certain words: the word is merely as it were the button of an electric bell that calls them up.

All words and all formulas do not possess the power of evoking images, while there are some which have once had this power, but lose it in the course of use, and cease to waken any response in the mind. They then become vain sounds, whose principal utility is to relieve the person who employs them of the obligation of thinking. Armed with a small stock of formulas and commonplaces learned while we are young, we possess all that is needed to traverse life without the tiring necessity of having to reflect on anything whatever.

If any particular language be studied, it is seen that the words of which it is composed change rather A lowly in the course of ages, while the images these words evoke or the meaning attached to them changes cease-lessly. This is the reason why, in another work, I have arrived at the conclusion that the absolute translation of a language, especially of a dead language, is totally impossible. What do we do in reality when we substitute a French for a Latin, Greek, or Sanscrit expression, or even when we endeavor to understand a book written in our own tongue two or three centuries back We merely put the images and ideas with which modern life has endowed our intelligence in the place of absolutely distinct notions and images which ancient life had brought into being in the mind of races submitted to conditions of existence having no analogy with our own. When the men of the Revolution imagined they were copying the Greeks and Romans, what were they doing except giving to ancient words a sense the latter had never had? What resemblance can possibly exist between the institutions of the Greeks and those designated today by corresponding words? A republic at that epoch was an essentially aristocratic institution, formed of a reunion of petty despots ruling over a crowd of slaves kept in the most absolute subjection. These communal aristocracies, based on slavery, could not have existed for a moment without it.

The word "liberty," again, what signification could it have in any way resembling that we attribute to it today at a period when the possibility of the liberty of thought was not even suspected, and when there was no greater and more exceptional crime than that of discussing the gods, the laws and the customs of the ? What did such a word as "fatherland" signify to an Athenian or Spartan unless it were the cult of Athens or Sparta, and in no wise that of Greece, composed of rival cities always at war with each other? What meaning had the same word " fatherland " among the ancient Gauls, divided into rival tribes and races, and possessing different languages and religions, and who were easily vanquished by Caesar because he always found allies among theme It was Rome that made a country of Gaul by endowing it with political and religious unity. Without going back so far, scarcely two centuries ago, is it to be believed that this same notion of a fatherland was conceived to have the same meaning as at present by French princes like the great Conde, who allied themselves with the foreigner against their sovereign. And yet again, the same word had it not a sense very different from the modern for the French royalist emigrants, who thought they obeyed the laws of honor in fighting against France, and who from their point of view did indeed obey them, since the feudal law bound the vassal to the lord and not to the soil, so that where the sovereign was there was the true fatherland?

Numerous are the words whose meaning has thus profoundly changed from age to age--words which we can only arrive at understanding in the sense in which they were formerly understood after a long effort. It has been said with truth that much study is necessary merely to arrive at conceiving what was signified to our great grandfathers by such words as the "king" and the "royal family." What, then, is likely to be the case with terms still more complex.

Words, then, have only mobile and transitory significations which change from age to age and people to people; and when we desire to exert an influence by their means on the crowd what it is requisite to know is the meaning given them by the crowd at a given moment, and not the meaning which they formerly had or may yet have for individuals of a different mental constitution.

Thus, when crowds have come, as the result of political upheavals or changes of belief, to acquire a profound antipathy for the images evoked by certain words, the first duty of the true statesman is to change the words without, of course, laying hands on the things themselves, the latter being too intimately bound up with the inherited constitution to be transformed. The judicious Tocqueville long ago made the remark that the work of the consulate and the empire consisted more particularly in the clothing with new words of the greater part of the institutions of the past--that is to say, in replacing words evoking disagreeable images in the imagination of the crowd by other words of which the novelty prevented such evocations. The "tattle" or tall age has become the land tax; the "gabells," the tax on salt; the " aids," the indirect contributions and the consolidated duties; the tax on trade companies and guilds, the license! etc.

One of the most essential functions of statesmen consists, then, in baptizing with popular or, at any rate, indifferent words things the crowd cannot endure under their old names. The power of words is so great that it suffices to designate in well-chosen terms the most odious things to make them acceptable to crowds. Taine justly observes that it was by invoking liberty and fraternity--words very popular at the time--that the Jacobians were able " to install a despotism worthy of Dahomey, a tribunal similar to that of the Inquisition, and to accomplish human hecatombs akin to those of ancient Mexico." The art of those who govern, as is the case with the art of advocates, consists above all in the science of employing words. One of the greatest difficulties of this art is, that in one and the same society the same words most often have very different meanings for the different social classes, who employ in appearance the same words, but never speak the same language.

In the preceding examples it is especially time that has been made to intervene as the principal factor in the changing of the meaning of words. If, however, we also make race intervene, we shall then see that, at the same period, among peoples equally civilized but of different race, the same words very often correspond to extremely dissimilar ideas. It is impossible to understand these differences without having travel led much, and for this reason I shall not insist upon them. I shall confine myself to observing that it is precisely the words most often employed by the masses which among different peoples possess the most different meanings. Such is the case, for instance, with the words "democracy" and "socialism" in such frequent use nowadays.

In reality they correspond to quite contrary ideas and images in the Latin and Anglo-Saxon mind. For the Latin peoples the word "democracy" signifies more especially the subordination of the will and the initiative of the individual to the will and the initiative of the community represented by the State. It is the State that is charged, to a greater and greater degree, with the direction of everything, the centralization, the monopoliza-tion, and the manufacture of everything. To the State it is that all parties without exception, radicals, socialists, or monar-chists, constantly appeal. Among the Anglo-Saxons and notably in America this same word "democracy" signifies, on the contrary, the intense development of the will of the individual, and as complete a subordination as possible of the State, which, with the exception of the police, the army, and diplomatic relations, is not allowed the direction of anything, not even of public instruction. It is seen, then, that the same word which signifies for one people the subordination of the will and the initiative of the individual and the preponderance of the State, signifies for another the excessive development of the will and the initiative of the individual and the complete subordination of the State. [1]

2. ILLUSIONS

From the dawn of civilization onwards crowds have always undergone the influence of illusions. It is to the creators of illusions that they have raised more temples, statues, and altars than to any other class of men. Whether it be the religious illusions of the past or the philosophic and social illusions of the present, these formidable sovereign powers are always found at the head of all the civilizations that have successively flourished on our planet. It is in their name that were built the temples of Chaldea and Egypt and the religious edifices of the Middle Ages, and that a vast upheaval shook the whole of Europe a century ago, and there is not one of our political, artistic, or social conceptions that is free from their powerful impress. Occasionally, at the cost of terrible disturbances, man overthrows them, but he seems condemned to always set them up again. Without them he would never have emerged from his primitive barbarian state, and without them again he would soon return to it. Doubtless they are futile shadows; but these children of our dreams have forced the nations to create whatever the arts may boast of splendor or civilizations of greatness.

"If one destroyed in museums and libraries, if one hurled down on the flagstones before the churches all the works and all the monuments of art that religions have inspired, what

1 In my book, " The Psychological Laws of the Evolution of Peoples," I have insisted at length on the differences which distinguish the Latin democratic ideal from the Anglo-Saxon democratic ideal. Independently, and as the result of his travels, M. Paul Bourget has arrived, in his quite recent book, " Outre-Mer," at conclusions almost identical with mine.

would remain of the great dreams of humanity? To give to men that portion of hope and illusion without which they cannot live, such is the reason for the existence of gods, heroes, and poets. During fifty years science appeared to undertake this task. But science has been compromised in hearts hungering after the ideal, because it does not dare to be lavish enough of promises, because it cannot lie." [1]

The philosophers of the last century devoted themselves with fervor to the destruction of the religious, political, and social illusions on which our forefathers had lived for a long tale of centuries. By destroying them they have dried up the springs of hope and resignation. Behind the immolated chimeras they came face to face with the blind and silent forces of nature, which are inexorable to weakness and ignore pity.

Notwithstanding all its progress, philosophy has been unable as yet to offer the masses any ideal that can charm them; but, as they must have their illusions at all cost, they turn instinctively, as the insect seeks the light, to the rhetoricians who accord them what they want. Not truth, but error has always been the chief factor in the evolution of nations, and the reason why socialism is so powerful today is that it constitutes the last illusion that is still vital. In spite of all scientific demonstrations it continues on the increase. Its principal strength lies in the fact that it is championed by minds sufficiently ignorant of things as they are in reality to venture boldly to promise mankind happiness. The social illusion reigns today upon all the heaped-up ruins of the past, and to it belongs the future. The masses have never thirsted after truth. They turn aside from evidence that is not to their taste, preferring to deify error, if error seduce them. Whoever can supply them with illusions is easily their master; whoever attempts to destroy their illusions is always their victim.

1 Daniel Lesueur.

3. EXPERIENCE.

Experience constitutes almost the only effective process by which a truth may be solidly established in the mind of the masses, and illusions grown too dangerous be destroyed. To this end, however, it is necessary that the experience should take place on a very large scale, and be very frequently repeated. The experiences undergone by one generation are useless, as a rule, for the generation that follows, which is the reason why historical facts, cited with a view to demonstration, serve no purpose. Their only utility is to prove to what an extent experiences need to be repeated from age to age to exert any influence, or to be successful in merely shaking an erroneous opinion when it is solidly implanted in the mind of the masses.

Our century and that which preceded it will doubtless be alluded to by historians as an era of curious experiments, which in no other age have been tried in such number.

The most gigantic of these experiments was the French Revolution. To find out that a society is not to be refashioned from top to bottom in accordance with the dictates of pure reason, it was necessary that several millions of men should be massacred and that Europe should be profoundly disturbed for a period of twenty years. To prove to us experimentally that dictators cost the nations who acclaim them dear, two ruinous experiences have been required in fifty years, and in spite of their clearness they do not seem to have been sufficiently convincing. The first, nevertheless, cost three millions of men and an invasion, the second involved a loss of territory, and carried in its wake the necessity for permanent armies. A third was almost attempted riot long since, and will assuredly be attempted one day. To bring an entire nation to admit that the huge German army was not, as was currently alleged thirty years ago, a sort of harmless national guard, the terrible war which cost us so dear had to take place. To bring about the recognition that Protection ruins the nations who adopt it, at least twenty years of disastrous experience will be needful.

4. REASON.

In enumerating the factors capable of making an impression on the minds of crowds all mention of reason might be dispensed with, were it not necessary to point out the negative value of its influence.

We have already shown that crowds are not to be influenced by reasoning, and can only comprehend rough-and-ready associations of ideas. The orators who know how to make an impression upon them always appeal in consequence to their sentiments and never to their reason.[2] The laws of logic have no action on crowds. To bring home conviction to crowds it is necessary first of all to thoroughly comprehend the sentiments by which they are animated, to pretend to share these sentiments, then to endeavor to modify them by calling up, by

1 The opinion of the crowd was formed in this case by those rough-and-ready associations of dissimilar things, the mechanism of which I have previously explained. The French national guard of that period, being composed of peaceable shopkeepers, utterly lacking in discipline and quite incapable of being taken seriously, whatever bore a similar name, evoked the same conception and was considered in consequence as harmless. The error of the crowd was shared at the time by its leaders, as happens so often in connection with opinions dealing with generalizations. In a speech made in the Chamber on the 31st of December, 1867, and quoted in a book by M. E. Ollivier that has appeared recently, a states-men who often followed the opinion of the crowd but was never in advance of it--I allude to M. Thiers--declared that Prussia only possessed a national guard analogous to that of France, and in consequence without importance, in addition to a regular army about equal to the French regular army; assertions about as accurate as the predictions of the same statesman as to the insignificant future reserved for railways.

2 My first observations with regard to the art of impressing crowds and touching the slight assistance to be derived in this connection from the rules of logic date back to the siege of Paris, to the day when I saw conducted to the Louvre, where the Government was then sitting, Marshal V--, whom a furious crowd asserted they had surprised in the act of taking the plans of the fortifications to sell them to the Prussians. A member of the Government (G. P--), a very celebrated orator, came out to harangue the crowd, which was demanding the immediate execution of the prisoner. I had expected that the speaker would point out the absurdity of the accusation by remarking that the accused Marshal was positively one of those who had constructed the fortifications, the plan of which, more-over, was on sale at every bookseller's. To my immense stupefaction--I was very young men--the speech was on quite different lines. " Justice shall be done," exclaimed the orator, advancing towards the prisoner, " and pitiless justice. Let the Government of the National Defence conclude your inquiry. In the meantime we will keep the prisoner in custody." At once calmed by this apparent concession, the crowd broke up, and a quarter of an hour later the Marshal was able to return home. He would infallibly have been torn in pieces had the speaker treated the infuriated crowd to the logical arguments that my extreme youth induced me to consider as very convincing

means of rudimentary associations, certain eminently suggestive notions, to be capable, if need be, of going back to the
point of view from which a start was made, and, above all, to
divine from instant to instant the sentiments to which one's
discourse is giving birth. This necessity of ceaselessly varying
one's language in accordance with the effect produced at the
moment of speaking deprives from the outset a prepared and
studied harangue of all efficaciousness. In such a speech the
orator follows his own line of thought, not that of his hearers,
and from this fact alone his influence is annihilated.

Logical minds, accustomed to be convinced by a chain of
somewhat close reasoning, cannot avoid having recourse to
this mode of persuasion when addressing crowds, and the
inability of their arguments always surprises them. "The usual
mathematical consequences based on the syllogism--that is, on
associations of identities--are imperative . . ." writes a logician.
" This imperativeness would enforce the assent even of an
inorganic mass were it capable of following associations of
identities." This is doubtless true, but a crowd is no more
capable than an inorganic mass of following such associations,
nor even of understanding them. If the attempt be made to
convince by reasoning primitive minds--savages or children,
for instance--the slight value possessed by this method of
arguing will be understood. It is not even necessary to descend
so low as primitive beings to obtain an insight into the utter
powerlessness of reasoning when it has to fight against
sentiment. Let us merely call to mind how tenacious, for
centuries long, have been religious superstitions in contradiction with the simplest logic. For nearly two thousand years the
most luminous geniuses have bowed before their laws, and
modern times have to be reached for their veracity to be merely
contested. The Middle Ages and the Renaissance possessed
many enlightened men, but not a single man who attained by
reasoning to an appreciation of the childish side of his
superstitions, or who promulgated even a slight doubt as to the
misdeeds of the devil or the necessity of burning sorcerers.

Should it be regretted that crowds are never guided by

reason? We would not venture to affirm it. Without a doubt human reason would not have availed to spur humanity along the path of civilization with the ardor and hardihood its illusions have done. These illusions, the offspring of those unconscious forces by which we are led, were doubtless necessary. Every race carries in its mental constitution the laws of its destiny, and it is, perhaps, these laws that it obeys with a resist less impulse, even in the case of those of its impulses which apparently are the most unreasoned. It seems at times as if nations were submitted to secret forces analogous to those which compel the acorn to transform itself into an oak or a comet to follow its orbit.

What little insight we can get into these forces must be sought for in the general course of the evolution of a people, and not in the isolated facts from which this evolution appears at times to proceed. Were these facts alone to be taken into consideration, history would seem to be the result of a series of improbable chances. It was improbable that a Galilean carpenter should become for two thousand years an all-powerful God in whose name the most important civilizations were founded; improbable, too, that a few bands of Arabs, emerging from their deserts, should conquer the greater part of the old Greeco-Roman world, and establish an empire greater than that of Alexander; improbable, again, that in Europe, at an advanced period of its development, and when authority throughout it had been systematically hierarchized, an obscure lieutenant of artillery should have succeeded in reigning over a multitude of peoples and kings.

Let us leave reason, then, to philosophers, and not insist too strongly on its intervention in the governing of men. It is not by reason, but most often in spite of it, that are created those sentiments that are the main-springs of all civilization--sentiments such as honor, self-sacrifice, religious faith, patriotism, and the love of glory.

CHAPTER III.

LEADERS OF CROWDS AND THEIR MEANS OF PERSUASION

WE are now acquainted with the mental constitution of crowds, and we also know what are the motives capable of making an impression on their mind. It remains to investigate how these motives may be set in action, and by whom they may usefully be turned to practical account.

1. THE LEADERS OF CROWDS

As soon as a certain number of living beings are gathered together, whether they be animals or men, they place themselves instinctively under the authority of a chief. In the case of human crowds the chief is often nothing more than a ringleader or agitator, but as such he plays a considerable part. His will is the nucleus around which the opinions of the crowd are grouped and attain to identity. He constitutes the first element towards the organization of heterogeneous crowds, and paves the way for their organization in sects; in the meantime he directs them. A crowd is a servile flock that is incapable of ever doing without a master.

The leader has most often started as one of the led. He has himself been hypnotized by the idea, whose apostle he has since become. It has taken possession of him to such a degree that everything outside it vanishes, and that every contrary opinion appears to him an error or a superstition. An example in point is Robespierre, hypnotized by the philosophical ideas of Rousseau, and employing the methods of the inquisition to propagate them.

The leaders we speak of are more frequently men of action than thinkers. They are not gifted with keen foresight, nor could they be, as this quality generally conduces to doubt and inactivity. They are especially recruited from the ranks of those morbidly nervous, excitable, half-deranged persons who are bordering on madness. However absurd may be the idea they uphold or the goal they pursue, their convictions are so strong that all reasoning is lost upon them. Contempt and persecution do not affect them, or only serve to excite them the more. They sacrifice their personal interest, their family—everything. The very instinct of self-preservation is entirely obliterated in them, and so much so that often the only recompense they solicit is that of martyrdom. The intensity of their faith gives great power of suggestion to their words. The multitude is always ready to listen to the strong-willed man, who knows how to impose himself upon it. Men gathered in a crowd lose all force of will, and turn instinctively to the person who possesses the quality they lack.

Nations have never lacked leaders, but all of the latter have by no means been animated by those strong convictions proper to apostles. These leaders are often subtle rhetoricians, seeking only their own personal interest, and endeavoring to persuade by flattering base instincts. The influence they can assert in this manner may be very great, but it is always ephemeral. The men of ardent convictions who have stirred the soul of crowds, the Peter the Hermits, the Luthers, the Savonarolas, the men of the French Revolution, have only exercised their fascination after having been themselves fascinated first of all by a creed. They are then able to call up in the souls of their fellows that formidable force known as faith, which renders a man the absolute slave of his dream. The arousing of faith—whether religious, political, or social, whether faith in a work, in a person, or an idea—has always been the function of the great leaders of crowds, and it is on this account that their influence is always very great. Of all the forces at the disposal of humanity, faith has always been one of the most tremendous, and the gospel rightly attributes to it the power of moving mountains. To endow a man with faith is to multiply his strength tenfold. The great events of history have been brought about by obscure believers, who have had little beyond their faith in their favor. It is not by the aid of the learned or of philosophers, and still less of skeptics, that have been built up the great religions which have swayed the world, or the vast empires which have spread from one hemisphere to the other.

In the cases just cited, however, we are dealing with great leaders, and they are so few in number that history can easily reckon them up. They form the summit of a continuous series, which extends from these powerful masters of men down to the workman who, in the smoky atmosphere of an inn, slowly fascinates his comrades by ceaselessly drumming into their ears a few set phrases, whose purport he scarcely comprehends, but the application of which, according to him, must surely bring about the realization of all dreams and of every hope.

In every social sphere, from the highest to the lowest, as soon as a man ceases to be isolated he speedily falls under the influence of a leader. The majority of men, especially among the masses, do not possess clear and reasoned ideas on any subject whatever outside their own speciality. The leader serves them as guide. It is just possible that he may be replaced, though very inefficiently, by the periodical publications which manufacture opinions for their readers and supply them with ready-made phrases which dispense them of the trouble of reasoning.

The leaders of crowds wield a very despotic authority, and this despotism indeed is a condition of their obtaining a following. It has often been remarked how easily they extort obedience, although without any means of backing up their authority, from the most turbulent section of the working classes. They fix the hours of labor and the rate of wages, and they decree strikes, which are begun and ended at the hour they ordain.

At the present day these leaders and agitators tend more and more to usurp the place of the public authorities in proportion as the latter allow themselves to be called in question and shorn of their strength. The tyranny of these new masters has for result that the crowds obey them much more docilely than they have obeyed any government. If in consequence of some accident or other the leaders should be removed from the scene the crowd returns to its original state of a collectivity without cohesion or force of resistance. During the last strike of the Parisian omnibus employes the arrest of the two leaders who were directing it was at once sufficient to bring it to an end. It is the need not of liberty but of servitude that is always predominant in the soul of crowds. They are so bent on obedience that they instinctively submit to whoever declares himself their master.

These ringleaders and agitators may be divided into two clearly defined classes. The one includes the men who are energetic and possess, but only intermittently, much strength of will, the other the men, far rarer than the preceding, whose strength of will is enduring. The first-mentioned are violent, brave, and audacious. They are more especially useful to direct a violent enterprise suddenly decided on, to carry the masses with them in spite of danger, and to transform into heroes the men who but yesterday were recruits. Men of this kind were Ney and Murat under the First Empire, and such a man in our own time was Garibaldi, a talent less but energetic adventurer who succeeded with a handful of men in laying hands on the ancient kingdom of Naples, defended though it was by a disciplined army.

Still, though the energy of leaders of this class is a force to be reckoned with, it is transitory, and scarcely outlasts the exciting cause that has brought it into play. When they have returned to their ordinary course of life the heroes animated by energy of this description often evince, as was the case with those I have just cited, the most astonishing weakness of character. They seem incapable of reflection and of conducting themselves under the simplest circumstances, although they had been able to lead others. These men are leaders who cannot exercise their function except on the condition that they be led themselves and continually stimulated, that they have always as their beacon a man or an idea, that they follow a line of conduct clearly traced. The second category of leaders, that of men of enduring strength of will, have, in spite of a less brilliant aspect, a much more considerable influence. In this category are to be found the true founders of religions and great undertakings; St. Paul, Mahomet, Christopher Columbus, and de Lesseps, for example. Whether they be intelligent or narrow-minded is of no importance: the world belongs to them. The persistent will-force they possess is an immensely rare and immensely powerful faculty to which everything yields. What a strong and continuous will is capable of is not always properly appreciated. Nothing resists it; neither nature, gods, nor man.

The most recent example of what can be effected by a strong and continuous will is afforded us by the illustrious man who separated the Eastern and Western worlds, and accomplished a task that during three thousand years had been attempted in vain by the greatest sovereigns. He failed later in an identical enterprise, but then had intervened old age, to which everything, even the will, succumbs.

When it is desired to show what may be done by mere strength of will, all that is necessary is to relate in detail the history of the difficulties that had to be surmounted in connection with the cutting of the Suez Canal. An ocular witness, Dr. Cazalis, has summed up in a few striking lines the entire story of this great work, recounted by its immortal author.

"From day to day, episode by episode, he told the stupendous story of the canal. He told of all he had had to vanquish, of the impossible he had made possible, of all the opposition he encountered, of the coalition against him, and the disappointments, the reverses, the defeats which had been unavailing to discourage or depress him. He recalled how England had combatted him, attacking him without cessation, how Egypt and France had hesitated, how the French Consul had been foremost in his opposition to the early stages of the work, and the nature of the opposition he had met with, the attempt to force his workmen to desert from thirst by refusing them fresh water; how the Minister of Marine and the engineers, all respon-sible men of experienced and scientific training, had naturally all been hostile, were all certain on scientific grounds that disaster was at hand, had calculated its coming, foretelling it for such a day and hour as an eclipse is foretold."

The book which relates the lives of all these great leaders would not contain many names, but these names have been bound up with the most important events in the history of civilization.

2. THE MEANS OF ACTION OF THE LEADERS: AFFIRMATION, REPETITION, CONTAGION.

When it is wanted to stir up a crowd for a short space of time, to induce it to commit an act of any nature—to pillage a palace, or to die in defense of a stronghold or a barricade, for instance—the crowd must be acted upon by rapid suggestion, among which example is the most powerful in its effect. To attain this end, however, it is necessary that the crowd should have been previously prepared by certain circumstances, and, above all, that he who wishes to work upon it should possess the quality to be studied farther on, to which I give the name of prestige.

When, however, it is proposed to imbue the mind of a crowd with ideas and beliefs—with modern social theories, for instance—the leaders have recourse to different expedients. The principal of them are three in number and clearly defined— affirmation, repetition, and contagion. Their action is somewhat slow, but its effects, once produced, are very lasting.

Affirmation pure and simple, kept free of all reasoning and all proof, is one of the surest means of making an idea enter the mind of crowds. The conciser an affirmation is, the more destitute of every appearance of proof and demonstration, the more weight it carries. The religious books and the legal codes of all ages have always resorted to simple affirmation. Statesmen called upon to defend a political cause, and commercial men pushing the sale of their products by means of advertising are acquainted with the value of affirmation.

Affirmation, however, has no real influence unless it be constantly repeated, and so far as possible in the same terms. It was Napoleon, I believe, who said that there is only one figure in rhetoric of serious importance, namely, repetition. The thing affirmed comes by repetition to fix itself in the mind in such a way that it is accepted in the end as a demonstrated truth.

The influence of repetition on crowds is comprehensible when the power is seen which it exercises on the most enlightened minds. This power is due to the fact that the repeated statement is embedded in the long run in those profound regions of our unconscious selves in which the motives of our actions are forged. At the end of a certain time we have forgotten who is the author of the repeated assertion, and we finish by believing it. To this circumstance is due the astonishing power of advertisements. When we have read a hundred, a thousand times that X's chocolate is the best, we imagine we have heard it said in many quarters, and we end by acquiring the certitude that such is the fact. When we have read a thousand time that Y's flour has cured the most illustrious persons of the most obstinate maladies, we are tempted at last to try it when suffering from an illness of a similar kind. If we always read in the same papers that A is an arrant scamp and B a most honest man we finish by being convinced that this is the truth, unless, indeed, we are given to reading another paper of the contrary opinion, in which the two qualifications are reversed. Affirmation and repetition are alone powerful enough to combat each other.

When an affirmation has been sufficiently repeated and there is unanimity in this repetition—as has occurred in the case of certain famous financial undertakings rich enough to purchase every assistance—what is called a current of opinion is formed and the powerful mechanism of contagion intervenes. Ideas, sentiments, emotions, and beliefs possess in crowds a contagious power as intense as that of microbes. This phenomenon is very natural, since it is observed even in animals when they are together in number. Should a horse in a stable take to biting his manager the other horses in the stable will imitate him. A panic that has seized on a few sheep will soon extend to the whole nook. In the course of men collected in a crowd all emotions are very rapidly contagious, which explains the suddenness of panics. Brain disorders, like madness, are themselves contagious. The frequency of madness among doctors who are specialists for the mad is notorious. Indeed, forms of madness have recently been cited—agoraphobia, for instance—which are communicable from men to animals.

For individuals to succumb to contagion their simultaneous presence on the same spot is not indispensable. The action of contagion may be felt from a distance under the influence of events which give all minds an individual trend and the characteristics peculiar to crowds. This is especially the case when men's minds have been prepared to undergo the influence in question by those remote factors of which I have made a study above. An example in point is the revolutionary movement of 1848, which, after breaking out in Paris, spread rapidly over a great part of Europe and shook a number of thrones.

Imitation, to which so much influence is attributed in social phenomena, is in reality a mere effect of contagion. Having shown its influence elsewhere, I shall confine myself to reproducing what I said on the subject fifteen years ago. My remarks have since been developed by other writers in recent publications.

"Man, like animals, has a natural tendency to imitation. Imitation is a necessity for him, provided always that the imitation is quite easy. It is this necessity that makes the influence of what is called fashion so powerful. Whether in the matter of opinions, ideas, literary manifestations, or merely of dress, how many persons are bold enough to run counter to the fashion. It is by examples not by arguments that crowds are guided. At every period there exists a small number of individuals which react upon the remainder and are imitated by the unconscious mass. It is needful, however, that these individualities should not be in too pronounced disagreement with received ideas. Were they so, to imitate them would be too difficult and their influence would be nil. For this very reason men who are too superior to their epoch are generally without influence upon it. The line of separation is too strongly marked. For the same reason, too, Europeans, in spite of all the advantages of their civilization, have so insignificant an influence on Eastern people; they differ from them to too great an extent.

"The dual action of the past and of reciprocal imitation renders, in the long run, all the men of the same country and the same period so alike that even in the case of individuals who would seem destined to escape this double influence, such as philosophers, learned men, and men of letters, thought and style have a family air which enables the age to which they belong to be immediately recognized. It is not necessary to talk for long with an individual to attain to a thorough knowledge of what he reads, of his habitual occupations, and of the surroundings amid which he lives."

Contagion is so powerful that it forces upon individuals not only certain opinions, but certain modes of feeling as well. Contagion is the cause of the contempt in which, at a given

1 Gustave le Bon, "L'Honune et les Societes, " vol. ii. p.116. 1881.

period, certain works are held—the example of "Tannhauser" may be cited —which, a few years later, for the same reason are admired by those who were foremost in criticizing them.

The opinions and beliefs of crowds are specially propagated by contagion, but never by reasoning. The conceptions at present rife among the working classes have been acquired at the public-house as the result of affirmation, repetition, and contagion, and indeed the mode of creation of the beliefs of crowds of every age has scarcely been different. Renan justly institutes a comparison between the first founders of Christianity and "the socialist working men spreading their ideas from public-house to public-house"; while Voltaire had already observed in connection with the Christian religion that "for more than a hundred years it was only embraced by the vilest riff-raff."

It will be noted that in cases analogous to those I have just cited, contagion, after having been at work among the popular classes, has spread to the higher classes of society. This is what we see happening at the present day with regard to the socialist doctrines which are beginning to be held by those who will yet be their first victims. Contagion is so powerful a force that even the sentiment of personal interest disappears under its action.

This is the explanation of the fact that every opinion adopted by the populace always ends in implanting itself with great vigor in the highest social strata, however obvious be the absurdity of the triumphant opinion. This reaction of the lower upon the higher social classes is the more curious, owing to the circumstance that the beliefs of the crowd always have their origin to a greater or less extent in some higher idea, which has often remained without influence in the sphere in which it was evolved. Leaders and agitators, subjugated by this higher idea, take hold of it, distort it and create a sect which distorts it afresh, and then propagates it amongst the masses, who carry the process of deformation still further. Become a popular truth the idea returns, as it were, to its source and exerts an influence on the upper classes of a nation. In the long run it is intelligence that shapes the destiny of the world, but very indirectly. The philosophers who evolve ideas have long since returned to dust, when, as the result of the process I have just described, the fruit of their reaction ends by triumphing.

3. PRESTIGE

Great power is given to ideas propagated by affirmation, repetition, and contagion by the circumstance that they acquire in time that mysterious force known as prestige.

Whatever has been a ruling power in the world, whether it be ideas or men, has in the main enforced its authority by means of that irresistible force expressed by the word "prestige." The term is one whose meaning is grasped by everybody, but the word is employed in ways too different for it to be easy to define it.

Prestige may involve such sentiments as admiration or fear. Occasionally even these sentiments are its basis, but it can perfectly well exist without them. The greatest measure of prestige is possessed by the dead, by beings, that is, of whom we do not stand in fear—by Alexander, Caesar, Mahomet, and Buddha, for example. On the other hand, there are fictive beings whom we do not admire—the monstrous divinities of the subterranean temples of India, for instance—but who strike us nevertheless as endowed with a great prestige. Prestige in reality is a sort of domination exercised on our mind by an individual, a work, or an idea. This domination entirely paralysis our critical faculty, and fills our soul with astonishment and respect. The sentiment provoked is inexplicable, like all sentiments, but it would appear to be of the same kind as the fascination to which a magnetized person is subjected. Prestige is the mainspring of all authority. Neither gods, kings, nor women have ever reigned without it.

The various kinds of prestige may be grouped under two principal heads: acquired prestige and personal prestige. Acquired prestige is that resulting from name, fortune, and reputation. It may be independent of personal prestige.

Personal prestige, on the contrary, is something essentially peculiar to the individual; it may coexist with reputation, glory, and fortune, or be strengthened by them, but it is perfectly capable of existing in their absence.

Acquired or artificial prestige is much the most common. The mere fact that an individual occupies a certain position, possesses a certain fortune, or bears certain titles, endows him with prestige, however slight his own personal worth. A soldier in uniform, a judge in his robes, always enjoys prestige. Pascal has very properly noted the necessity for judges of robes and wigs. Without them they would be stripped of half their authority. The most unbending socialist is always somewhat impressed by the sight of a prince or a marquis; and the assumption of such titles makes the robbing of tradesmen an easy matter.

The prestige of which I have just spoken is exercised by persons; side by side with it may be placed that exercised by opinions, literary and artistic works, etc. Prestige of the latter kind is most often merely the result of accumulated repetition a History, literary and artistic history especially, being nothing more than the repetition of identical judgements, which nobody endeavors to verify, every one ends by repeating what he learned at school, till there come to be names and things which nobody would venture to meddle with. For a modern

---

1 The influence of titles, decorations, and uniforms on crowds is to be traced in all countries, even in those in which the sentiment of personal independence is the most strongly developed. I quote in this connection a curious passage from a recent book of travel, on the prestige enjoyed in England by great persons. "I had observed, under various circumstances, the peculiar sort of intoxication produced in the most reasonable Englismen by the contact or sight of an English peer. "Provided his fortune enables him to keep up his rank, he is sure of their affection in advance, and brought into contact with him they are so enchanted as to put up with anything at his hands. They may be seen to redden with pleasure at his approach, and if he speaks to them their suppressed joy increases their redness, and causes their eyes to gleam with unusual brilliance. Respect for nobility is in their blood, so to speak, as with Spaniards the love of dancing, with Germans that of music, and with Frenchmen the liking for revolutions. Their passion for horses and Shakespeare is less violent, the satisfaction and pride they derive from these sources a less integral part of their being. There is a considerable sale for books dealing with the peerage, and go where one will they are to be found, like the Bible, in all hands."

reader the perusal of Homer results incontestably in immense boredom; but who would venture to say so? The Parthenon, in its present state, is a wretched ruin, utterly destitute of interest, but it is endowed with such prestige that it does not appear to us as it really is, but with all its accompaniment of historic memories. The special characteristic of prestige is to prevent us seeing things as they are and to entirely paralyze our judgment. Crowds always, and individuals as a rule, stand in need of ready-made opinions on all subjects. The popularity of these opinions is independent of the measure of truth or error they contain, and is solely regulated by their prestige.

I now come to personal prestige. Its nature is very different from that of artificial or acquired prestige, with which I have just been concerned. It is a faculty independent of all titles, of all authority, and possessed by a small number of persons whom it enables to exercise a veritably magnetic fascination on those around them, although they are socially their equals, and lack all ordinary means of domination. They force the acceptance of their ideas and sentiments on those about them, and they are obeyed as is the tamer of wild beasts by the animal that could easily devour him.

The great leaders of crowds, such as Buddha, Jesus, Mahomet, Joan of Arc, and Napoleon, have possessed this form of prestige in a high degree, and to this endowment is more particularly due the position they attained. Gods, heroes, and dogmas win their way in the world of their own inward strength. They are not to be discussed: they disappear, indeed, as soon as discussed.

The great personages I have just cited were in possession of their power of fascination long before they became illustrious, and would never have become so without it. It is evident, for instance, that Napoleon at the zenith of his glory enjoyed an immense prestige by the mere fact of his power, but he was already endowed in part with this prestige when he was without power and completely unknown. When, an obscure general, he was sent, thanks to influential protection, to command the army of Italy, he found himself among rough generals who were of a mind to give a hostile reception to the young intruder dispatched them by the Directory. From the very beginning, from the first interview, without the aid of speeches, gestures, or threats, at the first sight of the man who was to become great they were vanquished. Taine furnished a curious account of this interview taken from contemporary memoirs.

"The generals of division, amongst others Augereau, a sort of swashbuckler, uncouth and heroic, proud of his height and his bravery, arrive at the staff quarters very badly disposed towards the little upstart dispatched them from Paris. On the strength of the description of him that has been given them, Augereau is inclined to be insolent and insubordinate; a favorite of Barras, a general who owes his rank to the events of Vendemiaire, who has won his grade by street-fighting, who is looked upon as bearish, because he is always thinking in solitude, of poor aspect, and with the reputation of a mathematician and dreamer. They are introduced, and Bonaparte keeps them waiting. At last he appears, girt with his sword; he puts on his hat, explains the measures he has taken, gives his orders, and dismisses them. Augereau has remained silent; it is only when he is outside that he regains his self-possession and is able to deliver himself of his customary oaths. He admitted with Massena that this little devil of a general has inspired him with awe; he cannot understand the ascendancy by which from the very first he has felt himself overwhelmed."

Become a great man, his prestige increased in proportion as his glory grew, and came to be at least equal to that of a divinity in the eyes of those devoted to him. General Vandamme, a rough, typical soldier of the Revolution, even more brutal and energetic than Augereau, said of him to Marshal d'Arnano in 1815, as on one occasion they mounted together the stairs of the Tuileries: "That devil of a man exercises a fascination on me that I cannot explain even to myself, and in such a degree that, though I fear neither God nor devil, when I am in his presence I am ready to tremble like a child, and he could make me go through the eye of a needle to throw myself into the fire."

Napoleon exercised a like fascination on all who came into contact with him.

Davoust used to say, talking of Maret's devotion and of his own: "Had the Emperor said to us, 'It is important in the interest of my policy that Paris should be destroyed without a single person leaving it or escaping,' Maret I am sure would have kept the secret, but he could not have abstained from compromising himself by seeing that his family got clear of the city. On the other hand, I, for fear of letting the truth leak out, would have let my wife and children stay."[1]

It is necessary to bear in mind the astounding power exerted by fascination of this order to understand that marvellous return from the Isle of Elba, that lightning-like conquest of France by an isolated man confronted by all the organized forces of a great country that might have been supposed weary of his tyranny. He had merely to cast a look at the generals sent to lay hands on him, and who had sworn to accomplish their mission. All of them submitted without discussion.

"Napoleon," writes the English General Wolseley, "lands in France almost alone, a fugitive from the small island of Elba which was his kingdom, and succeeded in a few weeks, without bloodshed, in upsetting all organized authority in France under its legitimate king; is it possible for the personal ascendancy of a man to affirm itself in a more astonishing manner? But from the beginning to the end of this campaign, which was his last, how remarkable too is the ascendancy he exercised over the Allies, obliging them to follow his initiative, and how near he came to crushing them!"

His prestige outlived him and continued to grow. It is

1 Thoroughly conscious of his prestige, Napoleon was aware that personages around him, and among whom figured some of those celebrated men of the convention of whom Europe had stood in dread. The gossip of the period abounds in illustrations of this fact. One day, in the midst of a Council of State, Napoleon grossly insults Beugnot, treating him as one might an unmannerly valet. The effect produced, he goes up to him and says, " Well, stupid, have you found your head again?" Whereupon Beugnot, tall as a drum-major, bows very low, and the little man raising his hand, bakes the tall one by the ear, "an intoxicating sign of favour," writes Beugnot, " the familiar gesture of the master who waxes gracious." Such examples give a clear idea of the degree of base platitude that prestige can provoke. They enable us to understand the immense contempt of the great despot for the men surrounding him—men whom he merely looked upon as " food for powder."

his prestige that made an emperor of his obscure nephew. How powerful is his memory still is seen in the resurrection of his legend in progress at the present day. Ill-treat men as you will, massacre them by millions, be the cause of invasion upon invasion, all is permitted you if you possess prestige in a sufficient degree and the talent necessary to uphold it.

I have invoked, no doubt, in this case a quite exceptional example of prestige, but one it was useful to cite to make clear the genesis of great religions, great doctrines, and great empires. Were it not for the power exerted on the crowd by prestige, such growths would be incomprehensible.

Prestige, however, is not based solely on personal ascendancy, military glory, and religious terror; it may have a more modest origin and still be considerable. Our century furnishes several examples. One of the most striking ones that posterity will recall from age to age will be supplied by the history of the illustrious man who modified the face of the globe and the commercial relations of the nations by separating two continents. He succeeded in his enterprise owing to his immense strength of will, but also owing to the fascination he exercised on those surrounding him. To overcome the unanimous opposition he met with, he had only to show himself. He would speak briefly, and in face of the charm he exerted his opponents became his friends. The English in particular strenuously opposed his scheme; he had only to put in an appearance in England to rally all suffrages. In later years, when he passed Southampton, the bells were rung on his passage; and at the present day a movement is on foot in England to raise a statue in his honor.

"Having vanquished whatever there is to vanquish, men and things, marshes, rocks, and sandy wastes," he had ceased to believe in obstacles, and wished to begin Suez over again at Panama. He began again with the same methods as of old; but he had aged, and, besides, the faith that moves mountains does not move them if they are too lofty. The mountains resisted, and the catastrophe that ensued destroyed the glittering aureole of glory that enveloped the hero. His life teaches how prestige can grow and how it can vanish. After rivalling in greatness the most famous heroes of history, he was lowered by the magistrates of his country to the ranks of the Vilest criminals. When he died his coffin, unattended, traversed an indifferent crowd. Foreign sovereigns are alone in rendering homage to his memory as to that of one of the greatest men that history has known. [1]

Still, the various examples that have just been cited represent extreme cases. To fix in detail the psychology of prestige, it would be necessary to place them at the extremity of a series, which would range from the founders of religions and empires to the private individual who endeavors to dazzle his neighbors by a new coat or a decoration.

Between the extreme limits of this series would find a place all the forms of prestige resulting from the different elements composing a civilization--sciences, arts, literature, etc.--and it would be seen that prestige constitutes the fundamental element of persuasion. Consciously or not, the being, the idea, or the thing possessing prestige is immediately imitated in consequence of contagion, and forces an entire generation to adopt certain modes of feeling and of giving expression to its thought. This imitation, moreover, is, as a rule, unconscious, which accounts for the fact that it is perfect. The modern painters who copy the pale coloring and the stiff attitudes of some of the primitives are scarcely alive to the source of their inspiration. They believe in their own sincerity, whereas, if an eminent master had not revived this form of art, people would have continued blind to all but its naive and inferior sides. Those artists who, after the manner of another illustrious master, inundate their canvasses with violet shades do not see in nature more violet than was detected there fifty years ago; but they are influenced, "suggestions," by the personal and special impressions of a painter who, in spite of this eccentricity, was successful in acquiring great prestige. Similar examples might be brought forward in connection with all the elements of civilizations.

It is seen from what precedes that a number of factors may

be concerned in the genesia of prestige; among them success was always one of the most important. Every successful man, every idea that forces itself into recognition, ceases, *ipso facto*, to be called in question. The proof that success is one of the principal stepping-stones to prestige is that the disappearance of the one is almost always followed by the disappearance of the other. The hero whom the crowd acclaimed yesterday is insulted today should he have been overtaken by failure. The reaction, indeed, will be the stronger in proportion as the prestige has been great. The crowd in this case considers the fallen hero as an equal, and takes its revenge for having bowed to a superiority whose existence it no longer admits. While Robespierre was causing the execution of his colleagues and of a great number of his contemporaries, he possessed an immense prestige. When the transposition of a few votes deprived him of power, he immediately lost his prestige, and the crowd followed him to the guillotine with the selfsame imprecations with which shortly before it had pursued his victims. Believers always break the statues of their former gods with every symptom of fury.

Prestige lost by want of success disappears in a brief space of time. It can also be worn away, but more slowly by being subjected to discussion. This latter power, however, is exceedingly sure. From the moment prestige is called in question it ceases to be prestige. The gods and men who have kept their prestige for long have never tolerated discussion. For the crowd to admire, it must be kept at a distance.

CHAPTER IV

LIMITATIONS OF THE VARIABILITY OF THE BELIEFS AND OPINIONS OF CROWDS

1. *Fixed Beliefs.* The invariability of certain general beliefs —
They shape the course of a civilization—The difficulty of
uproot ing them—In what respect intolerance is a virtue in
a people—The philosophic absurdity of a belief cannot
interfere with its spreading. 2. *The Changeable of
Opinions of Crowds.* The extreme mobility of opinions
which do not arise from general beliefs—Apparent variations of ideas and beliefs in less than a century—The real
limits of these variations—The matters effected by the
variation—The disappearance at present in progress of
general beliefs, and the extreme diffusion of the newspa
per press, have for result that opinions are nowadays more
and more changeable—Why the opinions of crowds tend
on the majority of subjects towards indifference—Govern
ments now powerless to direct opinion as they formerly
did—Opinions prevented today from being tyrannical on
account of their exceeding divergency.

1. FIXED BELIEFS

A close parallel exists between the anatomical and psychological characteristics of living beings. In these anatomical
characteristics certain invariable, or slightly variable, elements
are met with, to change which the lapse is necessary of
geological ages. Side by side with these fixed, indestructible

features are to be found others extremely changeable, which the art of the breeder or horticulturist may easily modify, and at times to such an extent as to conceal the fundamental characteristics from an observer at all inattentive.

The same phenomenon is observed in the case of moral characteristics. Alongside the unalterable psychological elements of a race, mobile and changeable elements are to be encountered. For this reason, in studying the beliefs and opinions of a people, the presence is always detected of a fixed groundwork on which are in grafted opinions as changing as the surface sand on a rock.

The opinions and beliefs of crowds may be divided, then, into two very distinct classes. On the one hand we have great permanent beliefs, which endure for several centuries, and on which an entire civilization may rest. Such, for instance, in the past were feudalism, Christianity, and Protestantism; and such, in our own time, are the nationalist principle and contemporary democratic and social ideas. In the second place, there are the transitory, changing opinions, the outcome, as a rule, of general conceptions, of which every age sees the birth and disappearance; examples in point are the theories which mold literature and the arts—those, for instance, which produced romanticism, naturalism, mysticism, etc. Opinions of this order are as superficial, as a rule, as fashion, and as changeable. They may be compared to the ripples which ceaselessly arise and vanish on the surface of a deep lake.

The great generalized beliefs are very restricted in number. Their rise and fall form the culminating points of the history of every historic race. They constitute the real framework of civilization.

It is easy to imbue the mind of crowds with a passing opinion, but very difficult to implant therein a lasting belief. However, a belief of this latter description once established, it is equally difficult to uproot it. It is usually only to be changed at the cost of violent revolutions. Even revolutions can only avail when the belief has almost entirely lost its sway over men's minds. In that case revolutions serve to finally sweep away what had already been almost cast aside, though the force of habit prevented its complete abandonment. The beginning of a revolution is in reality the end of a belief.

The precise moment at which a great belief is doomed is easily recognizable; it is the moment when its value begins to be called in question. Every general belief being little else than a fiction, it can only survive on the condition that it be not subjected to examination.

But even when a belief is severely shaken, the institutions to which it has given rise retain their strength and disappear but slowly. Finally, when the belief has completely lost its force, all that rested upon it is soon involved in ruin. As yet a nation has never been able to change its beliefs without being condemned at the same time to transform all the elements of its civilization. The nation continues this process of transformation until it has alighted on and accepted a new general belief; until this juncture it is perforce in a state of anarchy. General beliefs are the indispensable pillars of civilizations; they determine the trend of ideas. They alone are capable of inspiring faith and creating a sense of duty.

Nations have always been conscious of the utility of acquiring general beliefs, and have instinctively understood that their disappearance would be the signal for their own decline. In the case of the Romans, the fanatical cult of Rome was the belief that made them masters of the world, and when the belief had died out Rome was doomed to die. As for the barbarians who destroyed the Roman civilization, it was only when they had acquired certain commonly accepted beliefs that they attained a measure of cohesion and emerged from anarchy.

Plainly it is not for nothing that nations have always displayed intolerance in the defense of their opinions. This intolerance, open as it is to criticism from the philosophic standpoint, represents in the life of a people the most necessary of virtues. It was to found or uphold general beliefs that so many victims were sent to the stake in the Middle Ages and that so many inventors and innovators have died in despair even if they have escaped martyrdom. It is in defense, too, of such beliefs that the world has been so often the scene of the direst disorder, and that so many millions of men have died on the battlefield, and will yet die there.

There are great difficulties in the way of establishing a general belief, but when it is definitely implanted its power is for a long time to come invincible, and however false it be philosophically it imposes itself upon the most luminous intelligence. Have not the European peoples regarded as incontrovertible for more than fifteen centuries religious legends which, closely examined, are as barbarous as those of Moloch? The frightful absurdity of the legend of a God who revenges himself for the disobedience of one of his creatures by inflicting horrible tortures on his son remained unperceived during many centuries. Such potent geniuses as a Galileo, a Newton, and a Leibnitz never supposed for an instant that the truth of such dogmas could be called in question. Nothing can be more typical than this fact of the hypnotizing effect of general beliefs, but at the same time nothing can mark more decisively the humiliating limitations of our intelligence.

As soon as a new dogma is implanted in the mind of crowds it becomes the source of inspiration whence are evolved its institutions, arts, and mode of existence. The sway it exerts over men's minds under these circumstances is absolute. Men of action have no thought beyond realizing the accepted belief, legislators beyond applying it, while philosophers, artists, and men of letters are solely preoccupied with its expression under various shapes.

From the fundamental belief transient accessory ideas may arise, but they always bear the impress of the belief from which they have sprung. The Egyptian civilization, the European civilization of the Middle Ages, the Mussulman civilization of the Arabs are all the outcome of a small number of religious beliefs which have left their mark on the least important

1 Barbarous, philosophically speaking, I mean. In practice they have created an entirely new civilization, and for fifteen centuries have given mankind a glimpse of those enchanted realms of generous dreams and of hope which he will know no more.

elements of these civilizations and allow of their immediate recognition.

Thus it is that, thanks to general beliefs, the men of every age are enveloped in a network of traditions, opinions, and customs which render them all alike, and from whose yoke they cannot extricate themselves. Men are guided in their conduct above all by their beliefs and by the customs that are the consequence of those beliefs. These beliefs and customs regulate the smallest acts of our existence, and the most independent spirit cannot escape their influence. The tyranny exercised unconsciously on men's minds is the only real tyranny, because it cannot be fought against. Tiberius, Ghengis Khan, and Napoleon were assuredly redoubtable tyrants, but from the depth of their graves Moses, Buddha, Jesus, and Mahomet have exerted on the human soul a far profounder despotism. A conspiracy may overthrow a tyrant, but what can it avail against a firmly established belief? In its violent struggle with Roman Catholicism it is the French Revolution that has been vanquished. and this in spite of the fact that the sympathy of the crowd was apparently on its side, and in spite of recourse to destructive measures as pitiless as those of the Inquisition. The only real tyrants that humanity has known have always been the memories of its dead or the illusions it has forged itself.

The philosophic absurdity that often marks general beliefs has never been an obstacle to their triumph. Indeed the triumph of such beliefs would seem impossible unless on the condition that they offer some mysterious absurdity. In consequence, the evident weakness of the socialist beliefs of today will not prevent them triumphing among the masses. Their real inferiority to all religious beliefs is solely the result of this consideration, that the ideal of happiness offered by the latter being realizable only in a future life, it was beyond the power of anybody to contest it. The socialist ideal of happiness being intended to be realized on earth, the vanity of its promises will at once appear as soon as the first efforts towards their realization are made, and simultaneously the new belief will entirely lose its prestige. Its strength, in consequence, will only increase until the day when, having triumphed, its practical realization shall commence. For this reason, while the new religion exerts to begin with, like all those that have preceded it, a destructive influence, it will be unable, in the future, to play a creative part.

2. THE CHANGEABLE OPINIONS OF CROWDS

Above the substratum of fixed beliefs, whose power we have just demonstrated, is found an overlying growth of opinions, ideas, and thoughts which are incessantly springing up and dying out. Some of them exist but for a day, and the more important scarcely outlive a generation. We have already noted that the changes which supervene in opinions of this order are at times far more superficial than real, and that they are always affected by racial considerations. When examining, for instance, the political institutions of France we showed that parties to all appearances utterly distinct—royalists, radical, imperialists, socialists, etc.—have an ideal absolutely identical, and that this ideal is solely dependent on the mental structure of the French race, since a quite contrary ideal is found under analogous names among other races. Neither the name given to opinions nor deceptive adaptations alter the essence of things. The men of the Great Revolution, saturated with Latin literature, who (their eyes fixed on the Roman Republic) adopted its laws, its fasces, and its togas, did not become Romans because they were under the empire of a powerful historical suggestion. The task of the philosopher is to investigate what it is which subsists of ancient beliefs beneath their apparent changes, and to identify amid the moving flux of opinions the part determined by general beliefs and the genius of the race.

In the absence of this philosophic test it might be supposed that crowds change their political or religious beliefs frequently and at will. All history, whether political, religious, artistic, or literary, seems to prove that such is the case.

As an example, let us take a very short period of French history, merely that from 1790 to 1820, a period of thirty years' duration, that of a generation. In the course of it we see the crowd at first monarchical become very revolutionary, then very imperialist, and again very monarchical. In the matter of religion it gravitates in the same lapse of time from Catholicism to atheism, then towards deism, and then returns to the most pronounced forms of Catholicism. These changes take place not only amongst the masses, but also amongst those who direct them. We observe with astonishment the prominent men of the Convention, the sworn enemies of kings, men who would have neither gods nor masters, become the humble servants of Napoleon, and afterwards, under Louis XVIII, piously carry candles in religious processions.

Numerous, too, are the changes in the opinions of the crowd in the course of the following seventy years. The "Perfidious Albion" of the opening of the century is the ally of France under Napoleon's heir; Russia, twice invaded by France, which looked on with satisfaction at French reverses, becomes its friend.

In literature, art, and philosophy the successive evolutions of opinion are more rapid still. Romanticism, naturalism, mysticism, etc., spring up and die out in turn. The artist and the writer applauded yesterday are treated on the morrow with profound contempt.

When, however, we analyze all these changes in appearance so far reaching, what do we find? All those that are in opposition with the general beliefs and sentiments of the race are of transient duration, and the diverted stream soon resumes its course. The opinions which are not linked to any general belief or sentiment of the race, and which in consequence cannot possess stability, are at the mercy of every chance, or, if the expression be preferred, of every change in the surrounding circumstances. Formed by suggestion and contagion, they are always momentary; they crop up and disappear as rapidly on occasion as the sandhills formed by the wind on the sea-coast. At the present day the changeable opinions of crowds are greater in number than they ever were, and for three different reasons.

The first is that as the old beliefs are losing their influence to a greater and greater extent, they are ceasing to shape the ephemeral opinions of the moment as they did in the past. The weakening of general beliefs clears the ground for a crop of haphazard opinions without a past or a future.

The second reason is that the power of crowds being on the increase, and this power being less and less counterbalanced, the extreme mobility of ideas, which we have seen to be a peculiarity of crowds, can manifest itself without let or hindrance.

Finally, the third reason is the recent development of the newspaper press, by whose agency the most contrary opinions are being continually brought before the attention of crowds. The suggestions that might result from each individual opinion are soon destroyed by suggestions of an opposite character. The consequence is that no opinion succeeds in becoming widespread, and that the existence of all of them is ephemeral. An opinion nowadays dies out before it has found a sufficiently wide acceptance to become general.

A phenomenon quite new in the world's history, and most characteristic of the present age, has resulted from these different causes; I allude to the powerlessness of governments to direct opinion.

In the past, and in no very distant past, the action of governments and the influence of a few writers and a very small number of newspapers constituted the real reflectors of public opinion. Today the writers have lost all influence, and the newspapers only reflect opinion. As for statesmen, far from directing opinion, their only endeavor is to follow it. They have a dread of opinion which amounts at times to terror and causes them to adopt an utterly unstable line of conduct.

The opinion of crowds tends, then, more and more to become the supreme guiding principle in politics. It goes so far to-day as to force on alliances, as has been seen recently in the case of the Franco-Russian alliance, which is solely the outcome of a popular movement. A curious symptom of the present time is to observe popes, kings, and emperors consent to be interviewed as a means of submitting their views on a given subject to the judgement of crowds. Formerly it might have been correct to say that politics were not a matter of sentiment. Can the same be said today, when politics are more and more swayed by the impulse of changeable crowds, who are uninfluenced by reason and can only be guided by sentiment?

As to the press, which formerly directed opinion, it has had, like governments, to humble itself before the power of crowds. It wields, no doubt, a considerable influence, but only because it is exclusively the reflection of the opinions of crowds and of their incessant variations. Become a mere agency for the supply of information, the press has renounced all endeavor to enforce an idea or a doctrine. It follows all the changes of public thought, obliged to do so by the necessities of competition under pain of losing its readers. The old staid and influential organs of the past, such as the *Constitutionnel,* the *Debats*, or the *Siecle*, which were accepted as oracles by the preceding generation, have disappeared or have become typical modern papers, in which a maximum news is sandwiched in between light articles, society gossip, and financial puffs. There can be no question today of a paper rich enough to allow its contributors to air their personal opinions, and such opinions would be of slight weight with readers who only ask to be kept informed or to be amused, and who suspect every affirmation of being prompted by motives of speculation. Even the critics have ceased to be able to assure the success of a book or a play. They are capable of doing harm, but not of doing a service. The papers are so conscious of the uselessness of everything in the shape of criticism or personal opinion, that they have reached the point of suppressing literary criticism, confining themselves to citing the title of a book, and appending a "puff" of two or three lines.   In twenty years' time the same fate will probably have overtaken theatrical criticism.[1]

The close watching of the course of opinion has become

[1]These remarks refer to the French newspaper press.—*Note of the Translator.*

today the principal preoccupation of the press and of governments. The effect produced by an event, a legislative proposal,
a speech, is without intermission what they require to know,
and the task is not easy, for nothing is more mobile and
changeable than the thought of crowds, and nothing more
frequent than to see them execrate today what they applauded
yesterday.

This total absence of any sort of direction of opinion, and at
the same time the destruction of general beliefs, have had for
final result an extreme divergency of convictions of every
order, and a growing indifference on the part of crowds to
everything that does not plainly touch their immediate interests.
Questions of doctrine, such as socialism, only recruit champions
boasting genuine convictions among the quite illiterate classes,
among the workers in mines and factories, for instance.
Members of the lower middle class, and working men possessing
some degree of instruction, have either become utterly skeptical
or extremely unstable in their opinions.

The evolution which has been effected in this direction in the
last twenty-five years is striking. During the preceding period,
comparatively near us though it is, opinions still had a certain
general trend; they had their origin in the acceptance of some
fundamental belief. By the mere fact that an individual was a
monarchist he possessed inevitably certain clearly defined
ideas in history as well as in science, while by the mere fact that
he was a republican, his ideas were quite contrary. A monarchist
was well aware that men are not descended from monkeys,
and a republican was not less well aware that such is in truth
their descent. It was the duty of the monarchist to speak with
horror, and of the republican to speak with veneration, of the
great Revolution. There were certain names, such as those of
Robespierre and Marat, that had to be uttered with an air of
religious devotion, and other names, such as those of Caesar,
Augustus, or Napoleon, that ought never to be mentioned
unaccompanied by a torrent of invective. Even in the French
Sorbonne this ingenuous fashion of conceiving history was
general. [1]

At the present day, as the result of discussion and analysis, all opinions are losing their prestige; their distinctive features are rapidly worn away, and few survive capable of arousing our enthusiasm. The man of modern times is more and more a prey to indifference.

The general wearing away of opinions should not be too greatly deplored. That it is a symptom of decadence in the life of a people cannot be contested. It is certain that men of immense, of almost supernatural insight, that apostles, leaders of crowds—men, in a word, of genuine and strong convictions—exert a far greater force than men who deny, who criticize, or who are indifferent, but it must not be forgotten that, given the power possessed at present by crowds, were a single opinion to acquire sufficient prestige to enforce its general acceptance, it would soon be endowed with so tyrannical a strength that everything would have to bend before it, and the era of free discussion would be closed for a long time. Crowds are occasionally easy-going masters, as were Heliogabalus and Tiberius, but they are also violently capricious. A civilization, when the moment has come for crowds to acquire a high hand over it, is at the mercy of too many chances to endure for long. Could anything postpone for a while the hour of its ruin, it would be precisely the extreme instability of the opinions of crowds and their growing indifference with respect to all general beliefs. [1]

1 These are pages in the books of the French official professors of history that are very curious from this point of view. They prove too how little the critical spirit is developed by the system of university education in vogue in France. I cite as an example the following extractes from the "French Revolution" of M. Rambaud, professor of history at the Sorbonne:

"The taking of the Bastille was a culminating event in the history not only of France, but of all Europe; and inaugurated a new epoch in the history of the world!"

With respect to Robespierre, we learn with stupefaction that "his dictatorship was based more especially on opinion, 'persuasion, and moral authority; it was a sort of pontificate in the hands of a virtuous man!" (pp.91 and 220).

BOOK III

THE CLASSIFICATION AND DESCRIPTION OF THE DIFFERENT KINDS OF CROWDS

CHAPTER I

THE CLASSIFICATION OF CROWDS

The general divisions of crowds—Their classification. 1. Heterogeneous crowds. Different varieties of them—The influence of race—The spirit of the crowd is weak in proportion as the spirit of the race is strong—The spirit of the race represents the civilized state and the spirit of the crowd the barbarian state. 2. Heterogeneous crowds. Their different varieties—Sects, castes, and classes.

WE have sketched in this work the general characteristics common to psychological crowds. It remains to point out the particular characteristics which accompany those of a general order in the different categories of collectivities, when they are transformed into a crowd under the influences of the proper exciting causes. We will, first of all, set forth in a few words a classification of crowds.

Our starting-point will be the simple multitude. Its most inferior form is met with when the multitude is composed of individuals belonging to different races. In this case its only common bond of union is the will, more or less respected, of a chief. The barbarians of very diverse origin who during several centuries invaded the Roman Empire, may be cited as a specimen of multitudes of this kind.

On a higher level than these multitudes composed of

different races are those which under certain influences have acquired common characteristics, and have ended by forming a single race. They present at times characteristics peculiar to crowds, but these characteristics are overruled to a greater or less extent by racial considerations.

These two kinds of multitudes may, under certain influtransformed into organized or psychological crowds. We shall break up these organized crowds into the following divisions:—

A. Heterogeneous crowds
{
1. Anonymous crowds (street crowds, for example).
2. Crowds not anonymous (juries, parliamentary assemblies, etc.).
}

B. Homogeneous crowds
{
1. Sects (political sects, religious sects, etc.).
2. Castes (the military caste, the priestly caste, the working caste, etc.).
3. Classes (the middle classes, the peasant classes, etc.).
}

We will point out briefly the distinguishing characteristics of these different categories of crowds.

1. HETEROGENEOUS CROWDS

It is these collectivities whose characteristics have been studied in this volume. They are composed of individuals of any description, of any profession, and any degree of intelligence.

We are now aware that by the mere fact that men form part of a crowd engaged in action, their collective psychology differs essentially from their individual psychology, and their intelligence is affected by this differentiation. We have seen that intelligence is without influence in collectivities, they being solely under the sway of unconscious sentiments.

A fundamental factor, that of race, allows of a tolerably thorough differentiation of the various heterogeneous crowds.

We have often referred already to the part played by race, and have shown it to be the most powerful of the factors capable of determining men's actions. Its action is also to be traced in the character of crowds. A crowd composed of individuals assembled at haphazard, but all of them Englishmen or Chinamen, will differ widely from another crowd also composed of individuals of any and every description, but of other races—Russians, Frenchmen, or Spaniards, for example.

The wide divergencies which their inherited mental constitution creates in men's modes of feeling and thinking at once come into prominence when, which rarely happens, circumstances gather together in the same crowd and in fairly equal proportions individuals of different nationality, and this occurs, however identical in appearance be the interests which provoked the gathering. The efforts made by the socialists to assemble in great congresses the representatives of the working-class populations of different countries, have always ended in the most pronounced discord. A Latin crowd, however revolutionary or however conservative it be supposed, will invariably appeal to the intervention of the State to realize its demands. It is always distinguished by a marked tendency towards centralization and by a leaning, more or less pronounced, in favor of a dictatorship. An English or an American crowd, on the contrary, sets no store on the State, and only appeals to private initiative. A French crowd lays particular weight on equality and an English crowd on liberty. These differences of race explain how it is that there are almost as many different forms of socialism and democracy as there are nations.

The genius of the race, then, exerts a paramount influence upon the dispositions of a crowd. It is the powerful underlying force that limits its changes of humor. It should be considered as an essential law that the *inferior characteristics of crowds are the less accentuated in proportion as the spirit of a race is strong.* The crowd state and the domination of crowds is equivalent to the barbarian state, or to a return to it. It is by the acquisition of a solidly constituted collective spirit that the race frees itself to a greater and greater extent from the unreflecting over of crowds, and emerges from the barbarian state. The only important classification to be made of heterogeneous crowds, apart from that based on racial considerations, is to separate them into anonymous crowds, such as street crowds, and crowds not anonymous—deliberative assemblies and juries, for example. The sentiment of responsibility absent from crowds of the first description and developed in those of the second often gives a very different tendency to their respective acts.

2. HOMOGENEOUS CROWD.

Homogeneous crowds include: 1. Sects; 2. Castes; 3. Classes.

The *sect* represents the first step in the process of organization of homogeneous crowds. A sect includes individuals differing greatly as to their education, their professions, and the class of society to which they belong, and with their common beliefs as the connecting link. Examples in point are religious and political sects.

The *caste* represents the highest degree of organization of which the crowd is susceptible. While the sect includes individuals of very different professions, degrees of education and social surrounding, who are only linked together by the beliefs they hold in common, the caste is composed of individuals of the same profession, and in consequence similarly educated and of much the same social status. Examples in point are the military and priestly castes.

The *class* is formed of individuals of diverse origin, linked together not by a community of beliefs, as are the members of a sect, or by common professional occupations, as are the members of a caste, but by certain interests and certain habits of life and education almost identical. The middle class and the agricultural class are examples.

Being only concerned in this work with heterogeneous crowds, and reserving the study of homogeneous crowds (sects, castes, and classes) for another volume, I shall not insist here on the characteristics of crowds of this latter kind. I shall conclude this study of heterogeneous crowds by the examination of a few typical and distinct categories of crowds.

CHAPTER II

CROWDS TERMED CRIMINAL CROWDS

Crowds termed criminal crowds—A crowd may be legally yet not
psychologically criminal—The absolute unconsciousness of the
acts of crowds—Various examples—Psychology of the authors of
the September massacres—Their reasoning, their sensibility,
their ferocity, and their morality.

OWING to the fact that crowds, after a period of excitement, enter upon a purely automatic and unconscious state,
in which they are guided by suggestion, it seems difficult to
qualify them in any case as criminal. I only retain this
erroneous qualification because it has been definitely brought
into vogue by recent psychological investigations. Certain
acts of crowds are assuredly criminal, if considered merely in
themselves, but criminal in that case in the same way as the
act of a tiger devouring a Hindu, after allowing its young to
maul him for their amusement.

The usual motive of the crimes of crowds is a powerful
suggestion, and the individuals who take part in such crimes
are afterwards convinced that they have acted in obedience
to duty, which is far from being the case with the ordinary
criminal.

The history of the crimes committed by crowds illustrates
what precedes.

The murder of M. de Launay, the governor of the Bastille,
may be cited as a typical example. After the taking of the
fortress the governor, surrounded by a very excited crowd,
was dealt blows from every direction. It was proposed to hang

him, to cut off his head, to tie him to a horse's tail. While struggling, he accidentally kicked one of those present. Some one proposed, and his suggestion was at once received with acclamation by the crowd, that the individual who had been kicked should cut the governor's throat.

"The individual in question, a cook out of work, whose chief reason for being at the Bastille was idle curiosity as to what was going on, esteems, that since such is the general opinion, the action is patriotic and even believes he deserves a medal for having destroyed a monster. With a sword that is lent him he strikes the bared neck, but the weapon being somewhat blunt and not cutting, he takes from his pocket a small black-handled knife and (in his capacity of cook he would be experienced in cutting up meat) successfully effects the operation."

The working of the process indicated above is clearly seen in this example. We have obedience to a suggestion, which is all the stronger because of its collective origin, and the murderer's conviction that he has committed a very meritorious act, a conviction the more natural seeing that he enjoys the unanimous approval of his fellow-citizens. An act of this kind may be considered crime legally but not psychologically.

The general characteristics of criminal crowds are precisely the same as those we have met with in all crowds: openness to suggestion, credulity, mobility, the exaggeration of the sentiments good or bad, the manifestation of certain forms of morality, etc.

We shall find all these characteristics present in a crowd which has left behind it in French history the most sinister memories—the crowd which perpetrated the September massacres. In point of fact it offers much similarity with the crowd that committed the Saint Bartholomew massacres. I borrow the details from the narration of M. Taine, who took them from contemporary sources.

It is not known exactly who gave the order or made the suggestion to empty the prisons by massacring the prisoners. Whether it was Danton, as is probable, or another does not matter; the one interesting fact for us is the powerful suggestion received by the crowd charged with the massacre.

The crowd of murderers numbered some three hundred persons, and was a perfectly typical heterogeneous crowd. With the exception of a very small number of professional scoundrels, it was composed in the main of shopkeepers and artisans of every trade: bootmakers, locksmiths, hairdressers, masons, clerks, messengers, etc. Under the influence of the suggestion received they are perfectly convinced, as was the cook referred to above, that they are accomplishing a patriotic duty. They fill a double office, being at once judge and executioner, but they do not for a moment regard themselves as criminals.

Deeply conscious of the importance of their duty, they begin by forming a sort of tribunal, and in connection with this act the ingenuousness of crowds and their rudimentary conception of justice are seen immediately. In consideration of the large number of the accused, it is decided that, to begin with, the nobles, priests, officers, and members of the king's household—in a word, all the individuals whose mere profession is proof of their guilt in the eyes of a good patriot—shall be slaughtered in a body, there being no need for a special decision in their case. The remainder shall be judged on their personal appearance and their reputation. In this way the rudimentary conscience of the crowd is satisfied. It will now be able to proceed legally with the massacre, and to give free scope to those instincts of ferocity whose genesis I have set forth elsewhere, they being instincts which collectivities always have in them to develop to a high degree. These instincts, however—as is regularly the case in crowds—will not prevent the manifestation of other and contrary sentiments, such as a tenderheartedness often as extreme as the ferocity.

"They have the expansive sympathy and prompt sensibility of the Parisian working man. At the Abbey, one of the federates, learning that the prisoners had been left without water for twenty-six hours, was bent on putting the gaoler to death, and would have done so but for the prayers of the prisoners themselves. When a prisoner is acquitted (by the improvised tribunal) every one, guards and slaughterers included, embraces him with transports of joy and applauds frantically," after which the wholesale massacre is recommenced. During its progress a pleasant gaiety never ceases to reign. There is dancing and singing around the corpses, and benches are arranged "for the ladies," delighted to witness the killing of aristocrats. The exhibition continues, moreover, of a special description of justice.

A slaughterer at the Abbey having complained that the ladies placed at a little distance saw badly, and that only a few of those present had the pleasure of striking the aristocrats, the justice of the observation is admitted, and it is decided that the victims shall be made to pass slowly between two rows of slaughterers, who shall be under the obligation to strike with the back of the sword only so as to prolong the agony. At the prison de la Force the victims are stripped stark naked and literally "carved" for half an hour, after which, when every one has had a good view, they are finished off by a blow that lays bare their entrails.

The slaughterers, too, have their scruples and exhibit that moral sense whose existence in crowds we have already pointed out. They refuse to appropriate the money and jewels of the victims, taking them to the table of the committees.

Those rudimentary forms of reasoning, characteristic of the mind of crowds, are always to be traced in all their acts. Thus, after the slaughter of the 1,200 or 1,500 enemies of the nation, some one makes the remark, and his suggestion is at once adopted, that the other prisons, those containing aged beggars, vagabonds, and young prisoners, hold in reality useless mouths, of which it would be well on that account to get rid. Besides, among them there should certainly be enemies of the people, a woman of the name of Delarue, for instance, the widow of a poisoner: " She must be furious at being in prison; if she could she would set fire to Paris: she must have said so, she has said so. Another good riddance." The demonstration appears convincing, and the prisoners are massacred without exception, included in the number being some fifty children of from twelve to seventeen years of age, who, of course, might themselves have become enemies of the nation, and of whom in consequence it was clearly well to be rid.

At the end of a week's work, all these operations being brought to an end, the slaughterers can think of reposing themselves. Profoundly convinced that they have deserved well of their country, they went to the authorities and demanded a recompense. The most zealous went so far as to claim a medal.

The history of the Commune of 1871 affords several facts analogous to those which precede. Given the growing influence of crowds and the successive capitulations before them of those in authority, we are destined to witness many others of a like nature.

CHAPTER III

CRIMINAL JURIES

Criminal juries—General characteristics of juries—Statistics show that their decisions are independent of their composition—The manner in which an impression may be made on juries—The style and influence of argument—The methods of persuasion of celebrated counsel—The nature of those crimes for which juries are respectively indulgent or severe—The utility of the jury as an institution, and the danger that would result from its place being taken by magistrates.

Being unable to study here every category of jury, I shall only examine the most important—that of the juries of the Court of Assize. These juries afford an excellent example of the heterogeneous crowd that is not anonymous. We shall find them display suggestibility and but slight capacity for reasoning, while they are open to the influence of the leaders of crowds, and they are guided in the main by unconscious sentiments. In the course of this investigation we shall have occasion to observe some interesting examples of the errors that may be made by persons not versed in the psychology of crowds.

Juries, in the first place, furnish us a good example of the slight importance of the mental level of the different elements composing a crowd, so far as the decisions it comes to are concerned. We have seen that when a deliberative assembly is called upon to give its opinion on a question of a character not entirely technical, intelligence stands for nothing. For instance, a gathering of scientific men or of artists, owing to the mere fact that they form an assemblage, will not deliver judgements on general subjects sensibly different from those rendered by a gathering of masons or grocers. At various periods, and in particular previous to 1848, the French administration instituted a careful choice among the persons summoned to form a jury, picking the jurors from among the enlightened classes; choosing professors, functionaries, men of letters, etc. At the present day jurors are recruited for the most part from among small tradesmen, petty capitalists, and employees. Yet, to the great astonishment of specialist writers, whatever the composition of the jury has been, its decisions have been identical. Even the magistrates, hostile as they are to the institution of the jury, have had to recognize the exactness of the assertion. M. Berard des Glajeux, a former President of the Court of Assizes, expresses himself on the subject in his " Memoirs " in the following terms:—

"The selection of jury men is today in reality in the hands of the municipal councillors, who put people down on the list or eliminate them from it in accordance with the political and electoral preoccupations inherent in their situation. . . . The majority of the jurors chosen are persons engaged in trade, but persons of less importance than formerly, and employees belonging to certain branches of the administration. . . . Both opinions and professions counting for nothing once the role of judge assumed, many of the jury men having the ardor of neophytes, and men of the best intentions being similarly disposed in humble situations, the spirit of the jury has not changed: *its verdicts have remained the same.*"

Of the passage just cited the conclusions, which are just, are to be borne in mind and not the explanations, which are weak. Too much astonishment should not be felt at this weakness, for, as a rule, counsel equally with magistrates seem to be ignorant of the psychology of crowds and, in consequence, of juries. I find a proof of this statement in a fact related by the author just quoted. He remarks that Lachaud, one of the most illustrious barristers practicing in the Court of Assize, made systematic use of his right to object to a juror in the case of all individuals of intelligence on the list. Yet experience—and experience alone—has ended by acquainting us with the utter uselessness of these objections. This is proved by the fact that at the present day public prosecutors and barristers, at any rate those belonging to the Parisian bar, have entirely renounced their right to object to a juror; still, as M. des Glajeux remarks, the verdicts have not changed, "they are neither better nor worse."

Like all crowds, juries are very strongly impressed by sentimental considerations, and very slightly by argument. "They cannot resist the sight," writes a barrister, " of a mother giving its child the breast, or of orphans." "It is sufficient that a woman should be of agreeable appearance," says M. des Glajeux, "to win the benevolence of the jury."

Without pity for crimes of which it appears possible they might themselves be the victims—such crimes, moreover, are the most dangerous for society—juries, on the contrary, are very indulgent in the case of breaches of the law whose motive is passion. They are rarely severe on infanticide by girl-mothers, or hard on the young woman who throws vitriol at the man who has seduced and deserted her, for the reason that they feel instinctively that society runs but slight danger from such crimes, and that in a country in which the law does not protect deserted girls the crime of the girl who avenges herself is rather useful than harmful, inasmuch as it frightens future seducers in advance.[1]

Juries, like all crowds, are profoundly impressed by prestige,

1 It is to be remarked, in passing, that this division of crimes into those dangerous and those not dangerous for society, which is well and instinctively made by juries, is far from being unjust. The object of criminal laws is evidently to protect society against dangerous criminals and not to avenge it. On the other hand, the French code, and above all the minds of the French magistrates, are still deeply imbued with the spirit of vengeance characteristic of the old primitive law, and the term "vindicte" (prosecution, from the Latin vindicta, vengeance) is still in daily use. A proof of this tendency on the part of the magistrates is found in the refusal by many of them to apply Berenger's law, which allows of a condemned person not undergoing his sentence unless he repeats his crime. Yet no magistrate can be ignorant, for the fact is proved by statistics, that the application of a punish-ment inflicted for the first time infallibly leads to further crime on the part of the person punished. When judges set free a sentenced person it always seems to them that society has not been avenged. Rather than not avenge it they prefer to create a dangerous, confirmed criminal.

and President des Glajeux very properly remarks that, very democratic as juries are in their composition, they are very aristocratic in their likes and dislikes: "Name, birth, great wealth, celebrity, the assistance of an illustrious counsel, everything in the nature of distinction or that lends brilliancy to the accused, stands him in extremely good stead."

The chief concern of a good counsel should be to work upon the feelings of the jury, and, as with all crowds, to argue but little, or only to employ rudimentary modes of reasoning. An English barrister, famous for his successes in the Assize courts, has well set forth the line of action to be followed:—

"While pleading he would attentively observe the jury. The most favour able opportunity has been reached. By dint of insight and experience the counsel reads the effect of each phrase on the faces of the jury men, and draws his conclusions in consequence. His first step is to be sure which members of the jury are already favourable to his cause. It is short work to definitely gain their adhesion, and having done so he turns his attention to the members who seem, on the contrary, ill disposed, and endeavors to discover why they are hostile to the accused. This is the delicate part of his task, for there may be an infinity of reasons for condemning a man, apart from the sentiment of justice."

These few lines resume the entire mechanism of the art of oratory, and we see why the speech prepared in advance has so slight an effect, it being necessary to be able to modify the terms employed from moment to moment in accordance with the impression produced.

The orator does not require to convert to his views all the members of a jury, but only the leading spirits among it who will determine the general opinion. As in all crowds, so in juries there are a small number of individuals who serve as guides to the rest. " I have, found by experience," says the counsel cited above, " that one or two energetic men suffice to carry the rest of the jury with them." It is those two or three whom it is necessary to convince by skillful suggestions. First of all, and above all, it is necessary to please them. The man forming part of a crowd whom one has succeeded in pleasing is on the point of being convinced, and is quite disposed to accept as excellent any arguments that may be offered him. I detach the following anecdote from an interesting account of M. Lachaud, alluded to above:—

"It is well known that during all the speeches he would deliver in the course of an assize sessions, Lachaud never lost sight of the two or three jury men whom he knew or felt to be influential but obstinate. As a rule he was successful in winning over these refractory jurors. On one occasion, however, in the provinces, he had to deal with a jury man whom he plied in vain for three-quarters of an hour with his most cunning arguments; the man was the seventh jury man, the first on the second bench. The case was desperate. Suddenly, in the middle of a passionate demonstration, Lachaud stopped short, and addressing the President of the court said: 'Would you give instructions for the curtain there in front to be drawn. The seventh jury man is blinded by the sun.' The jury man in question reddened, smiled, and expressed his thanks. He was won over for the defense."

Many writers, some of them most distinguished, have started of late a strong campaign against the institution of the jury, although it is the only protection we have against the errors, really very frequent, of a caste that is under no control.[1] A portion of these writers advocate a jury recruited solely from the ranks of the enlightened classes; but we have already

1 The magistracy is, in point of fact, the only administration whose acts are under no control. In spite of all its revolutions, democratic France does not possess that right of habeas corpus of which England is so proud. We have banished all the tyrants, but have set up a magistrate in each city who disposes at will of the honor and liberty of the citizens. An insignificant juge d'instruction (an examining magistrate who has no exact counterpart in England.—*Trans*.), fresh from the university, possesses the revolting power of sending to prison at will persons of the most considerable standing, on a simple supposition on his part of their guilt, and without being obliged to justify his act to any one. Under the pretext of pursuing his investigation he can keep these persons in prison for six months or even a year, and free them at last without owing them either an indemnity or excuses. The warrant in France is the exact equivalent of the *lettre de cachet*, with this difference, that the latter, with the use of which the monarchy was so justly reproached, could only be resorted to by persons occupying a very high position, while the warrant is an instrument in the hands of a whole class of citizens which is far from passing for being very enlightened or very independent.

proved that even in this case the verdicts would be identical with those returned under the present system. Other writers, taking their stand on the errors committed by juries, would abolish the jury and replace it by judges. It is difficult to see how these would-be reformers can forget that the errors for which the jury is blamed were committed in the first instance by judges,and that when the accused person comes before a jury he has already been held to be guilty by several magistrates, by the juge d'instruction, the public prosecutor, and the Court of Arraignment. It should thus be clear that were the accused to be definitely judged by magistrates instead of by jury men, he would lose his only chance of being admitted innocent. The errors of juries have always been first of all the errors of magistrates. It is solely the magistrates, then, who should be blamed when particularly monstrous judicial errors crop up, such, for instance, as the quite recent condemnation of Dr. L who, prosecuted by a juge d'instruction, of excessive stupidity, on the strength of the denunciation of a half-idiot girl, who accused the doctor of having performed an illegal operation upon her for thirty francs, would have been sent to penal servitude but for an explosion of public indignation, which had for result that he was immediately set at liberty by the Chief of the State. The honorable character given the condemned man by all his fellow-citizens made the grossness of the blunder self-evident. The magistrates themselves admitted it, and yet out of caste considerations they did all they could to prevent the pardon being signed. In all similar affairs the jury, confronted with technical details it is unable to understand, naturally hearkens to the public prosecutor, arguing that, after all, the affair has been investigated by magistrates trained to unravel the most intricate situations. Who, then, are the real authors of the error---the jurymen or the magistrates? We should cling vigorously to the jury. It constitutes, perhaps, the only category of crowd that cannot be replaced by any individuallity. It alone can temper the severity of the law, which, equal for all, ought in principle to be blind and to take no cognisance of particular cases. Inaccessible pity, and heeding nothing but the text of the law, the judge in his professional severity would visit with the same penalty the burglar guilty of murder and the wretched girl whom poverty and her abandonement by her seducer have driven to infanticide. The jury, on the other hand, instinctively feels that the seduced girl is much less guilty than the seducer, who, however, is not touched by the law, and that she deserves every indulgence.

Being well acquainted with the psychology of castes, and also with the psychology of other categories of crowds, I do not perceive a single case in which, wrongly accused of a crime, I should not prefer to have to deal with a jury rather than with magistrates. I should have some chance that my innocence would be recognized by the former and not the slightest chance that it would be admitted by the latter. The power of crowds is to be dreaded, but the power of certain castes is to be dreaded yet more. Crowds are open to conviction; castes are never.

CHAPTER IV

ELECTORAL CROWDS

ELECTORAL crowds—that is to say, collectivities invested
with the power of electing the holders of certain functions—
constitute heterogeneous crowds, but as their action is confined
to a single clearly determined matter, namely, to choosing
between different candidates, they present only a few of the
characteristics previously described. Of the characteristics
peculiar to crowds, they display in particular but slight aptitude
for reasoning, the absence of the critical spirit, irritability,
credulity, and simplicity. In their decision, moreover, is to be
traced the influence of the leaders of crowds and the part
played by the factors we have enumerated: affirmation,
repetition, prestige, and contagion.

Let us examine by what methods electoral crowds are to be
persuaded. It will be easy to deduce their psychology from the
methods that are most successful.

It is of primary importance that the candidate should possess prestige. Personal prestige can only be replaced by that resulting from wealth. Talent and even genius are not elements of success of serious importance.

Of capital importance, on the other hand, is the necessity for the candidate of possessing prestige, of being able, that is, to force himself upon the electorate without discussion. The reason why the electors, of whom a majority are working men or peasants, so rarely choose a man from their own ranks to represent them is that such a person enjoys no prestige among them. When, by chance, they do elect a man who is their equal, it is as a rule for subsidiary reasons—for instance, to spite an eminent man, or an influential employer of labor on whom the elector is in daily dependence, and whose master he has the illusion he becomes in this way for a moment.

The possession of prestige does not suffice, however, to assure the success of a candidate. The elector stickles in particular for the flattery of his greed and vanity. He must be overwhelmed with the most extravagant blandishments, and there must be no hesitation in making him the most fantastic promises.

If he is a working man it is impossible to go too far in insulting and stigmatizing employers of labor. As for the rival candidate, an effort must be made to destroy his chance by establishing by dint of affirmation, repetition, and contagion that he is an arrant scoundrel, and that it is a matter of common knowledge that he has been guilty of several crimes. It is, of course, useless to trouble about any semblance of proof. Should the adversary be ill-acquainted with the psychology of crowds he will try to justify himself by arguments instead of confining himself to replying to one set of affirmations by another; and he will have no chance whatever of being successful.

The candidate's written program should not be too categorical, since later on his adversaries might bring it up against him; in his verbal program, however, there cannot be too much exaggeration. The most important reforms may be fearlessly promised. At the moment they are made these exaggerations produce a great effect, and they are not binding for the future, it being a matter of constant observation that the elector never troubles himself to know how far the candidate he has returned has followed out the electoral program he applauded, and in virtue of which the election was supposed to have been secured.

In what precedes, all the factors of persuasion which we have described are to be recognized. We shall come across them again in the action exerted by words and formulas, whose magical sway we have already insisted upon. An orator who knows how to make use of these means of persuasion can do what he will with a crowd. Expressions such as infamous capital, vile exploiters, the admirable working man, the socialization of wealth, etc., always produce the same effect, although already somewhat worn by use. But the candidate who hits on a new formula as devoid as possible of precise meaning, and apt in consequence to flatter the most varied aspirations, infallibly obtains a success. The sanguinary Spanish revolution of 1873 was brought about by one of these magical phrases of complex meaning on which everybody can put his own interpretation. A contemporary writer has described the launching of this phrase in terms that deserve to be quoted:—

" The radicals have made the discovery that a centralized republic is a monarchy in disguise, and to humor them the Cortes had unanimously proclaimed a *federal republic*, though none of the voters could have explained what it was he had just voted for. This formula, however, delighted everybody; the joy was intoxicating, delirious. The reign of virtue and happiness had just been inaugurated on earth. A republican whose opponent refused him the title of federalist considered himself to be mortally insulted. People addressed each other in the streets with the words: 'Long live the federal republic !' After which the praises were sung of the mystic virtue of the absence of discipline in the army, and of the autonomy of the soldiers. What was understood by the 'federal republic?' There were those who took it to mean the emancipation of the provinces, institutions akin to those of the United States and administrative decentralization; others had in view the abolition of all authority and the speedy commencement of the great social liquidation. The socialists of Barcelona and Andalusia stood out for the absolute sovereignty of the communes; they proposed to endow Spain with ten thousand independent municipalities, to legislate on their own account, and their creation to be accompanied by the suppression of the police and the army. In the southern provinces the insurrection was soon seen to spread from town to town and village to village. Directly a village had made its *pronunciamiento* its first care was to destroy the telegraph wires and the railway lines so as to cut off all communication with its neighbors and Madrid. The sorriest hamlet was determined to stand on its own bottom. Federation had given place to cantonalism, marked by massacres, incendiarism, and every description of brutality, and bloody saturnalia were celebrated throughout the length and breadth of the land."

With respect to the influence that may be exerted by reasoning on the minds of electors, to harbor the least doubt on this subject can only be the result of never having read the reports of an electioneering meeting. In such a gathering affirmations, invectives, and sometimes blows are exchanged, but never arguments. Should silence be established for a moment it is because some one present, having the reputation of a "tough customer," has announced that he is about to heckle the candidate by putting him one of those embarrassing questions which are always the joy of the audience. The satisfaction, however, of the opposition party is short lived, for the voice of the questioner is soon drowned in the uproar made by his adversaries. The following reports of public meetings, chosen from hundreds of similar examples, and taken from the daily papers, may be considered as typical:—

"One of the organizers of the meeting having asked the assembly to elect a president, the storm bursts. The anarchists leap on to the platform to take the committee table by storm.

The socialists make an energetic defense; blows are exchanged, and each party accuses the other of being spies in the pay of the Government, etc... A citizen leaves the hall with a black eye. "The committee is at length installed as best it may be in the midst of the tumult, and the right to speak devolves upon 'Comrade' X.

"The orator starts a vigorous attack on the socialists, who interrupt him with shouts of 'Idiot, scoundrel, blackguard!' etc., epithets to which Comrade X. replies by setting forth a theory according to which the socialists are 'idiots' or 'jokers.'"

"The Allemanist party had organized yesterday evening, in the Hall of Commerce, in the Rue du Faubourg-du-Temple, a great meeting, preliminary to the workers' fete of the 1st of May. The watchword of the meeting was 'Calm and Tranquillity!'

"Comrade G--- alludes to the socialists as 'idiots' and 'humbugs.' "At these words there is an exchange of invectives and orators and audience come to blows. Chairs, tables, and benches are converted into weapons," etc., etc.

It is not to be imagined for a moment that this description of discussion is peculiar to a determined class of electors and dependent on their social position. In every anonymous assembly whatever, though it be composed exclusively of highly educated persons, discussion always assumes the same shape. I have shown that when men are collected in a crowd there is a tendency towards their mental leveling at work, and proof of this is to be found at every turn. Take, for example, the following extract from a report of a meeting composed exclusively of students, which I borrow from the Temps of 13th of February, 1895:—

"The tumult only increased as the evening went on; I do not believe that a single orator succeeded in uttering two sentences without being interrupted. At every instant there came shouts from this or that direction or from every direction at once. Applause was intermingled with hissing, violent discussions were in progress between individual members of the audience, sticks were brandished threateningly, others beat a tattoo on the floor, and the interrupters were greeted with yells of 'Put him out !' or 'Let him speak!'

"M. C— lavished such epithets as odious and cowardly, monstrous, vile, venal and vindictive, on the Association, which he declared he wanted to destroy," etc., etc.

How, it may be asked, can an elector form an opinion under such conditions? To put such a question is to harbor a strange delusion as to the measure of liberty that may be enjoyed by a collectivity. Crowds have opinions that have been imposed upon them, but they never boast reasoned opinions. In the case under consideration the opinions and votes of the electors are in the hands of the election committees, whose leading spirits are, as a rule, publicans, their influence over the working men, to whom they allow credit, being great. "Do you know what an election committee is?" writes M. Scherer, one of the most valiant champions of present-day democracy. "It is neither more nor less than the cornerstone of our institutions, the masterpiece of the political machine. France is governed today by the election committees."[1]

To exert an influence over them is not difficult, provided the candidate be in himself acceptable and possess adequate financial resources. According to the admissions of the donors, three millions of francs sufficed to secure the repeated elections of General Boulanger.

Such is the psychology of electoral crowds. It is identical with that of other crowds: neither better nor worse.

In consequence I draw no conclusion against universal suffrage from what precedes had I to settle its fate, I should

---

[1]'Committees under whatever name, clubs, syndicates, etc., constitute perhaps the most redoubtable danger resulting from the power of crowds. They represent in reality the most impersonal and, in consequence, the most oppressive form of tyranny. The leaders who direct the committees being supposed to speak and act in the name of a collectivity, are freed from all responsibility, and are in a position to do just as they choose. The most savage tyrant has never ventured even to dream of such prescriptions as those ordained by the committees of the Revolution. Barr as has declared that they decimated the Convention, picking off its members at their pleasure. So long as he was able to speak in their name, Robespierre wielded absolute power. The moment this frightful dictator separated himself from them, for reasons of personal pride, he was lost. The reign of crowds is the reign of committees, that is, of the leaders of crowds. A severer despotism cannot be imagined.

preserve it as it is for practical reasons, which are to be deduced in point of fact from our investigation of the psychology of crowds. On this account I shall proceed to set them forth.

No doubt the weak side of universal suffrage is too obvious to be overlooked. It cannot be gain said that civilization has been the work of a small minority of superior intelligences constituting the culminating point of a pyramid, whose stages, widening in proportion to the decrease of mental power, represent the masses of a nation. The greatness of a civilization cannot assuredly depend upon the votes given by inferior elements boasting solely numerical strength. Doubtless, too, the votes recorded by crowds are often very dangerous. They have already cost us several invasions, and in view of the triumph of socialism, for which they are preparing the way, it is probable that the vagaries of popular sovereignty will cost us still more dearly.

Excellent, however, as these objections are in theory, in practice they lose all force, as will be admitted if the invincible strength be remembered of ideas transformed into dogma. The dogma of the sovereignty of crowds is as little defensible, from the philosophical point of view, as the religious dogmas of the Middle Ages, but it enjoys at present the same absolute power they formerly enjoyed. It is as unattackable in consequence as in the past were our religious ideas. Imagine a modern freethinker miraculously transported into the midst of the Middle Ages. Do you suppose that, after having ascertained the sovereign power of the religious ideas that were then in force, he would have been tempted to attack them? Having fallen into the hands of a judge disposed to send him to the stake, under the imputation of having concluded a pact with the devil, or of having been present at the witches' sabbath, would it have occurred to him to call in question the existence of the devil or of the sabbath? It were as wise to oppose cyclones with discussion as the beliefs of crowds. The dogma of universal suffrage possesses today the power the Christian dogmas formerly possessed. Orators and writers allude to it with a respect and adulation that never fell to the share of Louis XIV. In consequence the same position must be taken up with regard to it as with regard to all religious dogmas. Time alone can act upon them.

Besides, it would be the more useless to attempt to undermine this dogma, inasmuch as it has an appearance of reasonableness in its favor. "In an era of equality," Tocqueville justly remarks, "men have no faith in each other on account of their being all alike; yet this same similitude gives them an almost limitless confidence in the judgment of the public, the reason being that it does not appear probable that, all men being equally enlightened, truth and numerical superiority should not go hand in hand."

Must it be believed that with a restricted suffrage—a suffrage restricted to those intellectually capable if it be desired—an improvement would be effected in the votes of crowds? I cannot admit for a moment that this would be the case, and that for the reasons I have already given touching the mental inferiority of all collectivities, whatever their composition. In a crowd men always tend to the same level, and, on general questions, a vote recorded by forty academicians is no better than that of forty water-carriers. I do not in the least believe that any of the votes for which universal suffrage is blamed— the reestablishment of the Empire, for instance—would have fallen out differently had the voters been exclusively recruited among learned and liberally educated men. It does not follow because an individual knows Greek or mathematics, is an architect, a veterinary surgeon, a doctor, or a barrister, that he is endowed with a special intelligence of social questions. All our political economists are highly educated, being for the most part professors or academicians, yet is there a single general question —protection, bimetallism, etc.—on which they have succeeded in agreeing? The explanation is that their science is only a very attenuated form of our universal ignorance. With regard to social problems, owing to the number of unknown quantities they offer, men are substantially, equally ignorant.

In consequence, were the electorate solely composed of

persons stuffed with sciences their votes would be no better than those emitted at present. They would be guided in the main by their sentiments and by party spirit. We should be spared none of the difficulties we now have to contend with, and we should certainly be subjected to the oppressive tyranny of castes.

Whether the suffrage of crowds be restricted or general, whether it be exercised under a republic or a monarchy, in France, in Belgium, in Greece, in Portugal, or in Spain, it is everywhere identical; and, when all is said and done, it is the expression of the unconscious aspirations and needs of the race. In each country the average opinions of those elected represent the genius of the race, and they will be found not to alter sensibly from one generation to another. It is seen, then, that we are confronted once more by the fundamental notion of race, which we have come across so often, and by this other notion, which is the outcome of the first, that institutions and governments play but a small part in the life of a people. Peoples are guided in the main by the genius of their race, that is, by that inherited residue of qualities of which the genius is the sum total. Race and the slavery of our daily necessities are the mysterious master-causes that rule our destiny.

CHAPTER V

PARLIAMENTARY ASSEMBLIES

Parliamentary crowds present most of the characteristics common to heterogeneous crowds that are not anonymous—The simplicity of
their opinions—Their suggestibility and its limits—Their indestruc
tible, fixed opinions and their changed opinions—The reason of
the predominance of indecision—The role of the leaders—The
reason of their prestige—They are the true masters of an assembly
whose votes, on that account, are merely those of a small
minority—The absolute power they exercise —The elements of
their oratorical art-- Phrases and images-- The psychological
necessity the leaders are under of being in a general way of
stubborn convictions and narrowminded—It is impossible for a
speaker without prestige to obtain recognition for his argu
ments—The exaggeration of the sentiments, whether good or
bad, of assemblies—At certain moments they become automatic
—The sittings of the Convention—Cases in which an assem
bly loses the characteristics of crowds—The influence of specialists
when technical questions arise—The advantages and dangers of a
parliamentary system in all countries—It is adapted to modern
needs; but it involves financial waste and the progressive
curtailment of all liberty-- Conclusion.

IN parliamentary assemblies we have an example of heterogeneous crowds that are not anonymous. Although the mode
of election of their members varies from epoch to epoch, and
from nation to nation, they present very similar characteristics. In this case the influence of the race makes itself felt to
weaken or exaggerate the characteristics common to crowds,
but not to prevent their manifestation. The parliamentary
assemblies of the most widely different countries, of Greece,
Italy, Portugal, Spain, France, and America present great

analogies in their debates and votes, and leave the respective governments face to face with identical difficulties.

Moreover, the parliamentary system represents the ideal of all modern civilized peoples. The system is the expression of the idea, psychologically erroneous, but generally admitted, that a large gathering of men is much more capable than a small number of coming to a wise and independent decision on a given subject.

The general characteristics of crowds are to be met with in parliamentary assemblies: intellectual simplicity, irritability, suggestibility, the exaggeration of the sentiments and the preponderating influence of a few leaders. In consequence, however, of their special composition parliamentary crowds offer some distinctive features, which we shall point out shortly.

Simplicity in their opinions is one of their most important characteristics. In the case of all parties, and more especially so far as the Latin peoples are concerned, an invariable tendency is met with in crowds of this kind to solve the most complicated social problems by the simplest abstract principles and general laws applicable to all cases. Naturally the principles vary with the party; but owing to the mere fact that the individual members are a part of a crowd, they are always inclined to exaggerate the worth of their principles, and to push them to their extreme consequences. In consequences parliaments are more especially representative of extreme opinions.

The most perfect example of the ingenuous simplification of opinions peculiar to assemblies is offered by the Jacobins of the French Revolution. Dogmatic and logical to a man, and their brains full of vague generalities, they busied themselves with the application of fixed principles without concerning themselves with events. It has been said of them, with reason, that they went through the Revolution without witnessing it. With the aid of the very simple dogmas that served them as guide, they imagined they could recast society from top to bottom, and cause a highly refined civilization to return to a very anterior phase of the social evolution. The methods they resorted to to realize their dream wore the same stamp of absolute ingenuousness. They confined themselves, in reality, to destroying what stood in their way. All of them, moreover— Girondists, the Men of the Mountain, the Thermidorians, etc.—were alike animated by the same spirit.

Parliamentary crowds are very open to suggestion; and, as in the case of all crowds, the suggestion comes from leaders possessing prestige; but the suggestibility of parliamentary assemblies has very clearly defined limits, which it is important to point out.

On all questions of local or regional interest every member of an assembly has fixed, unalterable opinions, which no amount of argument can shake. The talent of a Demosthenes would be powerless to change the vote of a Deputy on such questions as protection or the privilege of distilling alcohol, questions in which the interests of influential electors are involved. The suggestion emanating from these electors and undergone before the time to vote arrives, sufficiently outweighs suggestions from any other source to annul them and to maintain an absolute fixity of opinion.[1]

On general questions—the overthrow of a Cabinet, the imposition of a tax, etc.—there is no longer any fixity of opinion, and the suggestions of leaders can exert an influence, though not in quite the same way as in an ordinary crowd. Every party has its leaders, who possess occasionally an equal influence. The result is that the Deputy finds himself placed between two contrary suggestions, and is inevitably made to hesitate. This explains how it is that he is often seen to vote in contrary fashion in an interval of a quarter of an hour or to add to a law an article which nullifies it; for instance, to withdraw from employers of labour the right of choosing and dismissing their workmen, and then to very nearly annul this measure by

1 The following reflection of an English parliamentarian of long experience doubtless applies to these opinions, fixed beforehand, and rendered unalterable by electioneering necessities: " During the fifty years that I have sat at Westminster, I have listened to thousands of speeches; but few of them have changed my opinion, not one of them has changed my vote."

an amendment.

It is for the same reason that every Chamber that is returned has some very stable opinions, and other opinions that are very shifting. On the whole, the general questions being the more numerous, indecision is predominant in the Chamber—the indecision which results from the everpresent fear of the elector, the suggestion received from whom is always latent, rind tends to counterbalance the influence of the leaders.

Still, it is the leaders who are definitely the masters in those numerous discussions, with regard to the subject-matter of which the members of an assembly are without strong preconceived opinions.

The necessity for these leaders is evident, since, under the name of heads of groups, they are met with in the assemblies of every country. They are the real rulers of an assembly. Men forming a crowd cannot do without a master, whence it results that the votes of an assembly only represent, as a rule, the opinions of a small minority.

The influence of the leaders is due in very small measure to the arguments they employ, but in a large degree to their prestige. The best proof of this is that, should they by any circumstance lose their prestige, their influence disappears.

The prestige of these political leaders is individual, and independent of name or celebrity: a fact of which M. Jules Simon gives us some very curious examples in his remarks on the prominent men of the Assembly of 1848, of which he was a member:—

"Two months before he was all-powerful, Louis Napoleon was entirely without the least importance."

"Victor Hugo mounted the tribune. He failed to achieve success. He was listened to as Felix Pyat was listened to, but he did not obtain as much applause. 'I don't like his ideas,' Vaulabelle said to me, speaking of Felix Pyat, 'but he is one of the greatest writers and the greatest orator of France.' Edgar Quinet, in spite of his exceptional and powerful intelligence, was held in no esteem whatever. He had been popular for awhile before the opening of the Assembly; in the Assembly he had no popularity."

"The splendor of genius makes itself less felt in political assemblies than anywhere else. They only give heed to eloquence appropriate to the time and place and to party services, not to services rendered the country. For homage to be rendered Lamartine in 1848 and Thiers in 1871, the stimulant was needed of urgent, inexorable interest. As soon as the danger was passed the parliamentary world forgot in the same instant its gratitude and its fright."

I have quoted the preceding passage for the sake of the facts it contains, not of the explanations it offers, their psychology being somewhat poor. A crowd would at once lose its character of a crowd were it to credit its leaders with their services, whether of a party nature or rendered their country. The crowd that obeys a leader is under the influence of his prestige, and its submission is not dictated by any sentiment of interest or gratitude.

In consequence the leader endowed with sufficient prestige wields almost absolute power. The immense influence exerted during a long series of years, thanks to his prestige, by a celebrated Deputy, beaten at the last general election in consequence of certain financial events, is well known. He had only to give the signal and Cabinets were overthrown. A writer has clearly indicated the scope of his action in the following lines:—

"It is due, in the main, to M. X—— that we paid three times as dearly as we should have done for Tonkin, that we remained so long on a precarious footing in Madagascar, that we were defrauded of an empire in the region of the Lower Niger, and that we have lost the preponderating situation we used to occupy in Egypt. The theories of M. X—— have cost us more territories than the disasters of Napoleon I." [1]

We must not harbor too bitter a grudge against the leader in

1 M. Clemenceau.—*Note of the Translator.*

question. It is plain that he has cost us very dear; but a great part of his influence was due to the fact that he followed public opinion, which, in colonial matters, was far from being at the time what it has since become. A leader is seldom in advance of public opinion; almost always all he does is to follow it and to espouse all its errors.

The means of persuasion of the leaders we are dealing with, apart from their prestige, consist in the factors we have already enumerated several times. To make a skillful use of these resources a leader must have arrived at a comprehension, at least in an unconscious manner, of the psychology of crowds, and must know how to address them. He should be aware, in particular, of the fascinating influence of words, phrases, and images. He should possess a special description of eloquence, composed of energetic affirmations—unburdened with proofs—and impressive images, accompanied by very summary arguments. This is a kind of eloquence that is met with in all assemblies, the English Parliament included, the most serious though it is of all.

"Debates in the House of Commons," says the English philosopher Maine, "may be constantly read in which the entire discussion is confined to an exchange of rather weak generalities and rather violent personalities. General formulas of this description exercise a prodigious influence on the imagination of a pure democracy. It will always be easy to make a crowd accept general assertions, presented in striking terms, although they have never been verified, and are perhaps not susceptible of verification."

Too much importance cannot be attached to the "striking terms" alluded to in the above quotation. We have already insisted, on several occasions, on the special power of words and formulas. They must be chosen in such a way as to evoke very vivid images. The following phrase, taken from a speech by one of the leaders of our assemblies, affords an excellent example:—

"When the same vessel shall bear away to the fever-haunted lands of our penitentiary settlements the politician of shady reputation and the anarchist guilty of murder, the pair will be able to converse together, and they will appear to each other as the two complementary aspects of one and the same state of society."

The image thus evoked is very vivid, and all the adversaries of the speaker felt themselves threatened by it. They conjured up a double vision of the fever-haunted country and the vessel that may carry them away; for is it not possible that they are included in the somewhat ill-defined category of the politicians menaced? They experienced the lurking fear that the men of the Convention must have felt whom the vague speeches of Robespierre threatened with the guillotine, and who, under the influence of this fear, invariably yielded to him.

It is all to the interest of the leaders to indulge in the most improbable exaggerations. The speaker of whom I have just cited a sentence was able to affirm, without arousing violent protestations, that bankers and priests had subsidized the throwers of bombs, and that the directors of the great financial companies deserve the same punishment as anarchists. Affirmations of this kind are always effective with crowds. The affirmation is never too violent, the declamation never too threatening. Nothing intimidates the audience more than this sort of eloquence. Those present are afraid that if they protest they will be put down as traitors or accomplices.

As I have said, this peculiar style of eloquence has ever been of sovereign effect in all assemblies. In times of crisis its power is still further accentuated. The speeches of the great orators of the assemblies of the French Revolution are very interesting reading from this point of view. At every instant they thought themselves obliged to pause in order to denounce crime and exalt virtue, after which they would burst forth into imprecations against tyrants, and swear to live free men or perish. Those present rose to their feet, applauded furiously, and then, calmed, took their seats again.

On occasion, the leader may be intelligent and highly educated, but the possession of these qualities does him, as a rule, more harm than good. By showing how complex things are, by allowing of explanation and promoting comprehension, intelligence always renders its owner indulgent, and blunts, in a large measure, that intensity and violence of conviction needful for apostles. The great leaders of crowds of all ages, and those of the Revolution in particular, have been of lamentably narrow intellect; while it is precisely those whose intelligence has been the most restricted who have exercised the greatest influence.

The speeches of the most celebrated of them, of Robespierre, frequently astound one by their incoherence: by merely reading them no plausible explanation is to be found of the great part played by the powerful dictator:—

"The commonplaces and redundancies of pedagogic eloquence and Latin culture at the service of a mind childish rather than undistinguished, and limited in its notions of attack and defense to the defiant attitude of schoolboys. Not an idea, not a happy turn of phrase, or a telling hit: a storm of declamation that leaves us bored. After a dose of this unexhilarating reading one is tempted to exclaim 'Oh!' with the amiable Camille Desmoulins."

It is terrible at times to think of the power that strong conviction combined with extreme narrowness of mind gives a man possessing prestige. It is none the less necessary that these conditions should be satisfied for a man to ignore obstacles and display strength of will in a high measure. Crowds instinctively recognize in men of energy and conviction the masters they are always in need of.

In a parliamentary assembly the success of a speech depends almost solely on the prestige possessed by the speaker, and not at all on the arguments he brings forward. The best proof of this is that when for one cause or another a speaker loses his prestige, he loses simultaneously all his influence, that is, his power of influencing votes at will.

When an unknown speaker comes forward with a speech containing good arguments, but only arguments, the chances are that he will only obtain a hearing. A Deputy who is a psychologist of insight, M. Desaubes, has recently traced in the following lines the portrait of the Deputy who lacks prestige:—

"When he takes his place in the tribune he draws a document from his portfolio, spreads it out methodically before him, and makes a start with assurance.

"He flatters himself that he will implant in the minds of his audience the conviction by which he is himself animated. He has weighed and reweighed his arguments; he is well primed with figures and proofs; he is certain he will convince his hearers. In the face of the evidence he is to adduce all resistance would be futile. He begins, confident in the justice of his cause, and relying upon the attention of his colleagues, whose only anxiety, of course, is to subscribe to the truth.

"He speaks, and is at once surprised at the restlessness of the House, and a little annoyed by the noise that is being made.

"How is it silence is not kept? Why this general inattention? What are those Deputies thinking about who are engaged in conversation ? What urgent motive has induced this or that Deputy to quit his seat?"

"An expression of uneasiness crosses his face; he frowns and stops. Encouraged by the President, he begins again, raising his voice. He is only listened to all the less. He lends emphasis to his words, and gesticulates: the noise around him increases. He can no longer hear himself, and again stops; finally, afraid that his silence may provoke the dreaded cry, 'The Closure!' he starts off again. The clamour becomes unbearable."

When parliamentary assemblies reach a certain pitch of excitement they become identical with ordinary heterogeneous crowds, and their sentiments in consequence present the peculiarity of being always extreme. They will be seen to commit acts of the greatest heroism or the worst excesses. The individual is no longer himself, and so entirely is this the case that he will vote measures most adverse to his personal interests.

The history of the French Revolution shows to what an extent assemblies are capable of losing their self-consciousness, and of obeying suggestions most contrary to their interests. It was an enormous sacrifice for the nobility to renounce its privileges, yet it did so without hesitation on a famous night during the sittings of the Constituent Assembly. By renouncing their inviolability the men of the Convention placed themselves under a perpetual menace of death, and yet they took this step, and were not afraid to decimate their own ranks, though perfectly aware that the scaffold to which they were sending their colleagues today might be their own fate tomorrow. The truth is they had attained to that completely automatic state which I have described elsewhere, and no consideration would hinder them from yielding to the suggestions by which they were hypnotized. The following passage from the memoirs of one of them, Billaud-Varennes, is absolutely typical on this score: "The decisions with which we have been so reproached," he says, "*were not desired by us two days, a single day before they were taken: it was the crisis and nothing else that gave rise to them.*" Nothing can be more accurate.

The same phenomena of unconsciousness were to be witnessed during all the stormy sittings of the Convention.

"They approved and decreed measures," says Taine, "which they held in horror—measures which were not only stupid and foolish, but measures that were crimes —the murder of innocent men, the murder of their friends. The Left, supported by the Right, unanimously and amid loud applause, sent to the scaffold Danton, its natural chief, and the great promoter and leader of the Revolution. Unanimously and amid the greatest applause the Right, supported by the Left, votes the worst decrees of the revolutionary government. Unanimously and amid cries of admiration and enthusiasm, amid demonstrations of passionate sympathy for Collot d'Herbois, Couthon, and Robespierre, the Convention by spontaneous and repeated reelections keeps in office the homicidal government which the Plain detests because it is homicidal, and the Mountain detests because it is decimated by it. The Plain and the Mountain, the majority and the minority, finish by consenting to help on their own suicide. The 22 Prairial the entire Convention offered itself to the executioner; the Thermidor, during the first quarter of an hour that followed Robespierre's speech, it did the same thing again."

This picture may appear sombre. Yet it is accurate. Parliamentary assemblies, sufficiently excited and hypnotised, offer the same characteristics. They become an unstable flock, obedient to every impulsion. The following description of the Assembly of 1848 is due to M. Sputter, a parliamentarian whose faith in democracy is above suspicion. I reproduce it from the *Revue litteraire*, and it is thoroughly typical. It offers an example of all the exaggerated sentiments which I have described as characteristic of crowds, and of that excessive changeableness which permits of assemblies passing, from moment to moment, from one set of sentiments to another entirely opposite.

"The Republican party was brought to its perdition by its divisions, its jealousies, its suspicions, and, in turn, its blind confidence and its limitless hopes. Its ingenuousness and candor were only equalled by its universal mistrust. An absence of all sense of legality, of all comprehension of discipline, together with boundless terrors and illusions; the peasant and the child are on a level in these respects. Their calm is as great as their impatience; their ferocity is equal to their docility. This condition is the natural consequence of a temperament that is not formed and of the lack of education. Nothing astonishes such persons, and everything disconcerts them. Trembling with fear or brave to the point of heroism, they would go through fire and water or fly from a shadow.

"They are ignorant of cause, and effect and of the connecting links between events. They are as promptly discouraged as they are exalted, they are subject to every description of panic, they are always either too highly strung or too downcast, but never in the mood or the measure the situation would require. More fluid than water they reflect every line and assume every shape. What sort of foundation for a government can they be expected to supply?"

Fortunately all the characteristics just described as to be met with in parliamentary assemblies are in no wise constantly displayed. Such assemblies only constitute crowds at certain moments. The individuals composing them retain their individuality in a great number of cases, which explains how it is that an assembly is able to turn out excellent technical laws. It is true that the author of these laws is a specialist who has prepared them in the quiet of his study, and that in reality the law voted is the work of an individual and not of an assembly. These laws are naturally the best. They are, only liable to have disastrous results when a series of amendments has converted them into the outcome of a collective effort. The work of a crowd is always inferior, whatever its nature, to that of an isolated individual. It is specialists who safeguard assemblies from passing ill-advised or unworkable measures. The specialist in this case is a temporary leader of crowds. The Assembly is without influence on him, but he has influence over the Assembly.

In spite of all the difficulties attending their working, parliamentary assemblies are the best form of government mankind has discovered as yet, and more especially the best means it has found to escape the yoke of personal tyrannies. They constitute assuredly the ideal government at any rate for philosophers, thinkers, writers, artists, and learned men—in a word, for all those who form the cream of a civilization.

Moreover, in reality they only present two serious dangers, one being inevitable financial waste, and the other the progressive restriction of the liberty of the individual.

The first of these dangers is the necessary consequence of the exigencies and want of foresight of electoral crowds. Should a member of an assembly propose a measure giving apparent satisfaction to democratic ideas, should he bring, in a Bill, for instance, to assure old-age pensions to all workers, and to increase the wages of any class of State employees, the other Deputies, victims of suggestion in their dread of their electors, will not venture to seem to disregard the interests of the latter by rejecting the proposed measure, although well aware they are imposing a fresh strain on the Budget and necessitating the creation of new taxes. It is impossible for them to hesitate to give their votes. The consequences of the increase of expenditure are remote and will not entail disagreeable consequences for them personally, while the consequences of a negative vote might clearly come to light when they next present themselves for reelection.

In addition to this first cause of an exaggerated expenditure there is another not less imperative—the necessity of voting all grants for local purposes. A Deputy is unable to oppose grants of this kind because they represent once more the exigencies of the electors, and because each individual Deputy can only obtain what he requires for his own constituency on the condition of acceding to similar demands on the part of his colleagues. [1]

1 In its issue of April 6, 1895, the *Economiste* published a curious review of the figures that may be reached by expenditure caused solely by electoral considerations, and notably of the outlay on railways. To put Langayes (a town of 3,000 inhabitants, situated on a mountain) in communication with Puy, a railway is voted that will cost 15 millions of francs. Seven millions are to be spent to put Beaumont (3,500 in-habitants) in communication with Castel-Sarrazin; 7 millions to put Oust (a village of 523 inhabitants) in communication with Seix (1,200 inhabitants); 6 millions to put Prade in communication with the hamlet of Olette (747 inhabitant), etc. In 1895 alone 90 Millions of francs were voted for railways of only local utility. There is other no less important expenditure necessitated also by electioneering considerations. The law instituting working-men's pensions will soon involve a minimum annual outlay of 165 millions, according to the Minister of Finance, and of 800 millions according to the academician M. Leroy-Beaulieu. It is evident that the continued growth of expenditure of this kind must end in bankruptcy. Many European countries—Portugal, Greece, Spain, Turkey—have reached this stage, and others, such as Italy, will soon reduced to the same extremity. Still too much alarm need not be felt at this state of things, since the public has successively consented to put up with the reduction of four-fifths in the payment of their coupons by these different countries. Bankruptcy under these ingenious conditions allows the equilibrium of Budgets difficult to balance to be instantly restored. Moreover, wars, socialism, and economic conflicts hold in store for us a profusion of other catastrophes in the period of universal disintegration we are traversing, and it is necessary to be resigned to living from hand to mouth without too much concern for a future we cannot control.

The second of the dangers referred to above—the inevitable restrictions on liberty consummated by parliamentary assemblies—is apparently less obvious, but is, nevertheless, very real. It is the result of the innumerable laws—having always a restrictive action—which parliaments consider themselves obliged to vote and to whose consequences, owing to their shortsighted-ness, they are in a great measure blind.

The danger must indeed be most inevitable, since even England itself, which assuredly offers the most popular type of the parliamentary regime, the type in which the representative is most independent of his elector, has been unable to escape it. Herbert Spencer has shown, in a work already old, that the increase of apparent liberty must needs be followed by the decrease of real liberty. Returning to this contention in his recent book, "The Individual versus the State," he thus expresses himself with regard to the English Parliament:—

"Legislation since this period has followed the course I pointed out. Rapidly multiplying dictatorial measures have continually tended to restrict individual liberties, and this in two ways. Regulations have been established every year in greater number, imposing a constraint on the citizen in matters in which his acts were formerly completely free, and forcing him to accomplish acts which he was formerly at liberty to accomplish or not to accomplish at will. At the same time heavier and heavier public, and especially local, burdens have still further restricted his liberty by diminishing the portion of his profits he can spend as he chooses, and by augmenting the portion which is taken from him to be spent according to the good pleasure of the public authorities."

This progressive restriction of liberties shows itself in every country in a special shape which Herbert Spencer has not pointed out; it is that the passing of these innumerable series of legislative measures, all of them in a general way of a restrictive order, conduces necessarily to augment the number, the power, and the influence of the functionaries charged with their application. These functionaries tend in this way to become the veritable masters of civilized countries. Their power is all the greater owing to the fact that, amidst the incessant transfer of authority, the administrative caste is alone in being untouched by these changes, is alone in possessing irresponsibility, impersonality, and perpetuity. There is no more oppressive despotism than that which presents itself under this triple form.

This incessant creation of restrictive laws and regulations, surrounding the pettiest actions of existence with the most complicated formalities, inevitably has for its result thc confining within narrower and narrower limits of the sphere in which the citizen may move freely. Victims of the delusion that equality and liberty are the better assured by the multiplication of laws, nations daily consent to put up with trammels increasingly burdensome. They do not accept this legislation with impunity. Accustomed to put up with every yoke, they soon end by desiring servitude, and lose all spontaneousness and energy. They are then no more than vain shadows, passive, unresisting and powerless automata.

Arrived at this point, the individual is bound to seek outside himself the forces he no longer finds within him. The functions of governments necessarily increase in proportion as the indifference and helplessness of the citizens grow. They it is who must necessarily exhibit the initiative, enterprising, and guiding spirit in which private persons are lacking. It falls on them to undertake everything, direct everything, and take everything under their protection. The State becomes an all-powerful god. Still experience shows that the power of such gods was never either very durable or very strong.

This progressive restriction of all liberties in the case of certain peoples, in spite of an outward license that gives them the illusion that these liberties are still in their possession, seems at least as much a consequence of their old age as of any particular system. It constitutes one of the precursory symptoms of that decadent phase which up to now no civilization has escaped.

Judging by the lessons of the past, and by the symptoms that strike the attention on every side, several of our modern civilizations have reached that phase of extreme old age which precedes decadence. It seems inevitable that all peoples should pass through identical phases of existence, since history is so often seen to repeat its course.

It is easy to note briefly these common phases of the evolution of civilizations, and I shall terminate this work with a summary of them. This rapid sketch will perhaps throw some gleams of light on the causes of the power at present wielded by crowds.

If we examine in their main lines the genesis of the greatness and of the fall of the civilizations that preceded our own, what do we see?

At the dawn of civilization a swarm of men of various origin, brought together by the chances of migrations, invasions, and conquests. Of different blood, and of equally different languages and beliefs, the only common bond of union between these men is the half-recognized law of a chief. The psychological characteristics of crowds are present in an eminent degree in these confused agglomerations. They have the transient cohesion of crowds, their heroism, their weaknesses, their impulsiveness, and their violence. Nothing is stable in connection with them. They are barbarians.

At length time accomplishes its work. The identity of surroundings, the repeated intermingling of races, the necessities of life in common exert their influence. The assemblage of dissimilar units begins to blend into a whole, to form a race; that is, an aggregate possessing common characteristics and sentiments to which heredity will give greater and greater fixity. The crowd has become a people, and this people is able to emerge from its barbarous state. However, it will only entirely emerge therefrom when, after long efforts, struggles necessarily repeated, and innumerable recommencements, it shall have acquired an ideal. The nature of this ideal is of slight importance; whether it be the cult of Rome, the might of Athens, or the triumph of Allah, it will suffice to endow all the individuals of the race that is forming with perfect unity of sentiment and thought.

At this stage a new civilization, with its institutions, its beliefs, and its arts, may be born. In pursuit of its ideal, the race will acquire in succession the qualities necessary to give it splendour, vigor, and grandeur. At times no doubt it will still be a crowd, but henceforth, beneath the mobile and changing characteristics of crowds, is found a solid substratum, the genius of the race which confines within narrow limits the transformations of a nation and overrules the play of chance.

After having exerted its creative action, time begins that work of destruction from which neither gods nor men escape. Having reached a certain level of strength and complexity a civilization ceases to grow, and having ceased to grow it is condemned to a speedy decline. The hour of its old age has struck. This inevitable hour is always marked by the weakening of the ideal that was the mainstay of the race. In proportion as this ideal pales all the religious, political, and social structures inspired by it begin to be shaken.

With the progressive perishing of its ideal the race loses more and more the qualities that lent it its cohesion, its unity, and its strength. The personality and intelligence of the individual may increase, but at the same time this collective egoism of the race is replaced by an excessive development of the egoism of the individual, accompanied by a weakening of character and a lessening of the capacity for action. What constituted a people, a unity, a whole, becomes in the end an agglomeration of individualities lacking cohesion, and artificially held together for a time by its traditions and institutions. It is at this stage that men, divided by their interests and aspirations, and incapable any longer of self-government, require directing in their pettiest acts, and that the State exerts an absorbing influence.

With the definite loss of its old ideal the genius of the race entirely disappears; it is a mere swarm of isolated individuals and returns to its original state—that of a crowd. Without consistency and without a future, it has all the transitory characteristics of crowds. Its civilization is now without stability, and at the mercy of every chance. The populace is sovereign, and the tide of barbarism mounts. The civilization may still seem brilliant because it possesses an outward front, the work of a long past, but it is in reality an edifice crumbling to ruin, which nothing supports, and destined to fall in at the first storm.

To pass in pursuit of an ideal from the barbarous to the civilized state, and then, when this ideal has lost its virtue, to decline and die, such is the cycle of the life of a people.

EXTRAORDINARY
POPULAR DELUSIONS

AND THE
MADNESS OF CROWDS

By Charles Mackay

TM

TRADERS PRESS
P.O.BOX 6206
GREENVILLE, S.C. 29606

Books and Gifts
for Investors and Traders

PREFACE

THE object of the Author in the following pages has been to collect the most remarkable instances of those moral epidemics which have been excited, sometimes by one cause and some- times by another, and to show how easily the masses have been led astray, and how imitative and gregarious men are, even in their infatuations and crimes.

Some of the subjects introduced may be familiar to the reader; but the Author hopes that sufficient novelty of detail will be found even in these, to render them acceptable, while they could not be wholly omitted in justice to the subject of which it was proposed to treat. The memoirs of the South Sea madness and the Mississippi delusion are more complete and copious than are to be found elsewhere; and the same may be said of the history of the Witch Mania, which contains an account of its terrific progress in Germany, a part of the subject which has been left comparatively untouched by Sir Walter Scott, in his "Letters on Demonology and Witchcraft," the most important that have yet appeared on this fearful but most interesting subject.

Popular delusions began so early, spread so widely, and have lasted so long, that instead of two or three volumes, fifty would scarcely suffice to detail their history. The present may be considered more of a miscellany of delusions than a history, — a chapter only in the great and awful book of human folly which yet remains to be written, and which Porson once jestingly said he would write in five hundred volumes! Interspersed are sketches of some lighter matters,—amusing instances of the imitativeness and wrongheadedness of the people, rather than examples of folly and delusion.

Religious manias have been purposely excluded as incompatible with the limits prescribed to the present work;—a mere list of them would alone be sufficient to occupy a volume.

In another volume should these be favorably received, the Author will attempt a complete view of the progress of Alchemy and the philosophical delusions that sprang from it, including the Rosicrucians of a bygone, and the Magnetisers of the present, era. London, April 23rd, 1841.

PREFACE
TO EDITION OF 1852

IN reading the history of nations, we find that, like individuals, they have their whims and their peculiarities; their seasons of excitement and recklessness, when they care not what they do. We find that whole communities suddenly fix their minds upon one object, and go mad in its pursuit; that millions of people become simultaneously impressed with one delusion, and run after it, till their attention is caught by some new folly more captivating than the first. We see one nation suddenly seized, from its highest to its lowest members, with a fierce desire of military glory; another as suddenly becoming crazed upon a religious scruple; and neither of them recovering its senses until it has shed rivers of blood and sowed a harvest of groans and tears, to be reaped by its posterity. At an early age in the annals of Europe its population lost their wits about the sepulchre of Jesus, and crowded in frenzied multitudes to the Holy Land; another age went mad for fear of the devil, and offered up hundreds of thousands of victims to the delusion of witchcraft. At another time, the many became crazed on the subject of the philosopher's stone, and committed follies till then unheard of in the pursuit. It was once thought a venial offence, in very many countries of Europe, to destroy an enemy by slow poison. Persons who would have revolted at the idea of stabbing a man to the heart, drugged his potage without scruple. Ladies of gentle birth and manners caught the contagion of murder, until poisoning, under their auspices, became quite fashionable. Some delusions, though notorious to all the world, have subsisted for ages, flourishing as widely among civilized and polished nations as among the early barbarians with whom they originated,—that of duelling, for instance, and the belief in omens and divination of the future, which seem to defy the progress of knowledge to eradicate them entirely from the popular mind. Money, again, has often been a cause of the delusion of multitudes. Sober nations have all at once become desperate gamblers, and risked almost their existence upon the turn of a piece of paper. To trace the history of the most prominent of these delusions is the object of the present pages. Men, it has been well said, think in herds; it will be seen that they go mad in herds, while they only recover their senses slowly, and one by one.

Some of the subjects introduced may be familiar to the reader; but the Author hopes that sufficient novelty of detail will be found even in these, to render them acceptable, while they could not be wholly omitted in justice to the subject of which it was proposed to treat. The memoirs of the South Sea madness and the Mississippi delusion are more complete and copious than are to be found elsewhere; and the same may be said of the history of the Witch Mania, which contains an account of its terrific progress in Germany, a part of the subject which has been left comparatively untouched by Sir Walter Scott in his Letters on Demonology and Witchcraft, the most important that have yet appeared on this fearful but most interesting subject.

Popular delusions began so early, spread so widely, and have lasted so long, that instead of two or three volumes, fifty would scarcely suffice to detail their history. The present may be considered more of a miscellany of delusions than a history— a chapter only in the great and awful book of human folly which yet remains to be written, and which Porson once jestingly said he would write in five hundred volumes! Interspersed are sketches of some lighter matters,—amusing instances of the imitativeness and wrongheadedness of the people, rather than examples of folly and delusion.

JOHN LAW

MONEY MANIA—
THE MISSISSIPPI SCHEME

Some in clandestine companies combine;
Erect new stocks to trade beyond the line;
With air and empty names beguile the town,
And raise new credits first, then cry'em down;
Divide the empty nothing into shares,
And set the crowd together by the ears.—*Defoe.*

THE personal character and career of one man are so
intimately connected with the great scheme of the years 1719
and 1720, that a history of the Mississippi madness can have
no fitter introduction than a sketch of the life of its great author
John Law. Historians are divided in opinion as to whether
they should designate him a knave or a madman. Both
epithets were unsparingly applied to him in his lifetime, and
while the unhappy consequences of his projects were still
deeply felt. Posterity, however, has found reason to doubt the
justice of the accusation, and to confess that John Law was
neither knave nor madman, but one more deceived than
deceiving, more sinned against than sinning. He was thoroughly
acquainted with the philosophy and true principles of credit.
He understood the monetary question better than any man of
his day; and if his system fell with a crash so tremendous, it was
not so much his fault as that of the people amongst whom he
had erected it. He did not calculate upon the avaricious frenzy
of a whole nation; he did not see that confidence, like mistrust,
could be increased almost ad infinitum, and that hope was as
extravagant as fear. How was he to foretell that the French
people, like the man in the fable, would kill, in their frantic
eagerness, the fine goose he had brought to lay them so many

golden eggs? His fate was like that which may be supposed to have overtaken the first adventurous boatman who rowed from Erie to Ontario. Broad and smooth was the river on which he embarked; rapid and pleasant was his progress; and who was to stay him in his career? Alas for him! The cataract was nigh. He saw, when it was too late, that the tide which wafted him so joyously along was a tide of destruction; and when he endeavored to retrace his way, he found that the current was too strong for his weak efforts to stem, and that he drew nearer every instant to the tremendous falls. Down he went over the sharp rocks, and the waters with him. He was dashed to pieces with his bark; but the waters, maddened and turned to foam by the rough descent, only boiled and bubbled for a time, and then flowed on again as smoothly as ever. Just so it was with Law and the French people. He was the boatman, and they were the waters.

John Law was born at Edinburgh in the year 1671. His father was the younger son of an ancient family in Fife, and carried on the business of a goldsmith and banker. He amassed considerable wealth in his trade, sufficient to enable him to gratify the wish, so common among his countrymen, of adding a territorial designation to his name. He purchased with this view the estates of Lauriston and Randleston, on the Firth of Forth, on the borders of West and Mid Lothian, and was thenceforth known as Law of Lauriston. The subject of our memoir, being the eldest son, was received into his father's counting-house at the age of fourteen, and for three years labored hard to acquire an insight into the principles of banking as then carried on in Scotland. He had always manifested great love for the study of numbers, and his proficiency in the mathematics was considered extraordinary in one of his tender years. At the age of seventeen he was tall, strong, and well made; and his face, although deeply scarred with the smallpox, was agreeable in its expression, and full of intelligence. At this time he began to neglect his business, and becoming vain of his person, indulged in considerable extravagance of attire. He was a great favorite with the ladies, by whom he was called Beau Law; while the other sex, despising his foppery, nicknamed him Jessamy

John. At the death of his father, which happened in 1688, he withdrew entirely from the desk, which had become so irksome, and being possessed of the revenues of the paternal estate of Lauriston, he proceeded to London, to see the world.

He was now very young, very vain, good-looking, tolerably rich, and quite uncontrolled. It is no wonder that, on his ar-rival in the capital, he should launch out into extravagance. He soon became a regular frequenter of the gaming-houses, and by pursuing a certain plan, based upon some abstruse calculation of chances, he contrived to gain considerable sums. All the gamblers envied him his luck, and many made it a point to watch his play, and stake their money on the same chances. In affairs of gallantry he was equally fortunate; ladies of the first rank smiled graciously upon the handsome Scotchman—the young, the rich, the witty, and the obliging. But all these successes only paved the way for reverses. After he had been for nine years exposed to the dangerous attractions of the gay life he was leading, he became an irrecoverable gambler. As his love of play increased in violence, it diminished in prudence. Great losses were only to be repaired by still greater ventures, and one unhappy day he lost more than he could repay without mortgaging his family estate. To that step he was driven at last. At the same time his gallantry brought him into trouble. A love affair, or slight flirtation, with a lady of the name of Villiers,* exposed him to the resentment of a Mr. Wilson, by whom he was challenged to fight a duel. Law accepted, and had the ill fortune to shoot his antagonist dead upon the spot. He was arrested the same day, and brought to trial for murder by the relatives of Mr. Wilson. He was afterwards found guilty, and sentenced to death. The sentence was commuted to a fine, upon the ground that the of fence only amounted to manslaughter. An appeal being lodged by a brother of the de-ceased, Law was detained in the King's Bench, whence, by some means or other, which he never explained, he contrived to escape; and an action being instituted against the sheriffs, he was advertised in the Gazette,

* Miss Elizabeth Villiers, afterwards Countess of Orkney.

and a reward offered for his apprehension. He was described as "Captain John Law, a Scotchman, aged twenty-six; a very tall, black, lean man; well shaped, above six feet high, with large pock-holes in his face; big nosed, and speaking broad and loud." As this was rather a caricature than a description of him, it has been supposed that it was drawn up with a view to favour his escape. He succeeded in reaching the Continent, where he travelled for three years, and devoted much of his attention to the monetary and banking affairs of the countries through which he passed. He stayed a few months in Amsterdam, and speculated to some extent in the funds. His mornings were devoted to the study of finance and the principles of trade, and his evenings to the gaming-house. It is generally believed that he returned to Edinburgh in the year 1700. It is certain that he published in that city his *Proposals and Reasons for constituting a Council of Trade*. This pamphlet did not excite much attention.

In a short time afterwards he published a project for establishing what he called a Land-Bank,* the notes issued by which were never to exceed the value of the entire lands of the state, upon ordinary interest, or were to be equal in value to the land, with the right to enter into possession at a certain time. The project excited a good deal of discussion in the Scottish Parliament, and a motion for the establishment of such a bank was brought forward by a neutral party, called the Squadrone, whom Law had interested in his favor. The Parliament ultimately passed a resolution to the effect, that, to establish any kind of paper credit, so as to force it to pass, was an improper expedient for the nation.

Upon the failure of this project, and of his efforts to procure a pardon for the murder of Mr. Wilson, Law withdrew to the Continent, and resumed his old habits of gaming. For fourteen years he continued to roam about, in Flanders, Holland, Germany, Hungary, Italy, and France. He soon became intimately acquainted with the extent of the trade and resources of each, and daily more confirmed in his opinion that

* The wits of the day called it a sand-bank, which would wreck the vessel of the state.

no country could prosper without a paper currency. During the whole of this time he appears to have chiefly supported himself by successful play. At every gambling-house of note in the capitals of Europe he was known and appreciated as one better skilled in the intricacies of chance than any other man of the day. It is stated in the *Biographie Universelle* that he was expelled, first from Venice, and afterwards from Genoa, by the magistrates, who thought him a visitor too dangerous for the youth of those cities. During his residence in Paris he rendered himself obnoxious to D'Argenson, the lieutenant-general of the police, by whom he was ordered to quit the capital. This did not take place, however, before he had made the acquaintance, in the saloons, of the Duke de Vendome, the Prince de Conti, and of the gay Duke of Orleans, the latter of whom was destined afterwards to exercise so much influence over his fate. The Duke of Orleans was pleased with the vivacity and good sense of the Scottish adventurer, while the latter was no less pleased with the wit and amiability of a prince who promised to become his patron. They were often thrown into each other's society, and Law seized every opportunity to instill his financial doctrines into the mind of one whose proximity to the throne pointed him out as destined, at no very distant date, to play an important part in the government.

Shortly before the death of Louis XIV., or, as some say, in 1780, Law proposed a scheme of finance to Desmarets, the comptroller. Louis is reported to have inquired whether the projector were a Catholic, and on being answered in the negative, to have declined having any thing to do with him.*

It was after this repulse that he visited Italy. His mind being still occupied with schemes of finance, he proposed to Victor Amadeus, Duke of Savoy, to establish his land-bank in that country. The duke replied that his dominions were too circumscribed for the execution of so great a project, and that

*This anecdote, which is related in the correspondence of Madame de Baviere, Duchess of Orleans and mother of the Regent, is discredited by Lord John Russell in his History of the principal States of Europe from the Peace of Utrecht; for what reason he does not inform us. There is no doubt that Law proposed his scheme to Desmarets, and that Louis refused to hear it. The reason given for the refusal is quite consistent with the character of that bigoted and tyrannical monarch.

188 *Extraordinary Popular Delusions*

he was by far too poor a potentate to be ruined. He advised him, however, to try the king of France once more; for he was sure, if he knew any thing of the French character, that the people would be delighted with a plan, not only so new, but so plausible.

Louis XIV. died in 1715, and the heir to the throne being an infant only seven years of age, the Duke of Orleans assumed the reins of government, as regent, during his minority. Law now found himself in a more favorable position. The tide in his affairs had come, which, taken at the flood, was to waft him on to fortune. The regent was his friend, already acquainted with his theory and pretensions, and inclined, moreover, to aid him in any efforts to restore the wounded credit of France, bowed down to the earth by the extravagance of the long reign of Louis XIV.

Hardly was that monarch laid in his grave ere the popular hatred, suppressed so long, burst forth against his memory. He who, during his life, had been flattered with an excess of adulation, to which history scarcely offers a parallel, was now cursed as a tyrant, a bigot, and a plunderer. His statues were pelted and disfigured; his effigies torn down, amid the execrations of the populace, and his name rendered synonymous with selfishness and oppression. The glory of his arms was forgotten, and nothing was remembered but his reverses, his extravagance, and his cruelty.

The finances of the country were in a state of the utmost disorder. A profuse and corrupt monarch, whose profuseness and corruption were imitated by almost every functionary, from the highest to the lowest grade, had brought France to the verge of ruin. The national debt amounted to 3000 millions of livres, the revenue to 145 millions, and the expenses of government to 142 millions per annum; leaving only three millions to pay the interest upon 3000 millions. The first care of the regent was to discover a remedy for an evil of such magnitude, and a council was early summoned to take the matter into consideration. The Duke de St. Simon was of opinion that nothing could save the country from revolution but a remedy at once bold and dangerous. He advised the regent to convoke the states-general, and declare a national bankruptcy. The Duke de Noailles, a man of accommodating principles, an accomplished courtier, and totally averse from giving himself any trouble or annoyance that ingenuity could escape from, opposed the project of St. Simon with all his influence. He represented the expedient as alike dishonest and ruinous. The regent was of the same opinion, and this desperate remedy fell to the ground.

The measures ultimately adopted, though they promised fair, only aggravated the evil. The first and most dishonest measure was of no advantage to the state. A recoin age was ordered, by which the currency was depreciated one-fifth; those who took a thousand pieces of gold or silver to the mint received back an amount of coin of the same nominal value, but only four-fifths of the weight of metal. By this contrivance the treasury gained seventy-two millions of livres, and all the commercial operations of the country were disordered. A trifling diminution of the taxes silenced the clamors of the people, and for the slight present advantage the great prospective evil was forgotten.

A Chamber of Justice was next instituted to inquire into the malversations of the loan-contractors and the farmers of the revenues. Tax-collectors are never very popular in any country, but those of France at this period deserved all the odium with which they were loaded. As soon as these farmers-general, with all their hosts of subordinate agents, called *maltotiers,** were called to account for their misdeeds, the most extravagant joy took possession of the nation. The Chamber of Justice, instituted chiefly for this purpose, was endowed with very extensive powers. It was composed of the presidents and councils of the parliament the judges of the Courts of Aid and of Requests, and the officers of the Chamber of Account, under the general presidence of the minister of finance. Informers were encouraged to give evidence against the offenders by the promise of one-fifth part of the fines and confiscations. A tenth of all concealed effects belonging to the

1 From maltote, an oppressive tax.

guilty was promised to such as should furnish the means of discovering them.

The promulgation of the edict constituting this court caused a degree of consternation among those principally concerned, which can only be accounted for on the supposition that their peculation had been enormous. But they met with no sympathy. The proceedings against them justified their terror. The Bastille was soon unable to contain the prisoners that were sent to it, and the gaols all over the country teemed with guilty or suspected persons. An order was issued to all innkeepers and postmasters to refuse horses to such as endeavoured to seek safety in flight; and all persons were forbidden, under heavy fines, to harbour them or favour their evasion. Some were condemned to the pillory, others to the galleys, and the least guilty to fine and imprisonment. One only, Samuel Bernard, a rich banker and farmer-general of a province remote from the capital, was sentenced to death. So great had been the illegal profits of this man,—looked upon as the tyrant and oppressor of his district,—that he offered six millions of livres, or 250,000L. sterling, to be allowed to escape.

His bribe was refused, and he suffered the penalty of death. Others, perhaps more guilty, were more fortunate. Confiscation, owing to the concealment of their treasures by the delinquents, often produced less money than a fine. The severity of the government relaxed, and fines, under the denomination of taxes, were indiscriminately levied upon all offenders; but so corrupt was every department of the administration, that the country benefited but little by the sums which thus flowed into the treasury. Courtiers and courtiers' wives and mistresses came in for the chief share of the spoils. One contractor had been taxed, in proportion to his wealth and guilt, at the sum of twelve millions of livres. The Count *, a man of some weight in the government, called upon him, and offered to procure a remission of the fine if he would give him a hundred thousand crowns. "*Vous êtes trop tart, mon ami;*" replied the financier; "I have already made a bargain with your wife for fifty thousand."*

About a hundred and eighty millions of livres were levied in this manner, of which eighty were applied in payment of the debts contracted by the government. The remainder found its way into the pockets of the courtiers. Madame de Maintenon, writing on this subject, says—"We hear every day of some new grant of the regent. The people murmur very much at this mode of employing the money taken from the peculators." The people, who, after the first burst of their resentment is over, generally express a sympathy for the weak, were indignant that so much severity should be used to so little purpose. They did not see the justice of robbing one set of rogues to fatten another. In a few months all the more guilty had been brought to punishment, and the Chamber of Justice looked for victims in humbler walks of life. Charges of fraud and extortion were brought against tradesmen of good character in consequence of the great inducements held out to common informers. They were compelled to lay open their affairs before this tribunal in order to establish their innocence. The voice of complaint resounded from every side; and at the expiration of a year the government found it advisable to discontinue further proceedings. The Chamber of Justice was suppressed, and a general amnesty granted to all against whom no charges had yet been preferred.

In the midst of this financial confusion Law appeared upon the scene. No man felt more deeply than the regent the deplorable state of the country, but no man could be more averse from putting his shoulders manfully to the wheel. He disliked business; he signed official documents without proper examination, and trusted to others what he should have undertaken himself. The cares inseparable from his high office were burdensome to him. He saw that something was necessary to be done; but he lacked the energy to do it, and had not virtue enough to sacrifice his ease and his pleasures in the attempt.

*This anecdote is related by M. de la Hode, in his *Life of Philippe of Orleans*. It would have looked more authentic if he had given the names of the dishonest contractor and the still more dishonest minister. But M.de la Hode, book is liable to the same objection as most of the French memoirs of that and of subsequent periods. It is sufficientwith most of them that an anecdote be *ben trovato*; the *vero* is but matter of secondary consideration.

No wonder that, with this character, he listened favourably to the mighty projects, so easy of execution, of the clever adventurer whom he had formerly known, and whose talents he appreciated.

When Law presented himself at court he was most cordially received. He offered two memorials to the regent, in which he set forth the evils that had befallen France, owing to an insufficient currency, at different times depreciated. He asserted that a metallic currency, unaided by a paper money, was wholly inadequate to the wants of a commercial country, and particularly cited the examples of Great Britain and Holland to shew the advantages of paper. He used many sound arguments on the subject of credit, and proposed as a means of restoring that of France, then at so low an ebb among the nations, that he should be allowed to set up a bank, which should have the man-agement of the royal revenues, and issue notes both on that and on landed security. He further proposed that this bank should be administered in the king's name, but subject to the control of commissioners to be named by the States General.

While these memorials were under consideration, Law translated into French his essay on money and trade, and used every means to extend through the nation his renown as a financier. He soon became talked of. The confidants of the regent spread abroad his praise, and every one expected great things of Monsieur Lass.*

On the 5th of May, 1716, a royal edict was published, by which Law was authorized, in conjunction with his brother, to establish a bank under the name of Law and Company, the notes of which should be received in payment of the taxes. The capital was fixed at six millions of livres, in twelve thousand shares of five hundred livres each, purchasable one fourth in specie, and the remainder in *billets d'état*. It was not thought expedient to grant him the whole of the privileges prayed for

---

* The French pronounced his name in this manner to avoid the ungallic sound, *aw*. After the failure of his scheme, the wags said the nation was *lasse de lui*, and proposed that he should in future be known by the name Of Monsieur *Hélas!*

in his memorials until experience should have shewn their safety and advantage.

Law was now on the high road to fortune. The study of thirty years was brought to guide him in the management of his bank. He made all his notes payable at sight, and in the coin current at the time they were issued. This last was a master-stroke of policy, and immediately rendered his notes more valuable than the precious metals. The latter were constantly liable to depreciation by the unwise tampering of the government. A thousand livres of silver might be worth their nominal value one day, and be reduced one-sixth the next, but a note of Law's bank retained its original value. He publicly declared at the same time, that a banker deserved death if he made issues without having sufficient security to answer all demands. The consequence was, that his notes advanced rapidly in public estimation, and were received at one percent more than specie. It was not long before the trade of the country felt the benefit. Languishing commerce began to lift up her head; the taxes were paid with greater regularity and less murmuring; and a degree of confidence was established that could not fail, if it continued, to become still more advantageous. In the course of a year, Law's notes rose to fifteen per cent premium, while the *billets d'état,* or notes issued by the government as security for the debts contracted by the extravagant Louis XIV., were at a discount of no less than seventy-eight and a half percent. The comparison was too great in favor of Law not to attract the attention of the whole kingdom, and his credit extended itself day by day. Branches of his bank were almost simultaneously established at Lyons, Rochelle, Tours, Amiens, and Orleans.

The regent appears to have been utterly astonished at his success, and gradually to have conceived the idea that paper, which could so aid a metallic currency, could entirely supercede it. Upon this fundamental error he afterwards acted. In the mean time, Law commenced the famous project which has handed his name down to posterity. He proposed to the regent (who could refuse him nothing) to establish a company that should have the exclusive privilege of trading to the great river Mississippi and the province of Louisiana, on its western bank. The country was supposed to abound in the precious metals; and the company, supported by the profits of their exclusive commerce, were to be the sole farmers of the taxes and sole coiners of money. Letters patent were issued, incorporating the company, in August 1717. The capital was divided into two hundred thousand shares of five hundred livres each, the whole of which might be paid in *billets d'état*, at their nominal value, although worth no more than a hundred and sixty livres in the market.

It was now that the frenzy of speculating began to seize upon the nation. Law's bank had effected so much good, that any promises for the future which he thought proper to make were readily believed. The regent every day conferred new privileges upon the fortunate projector. The bank obtained the monopoly of the sale of tobacco, the sole right of refinage of gold and silver, and was finally erected into the Royal Bank of France. Amid the intoxication of success, both Law and the regent forgot the maxim so loudly proclaimed by the former, that a banker deserved death who made issues of paper without the necessary funds to provide for them. As soon as the bank, from a private, became a public institution, the regent caused a fabrication of notes to the amount of one thousand millions of livres. This was the first departure from sound principles, and one for which Law is not justly blame able. While the affairs of the bank were under his control, the issues had never exceeded sixty millions. Whether Law opposed the inordinate increase is not known; but as it took place as soon as the bank was made a royal establishment, it is but fair to lay the blame on the change of system upon the regent.

Law found that he lived under a despotic government; but he was not yet aware of the pernicious influence which such a government could exercise upon so delicate a framework as that of credit. He discovered it afterwards to his cost, but in the meantime suffered himself to be impelled by the regent into courses which his own reason must have disapproved. With a weakness most culpable, he lent his aid in inundating the country with paper money, which, based upon no solid foundation, was sure to fall, sooner or later. The extraordinary present fortune dazzled his eyes, and prevented him from seeing the evil day that would burst over his head, when once, from any cause or other, the alarm was sounded. The parliament were from the first jealous of his influence as a foreigner, and had, besides, their misgivings as to the safety of his projects. As his influence extended, their animosity increased. D'Aguesseau, the chancellor, was unceremoniously dismissed by the regent for his opposition to the vast increase of paper money, and the constant depreciation of the gold and silver coin of the realm. This only served to augment the enmity of the parliament, and when D'Argenson, a man devoted to the interests of the regent, was appointed to the vacant chancellorship, and made at the same time minister of finance, they became more violent than ever. The first measure of the new minister caused a further depreciation of the coin. In order to extinguish the *billets d'état*, it was ordered that persons bringing to the mint four thousand livres in specie and one thousand livres in *billets d'état*, should receive back coin to the amount of five thousand livres. D'Argenson plumed himself mightily upon thus creating five thousand new and smaller livres out of the four thou-sand old and larger ones, being too ignorant of the true principles of trade and credit to be aware of the immense injury he was in-flicting upon both.

The parliament saw at once the impolicy and danger of such a system, and made repeated remonstrances to the regent. The latter refused to entertain their petitions, when the parliament, by a bold and very unusual stretch of authority, commanded that no money should be received in payment but that of the old standard. The regent summoned a *lit de justice*, and annulled the decree. The parliament resisted, and issued another. Again the regent exercised his privilege, and annulled it, till the parliament, stung to fiercer opposition, passed another decree, dated August 12th, 1718, by which they forbade the bank of Law to have any concern, either direct or indirect, in the administration of the revenue; and prohibited all foreigners, under heavy penalties, from interfering, either in their own names or in that of others, in the management of the finances of the state. The parliament considered Law to be the author of all the evil, and some of the councillors in the virulence of their enmity, proposed that he should be brought to trial, and, if found guilty, be hung at the gates of the Palais de Justice.

Law, in great alarm, fled to the Palais Royal, and threw himself on the protection of the regent, praying that measures might be taken to reduce the parliament to obedience. The regent had nothing so much at heart, both on that account and because of the disputes that had arisen relative to the legitimation of the Duke of Maine and the Count of Thoulouse, the sons of the late king. The parliament was ultimately overawed by the arrest of their president and two of the councillors, who were sent to distant prisons.

Thus the first cloud upon Law's prospects blew over; freed from apprehension of personal danger, he devoted his attention to his famous Mississippi project, the shares of which were rapidly rising, in spite of the parliament. At the commencement of the year 1719, an edict was published, granting to the Mississippi Company the exclusive privilege of trading to the East Indies, China, and the South Seas, and to all the possessions of the French East India Company, established by Colbert. The Company, in consequence of this great increase of their business, assumed, as more appropriate, the title of Company of the Indies, and created fifty thousand new shares. The prospects now held out by Law were most magnificent. He promised a yearly dividend of two hundred livres upon each share of five hundred, which, as the shares were paid for in *billets d'etat,* at their nominal value, but worth ony 100 livres, was at the rate of about 120 percent profit.

The public enthusiasm, which had been so long rising, could not resist a vision so splendid. At least three hundred thousand applications were made for the fifty thousand new shares, and

Law's house in the Rue de Quincampoix was beset from morning to night by the eager applicants. As it was impossible to satisfy them all, it was several weeks before a list of the fortunate new stockholders could be made out, during which time the public impatience rose to a pitch of frenzy. Dukes, marquises, counts, with their duchesses, marchionesses, and countesses, waited in the streets for hours every day before Mr. Law's door to know the result. At last, to avoid the jostling of the plebeian crowd, which, to the number of thousands, filled the whole thoroughfare, they took apartments in the adjoining houses, that they might be continually near the temple whence the new Plutus was diffusing wealth. Every day the value of the old shares increased, and the fresh applications, induced by the golden dreams of the whole nation, became so numerous that it was deemed advisable to create no less than three hundred thousand new shares, at five thousand livres each, in order that the regent might take advantage of the popular enthusiasm to pay off the national debt. For this purpose, the sum of fifteen hundred millions of livres was necessary. Such was the eagerness of the nation, that thrice the sum would have been subscribed if the government had authorized it.

Law was now at the zenith of his prosperity, and the people were rapidly approaching the zenith of their infatuation. The highest and the lowest classes were alike filled with a vision of boundless wealth. There was not a person of note among the aristocracy, with the exception of the Duke of St. Simon and Marshal Villars, who was not engaged in buying or selling stock. People of every age and sex and condition in life speculated in the rise and fall of the Mississippi bonds. The Rue de Quincampoix was the grand resort of the jobbers, and it being a narrow, inconvenient street, accidents continually occurred in it, from the tremendous pressure of the crowd. Houses in it, worth, in ordinary times, a thousand livres of yearly rent, yielded as much as twelve or sixteen thousand. A cobbler, who had a stall in it, gained about two hundred livres a day by letting it out, and furnishing writing materials to brokers and their clients. The story goes, that a hunchbacked man who stood in the street gained considerable sums by lending his hump as a writing-desk to the eager speculators! The great concourse of persons who assembled to do business brought a still greater concourse of spectators. These again drew all the thieves and immoral characters of Paris to the spot, and constant riots and disturbances took place. At nightfall, it was often found necessary to send a troop of soldiers to clear the street.

Law, finding the inconvenience of his residence, removed to the Place Vendome, whither the crowd of agioteurs followed him. That spacious square soon became as thronged as the Rue de Quincampoix: from morning to night it presented the appearance of a fair. Booths and tents were erected for the transaction of business and the sale of refreshments, and gamblers with their roulette-tables stationed themselves in the very middle of the place, and reaped a golden, or rather a paper, harvest from the throng. The boulevards and public gardens were forsaken; parties of pleasure took their walks in preference in the Place Vendome, which became the fashionable lounge of the idle as well as the general rendezvous of the busy. The noise was so great all day, that the chancellor, whose court was situated in the square, complained to the regent and the municipality that he could not hear the advocates. Law, when applied to, expressed his willingness to aid in the removal of the nuisance, and for this purpose entered into a treaty with the Prince de Carignan for the Hotel de Soissons, which had a garden of several acres in the rear. A bargain was concluded, by which Law became the purchaser of the hotel at an enormous price, the prince reserving to himself the magnificent gardens as a new source of profit. They contained some fine statues and several fountains, and were altogether laid out with much taste. As soon as Law was installed in his new abode, an edict was published, forbidding all persons to buy or sell stock any where but in the gardens of the Hotel de Soissons. In the midst, among the trees, about five hundred small tents and pavilions were erected, for the convenience of the stock-jobbers. Their various colors, the gay ribands and banners which floated from them, the busy crowds which passed continually in and out—the incessant hum of voices, the noise, the music, and the strange mixture of business and pleasure on the countenances of the throng, all combined to give the place an air of enchantment that quite enraptured the Parisians. The Prince de Carignan made enormous profits while the delusion lasted. Each tent was let at the rate of five hundred livres a month; and, as there were at least five hundred of them, his monthly revenue from this source alone must have amounted to 250,000 livres, or upwards of 10,000*l*. sterling.

The honest old soldier, Marshal Villars, was so vexed to see the folly which had smitten his countrymen, that he never could speak with temper on the subject. Passing one day through the Place Vendome in his carriage, the choleric gentleman was so annoyed at the infatuation of the people, that he abruptly ordered his coachman to stop, and, putting his head out of the carriage-window, harangued them for full half an hour on their "disgusting avarice." This was not a very wise proceeding on his part. Hisses and shouts of laughter resounded from every side, and jokes without number were aimed at him. There being at last strong symptoms that something more tangible was flying through the air in the direction of his head, the marshal was glad to drive on. He never again repeated the experiment.

Two sober, quiet, and philosophic men of letters, M. de la Motte and the Abbe Terrason, congratulated each other, that they, at least, were free from this strange infatuation. A few days afterward, as the worthy abbe was coming out of the Hotel de Soissons, whither he had gone to buy shares in the Mississippi, whom should he see but his friend La Motte entering for the same purpose. "Ha!" said the abbe smiling, "is that *you*?" "Yes," said La Motte, pushing past him as fast as he was able; "and can that be *you*?" The next time the two scholars met, they talked of philosophy, of science, and of religion, but neither had courage for a long time to breathe one syllable about the Mississippi. At last, when it was mentioned, they agreed that a man ought never to swear against his doing any one thing, and that there was no sort of extravagance of which even a wise man was not capable.

During this time, Law, the new Plutus, had become all at once the most important personage of the state. The ante-chambers of the regent were forsaken by the courtiers. Peers, judges, and bishops thronged to the Hotel de Soissons; officers of the army and navy, ladies of title and fashion, and every one to whom hereditary rank or public employ gave a claim to precedence, were to be found waiting in his ante-chambers to beg for a portion of his India stock. Law was so pestered that he was unable to see one-tenth part of the applicants, and every manuvere that ingenuity could suggest was employed to gain access to him. Peers, whose dignity would have been outraged if the regent had made them wait half an hour for an interview, were content to wait six hours for the chance of seeing Monsieur Law. Enormous fees were paid to his servants, if they would merely announce their names. Ladies of rank employed the blandishments of their smiles for the same object; but many of them came day after day for a fortnight before they could obtain an audience. When Law accepted an invitation, he was sometimes so surrounded by ladies, all asking to have their names put down in his lists as shareholders in the new stock, that, in spite of his well-known and habitual gallantry, he was obliged to tear himself away par force. The most ludicrous stratagems were employed to have an opportunity of speaking to him. One lady, who had striven in vain during several days, gave up in despair all attempts to see him at his own house, but ordered her coachman to keep a strict watch whenever she was out in her carriage, and if he saw Mr. Law coming, to drive against a post and upset her. The coachman promised obedience, and for three days the lady was driven incessantly through the town, praying inwardly for the opportunity to be overturned. At last she espied Mr. Law, and, pulling the string, called out to the coachman, "Upset us now! for God's sake, upset us now!" The coachman drove against a post, the lady screamed, the coach was overturned, and Law, who had seen the accident, hastened to the spot to render assistance. The cunning dame was led into the Hotel de Soissons, where she soon thought it advisable to recover from her fright, and, after apologizing to Mr. Law, confessed her stratagem. Law smiled, and entered the lady in his books as the purchaser of a quantity of India stock. Another story is told of a Madame de Boucha, who, knowing that Mr. Law was at dinner at a certain house, proceeded thither in her carriage, and gave the alarm of fire. The company started from table, and Law among the rest; but seeing one lady making all haste into the house towards him, while everybody else was scampering away, he suspected the trick, and ran off in another direction.

Many other anecdotes are related, which even though they may be a little exaggerated, are nevertheless worth preserving, as shewing the spirit of that singular period.* The regent was one day mentioning, in the presence of D'Argenson, the Abbe Dubois, and some other persons, that he was desirous of desputing some lady, of the rank at least of a duchess, to attend upon his daughter at Modena: "but," added he, "I do not exactly know where to find one." "No!" replied one, in affected surprise; "I can tell you where to find every duchess in France: you have only to go to Mr. Law's; you will see them every one in his ante-chamber."

M. de Chirac, a celebrated physician, had bought stock at an unlucky period, and was very anxious to sell out. Stock, however, continued to fall for two or three days, much to his alarm. His mind was filled with the subject, when he was suddenly called upon to attend a lady who imagined herself unwell. He arrived, was shewn up stairs, and felt the lady's pulse. "It falls! It falls! Good God! It falls continually!" said he musingly, while the lady looked up in his face all anxiety for his opinion. "Oh, M. de Chirac," said she, starting to her feet and

---

*The curious reader may find an anecdote of the eagerness of the French ladies to retain Law in their company, which will make him blush or smile according as he happens to be very modest or the reverse. It is related in the *Letters of Madame Charlotte Elizabeth de Baviere, Duchess of Orleans* .

ringing the bell for assistance; "I am dying! I am dying! It falls! It falls! It falls!" "What falls?" inquired the doctor in amazement. "My pulse! my pulse" said the lady; "I must be dying." "Calm your apprehensions, my dear madam," said M. de Chirac; "I was speaking of the stocks. The truth is, I have been a great loser, and my mind is so disturbed, I hardly know what I have been saying."

The price of shares sometimes rose ten or twenty percent in the course of a few hours, and many persons in the humbler walks of life, who had risen poor in the morning, went to bed in affluence. An extensive holder of stock, being taken ill, sent his servant to sell two hundred and fifty shares, at eight thousand livres each, the price at which they were then quoted. The servant went, and, on his arrival in the Jardin de Soissons, found that in the interval the price had risen to ten thousand livres. The difference of two thousand livres on the two hundred and fifty shares, amounting to 500,000 livres, or 20,000L. sterling, he very coolly transferred to his own use, and giving the remainder to his master, set out the same evening for another country. Law's coachman in a very short time made money enough to set up a carriage of his own, and requested permission to leave his service. Law, who esteemed the man, begged of him as a favour that he would endeavor, before he went, to find a substitute as good as himself. The coachman consented, and in the evening brought two of his former comrades, telling Mr. Law to choose between them, and he would take the other. Cook maids and footmen were now and then as lucky, and, in the full-blown pride of their easily-acquired wealth, made the most ridiculous mistakes. Preserving the language and manners of their old with the finery of their new station, they afforded continual subjects for the pity of the sensible, the contempt of the sober, and the laughter of everybody. But the folly and meanness of the higher ranks of society were still more disgusting. One instance alone, related by the Duke de St. Simon, will shew the unworthy avarice which infected the whole of society. A man of the name of Andre, without character or education, had, by a series of well-timed speculations in Mississippi bonds, gained enormous wealth in an incredibly short space of time. As St. Simon expresses it, "he had amassed mountains of gold." As he became rich, he grew ashamed of the lowness of his birth, and anxious above all things to be allied to nobility. He had a daughter, an infant only three years of age, and he opened a negotiation with the aristocratic and needy family of D'Oyse, that this child should, upon certain conditions, marry a member of that house. The Marquis D'Oyse, to his shame, consented, and promised to marry her himself on her attaining the age of twelve, if the father would pay him down the sum of a hundred thousand crowns, and twenty thousand livres every year until the celebration of the marriage. The Marquis was himself in his thirty-third year. This scandalous bargain was duly signed and sealed, the stock jobber furthermore agreeing to settle upon his daughter, on the marriage-day, a fortune of several millions. The Duke of Brancas, the head of the family, was present throughout the negotiation, and shared in all the profits. St. Simon, who treats the matter with the levity becoming what he thought so good a joke, adds, "that people did not spare their animadversions on this beautiful marriage," and further informs us "that the project fell to the ground some months afterwards by the overthrow of Law, and the ruin of the ambitious Monsieur Andre." It would appear, however, that the noble family never had the honesty to return the hundred thousand crowns.

Amid events like these, which, humiliating though they be, partake largely of the ludicrous, others occurred of a more serious nature. Robberies in the streets were of daily occurrence, in consequence of the immense sums, in paper, which people carried about with them. Assassinations were also frequent. One case in particular fixed the attention of the whole of France, not only on account of the enormity of the of fence, but of the rank and high connections of the criminal.

The Count d'Horn, a younger brother of the Prince d'Horn, and related to the noble families of D'Aremberg, DeLigne, and DeMontmorency, was a young man of dissipated character, extravagant to a degree, and unprincipled as he was extravagant. In connection with two other young men as reckless as himself, named Mille, a Piedmontese captain, and one Destampes, or Lestang, a Fleming, he formed a design to rob a very rich broker, who was known, unfortunately for himself, to carry great sums about his person. The count pretended a desire to purchase of him a number of shares in the Company of the Indies, and for that purpose appointed to meet him in a *cabaret,* or low public-house, in the neighborhood of the Place Vendome. The unsuspecting broker was punctual to his appointment; so were the Count d'Horn and his two associates, whom he introduced as his particular friends. After a few moments' conversation, the Count d'Horn suddenly sprang upon his victim, and stabbed him three times in the breast with a poniard. The man fell heavily to the ground, and, while the count was employed in rifling his portfolio of bonds in the Mississippi and Indian schemes to the amount of one hundred thousand crowns, Mille, the Piedmontese, stabbed the unfortunate broker again and again, to make sure of his death. But the broker did not fall without a struggle, and his cries brought the people of the cabaret to his assistance. Lestang, the other assassin, who had been set to keep watch at a staircase, sprang from a window and escaped; but Mille and the Count d'Horn were seized in the very act.

This crime, committed in open day, and in so public a place as a *cabaret,* filled Paris with consternation. The trial of the assassins commenced on the following day; and the evidence being so clear, they were ooth found guilty, and condemned to be broken alive on the wheel. The noble relatives of the Count d'Horn absolutely blocked up the ante-chambers of the regent, praying for mercy on the misguided youth, and alleging that he was insane. The regent avoided them as long as possible, being determined that, in a case so atrocious, justice should take its course. But the importunity of these influential suitors was not to be overcome so silently; and they at last forced themselves into the presence of the regent, and prayed him to save their house the shame of a public execution. They hinted that the Princes d'Horn were allied to the illustrious family of Orleans; and added, that the regent himself would be disgraced if a kinsman of his should die by the hands of a common executioner. The regent, to his credit, was proof against all their solicitations, and replied to their last argument in the words of Corneille:

"Le crime fâte la honte, et non pas l'échafaud:"

adding, that whatever shame there might be in the punishment he would very willingly share with the other relatives. Day after day they renewed their entreaties, but always with the same result. At last they thought, that if they could interest the Duke de St. Simon in their favour—a man for whom the regent felt sincere esteem—they might succeed in their object. The duke, a thorough aristocrat, was as shocked as they were that a noble assassin should die by the same death as a plebeian felon, and represented to the regent the impolicy of making enemies of so numerous, wealthy, and powerful a family. He urged, too, that in Germany, where the family of D'Aremberg had large possessions, it was the law, that no relative of a person broken on the wheel could succeed to any public office or employ until a whole generation had passed away. For this reason, he thought the punishment of the guilty might be transmuted into beheading, which was considered all over Europe as much less infamous. The regent was moved by this argument, and was about to consent, when Law, who felt peculiarly interested in the fate of the murdered man, confirmed him in his former resolution to let the law take its course.

The relatives of D'Horn were now reduced to the last extremity. The Prince de Robec Montmorency, despairing of other methods, found means to penetrate into the dungeon of the criminal, and offering him a cup of poison, implored him to save them from disgrace. The Count d'Horn turned away his head, and refused to take it. Montmorency pressed him once more; and losing all patience at his continued refusal, turned on his heel, and exclaiming, "Die, then, as thou wilt, mean-spirited wretch thou art fit only to perish by the hands of the hangman" left him to his fate.

D'Horn himself petitioned the regent that he might be beheaded; but Law, who exercised more influence over his mind than any other person, with the exception of the notorious Abbe Dubois, his tutor, insisted that he could not in justice succumb to the self-interested views of the D'Horns. The regent had from the first been of the same opinion: and within six days after the commission of their crime, D'Horn and Mille were broken on the wheel in the Place de Greve. The other assassin, Lestang, was never apprehended.

This prompt and severe justice was highly pleasing to the populace of Paris. Even M. de Quincampoix, as they called Law, came in for a share of their approbation for having induced the regent to show no favour to a patrician. But the number of robberies and assassinations did not diminish; no sympathy was shewn for rich jobbers when they were plundered. The general laxity of public morals, conspicuous enough before, was rendered still more so by its rapid pervasion of the middle classes, who had hitherto remained comparatively pure between the open vices of the class above and the hidden crimes of the class below them. The pernicious love of gambling diffused itself through society, and bore all public and nearly all private virtue before it.

For a time, while confidence lasted, an impetus was given to trade which could not fail to be beneficial. In Paris especially the good results were felt. Strangers flocked into the capital from every part, bent not only upon making money, but on spending it. The Duchess of Orleans, mother of the regent,

* The following squib was circulated on the occasion:
"Foin de ton zéle seraphique,
Malheureux Abbe de Tencin,
Depuis que Law eat Catholique,
Tout le royaume ête Capucinl"
Thus somewhat weakly and paraphrastically rendered by Justandsond, in histranslation of the *Memoirs of Louis XV.*:
"Tencin, a curse on thy seraphic zeal,
Which by persuasion hathcontrivedthmeans
To make the Scotchman at our altars kneel,
Since which we all are poor as Capucines!"

computes the increase of the population during this time, from the great influx of strangers from all parts of the world, at 305,000 souls. The housekeepers were obliged to make up beds in garrets, kitchens, and even stables, for the accommodation of lodgers; and the town was so full of carriages and vehicles of every description, that they were obliged, in the principal streets, to drive at a foot-pace for fear of accidents. The looms of the country worked with unusual activity to supply rich laces, silks, broad-cloth, and velvets, which being paid for in abundant paper, increased in price fourfold. Provisions shared the general advance. Bread, meat, and vegetables were sold at prices greater than had ever before been known; while the wages of lab our rose in exactly the same proportion. The artisan who formerly gained fifteen so us per diem now gained sixty. New houses were built in every direction; an illusory prosperity shone over the land, and so dazzled the eyes of the whole nation, that none could see the dark cloud on the horizon announcing the storm that was too rapidly approaching.

Law himself, the magician whose wand had wrought so surprising a change, shared, of course, in the general prosperity. His wife and daughter were courted by the highest nobility, and their alliance sought by the heirs of ducal and princely houses. He bought two splendid estates in different parts of France, and entered into a negotiation with the family of the Duke de Sully for the purchase of the marquisate of Rosny. His religion being an obstacle to his advancement, the regent promised, if he would publicly conform to the Catholic faith, to make him comptroller-general of the finances. Law, who had no more real religion than any other professed gambler, readily agreed, and was confirmed by the Abbe de Tencin in the cathedral of Melun, in presence of a great crowd of spectators.* On the following day he was elected honorary

---

*The Duke de la Force gained considerable sums, not only by jobbing in the stocks but in dealing in porcelain, spices, etc. It was debated for a length of time in the parliament of Paris whether he had not, in his quality of spice-merchant, forfeited his rank in the peerage. It was decided in the negative. A caricature of him was made, dressed as a street-porter, carrying a large bale of spices on his back, with the inscription, "Admirez LA FORCE."

church-warden of the parish of St. Roch, upon which occasion he made it a present of the sum of five hundred thousand livres. His charities, always magnificent, were not always so ostentatious. He gave away great sums privately, and no tale of real distress ever reached his ears in vain.

At this time he was by far the most influential person of the state. The Duke of Orleans had so much confidence in his sagacity and the success of his plans, that he always consulted him upon every matter of moment. He was by no means unduly elevated by his prosperity, but remained the same simple, affable, sensible man that he had shewn himself in adversity. His gallantry, which was always delightful to the fair objects of it, was of a nature so kind, so gentlemanly, and so respectful, that not even a lover could have taken offence at it. If upon any occasion he showed any symptoms of haughtiness, it was to the cringing nobles who lavished their adulation upon him till it became fulsome. He often took pleasure in seeing how long he could make them dance attendance upon him for a single favour. To such of his own countrymen as by chance visited Paris, and sought an interview with him, he was, on the contrary, all politeness and attention. When Archibald Campbell, Earl of Islay, and afterwards Duke of Argyle, called upon him in the Place Vendome, he had to pass through an antechamber crowded with persons of the first distinction, all anxious to see the great financier, and have their names put down as first on the list of some new subscription. Law himself was quietly sitting in his library, writing a letter to the gardener at his paternal estate of Lauriston, about the planting of some cabbages! The earl stayed a considerable time, played a game of piquet with his countryman, and left him charmed with his ease, good sense, and good breeding.

Among the nobles who, by means of the public credulity at this time, gained sums sufficient to repair their ruined fortunes, may be mentioned the names of the Dukes de Bourbon, de Guiche, de la Force,* de Chaulnes, and d'Antin; the Marechal d'Estrées; the Princes de Rohan, de Poix, and de Leon. The Duke de Bourbon, son of Louis XIV. by Madame de Montespan, was peculiarly fortunate in his speculations in Mississippi paper. He rebuilt the royal residence of Chantilly in a style of unwonted magnificence; and being passionately fond of horses, he erected a range of stables, which were long renowned throughout Europe, and imported a hundred and fifty of the finest racers from England to improve the breed in France. He bought a large extent of country in Picardy, and became possessed of nearly all the valuable lands lying between the Oise and the Somme.

When fortunes such as these were gained, it is no wonder that Law should have been almost worshipped by the mercurial population. Never was monarch more flattered than he was. All the small poets and litterateurs of the day poured floods of adulation upon him. According to them, he was the savior of the country, the tutelary divinity of France; wit was in all his words, goodness in all his looks, and wisdom in all his actions. So great a crowd followed his carriage whenever he went abroad, that the regent sent him a troop of horse as his permanent escort to clear the streets before him.

It was remarked at this time that Paris had never before been so full of objects of elegance and luxury. Statues, pictures, and tapestries were imported in great quantities from foreign countries, and found a ready market. All those pretty trifles in the way of furniture and ornament which the French excel in manufacturing were no longer the exclusive playthings of the aristocracy, but were to be found in abundance in the houses of traders and the middle classes in general. Jewellery of the most costly description was brought to Paris as the most favourable mart; among the rest, the famous diamond bought by the regent, and called by his name, and which long adorned the crown of France. It was purchased for the sum of two millions of livres, under circumstances which shew that the regent was not so great a gainer as some of his subjects by the impetus which trade had received. When the diamond was first offered to him, he refused to buy it. although he desired above all things to possess it, alleging as his reason, that his duty to the country he governed would not allow him to spend so large a sum of the public money for a mere jewel. This valid and honorable excuse threw all the ladies of the court into alarm, and nothing was heard for some days but expressions of regret that so rare a gem should be allowed to go out of France, no private individual being rich enough to buy it. The regent was continually importuned about it, but all in vain, until the Duke de St. Simon, who with all his ability, was something of a twaddler, undertook the weighty business. His entreaties being seconded by Law, the good-natured regent gave his consent, leaving to Law's ingenuity to find the means to pay for it. The owner took security for the payment of the sum of two millions of livres within a stated period, receiving in the mean time the interest of five per cent upon that amount, and being allowed, besides, all the valuable clippings of the gem. St. Simon, in his *Memoirs,* relates with no little complacency his share in this transaction. After describing the diamond to be as large as a greengage, of a form nearly round, perfectly white, and without flaw, and weighing more than five hundred grains, he concludes with a chuckle, by telling the world "that he takes great credit to himself for having induced the regent to make so illustrious a purchase." In other words; he was proud that he had induced him to sacrifice his duty, and buy a bauble for himself at an extravagant price out of the public money.

Thus the system continued to flourish till the commencement of the year 1720. The warnings of the Parliament, that too great a creation of paper money would, sooner or later, bring the country to bankruptcy, were disregarded. The regent, who knew nothing whatever of the philosophy of finance, thought that a system which had produced such good effects could never be carried to excess. If five hundred millions of paper had been of such advantage, five hundred millions additional would be of still greater advantage. This was the grand error of the regent, and which Law did not attempt to dispel. The extraordinary avidity of the people kept up the delusion; and the higher the price of Indian and Mississippi stock, the more *billets de banque* were issued to keep pace with it. The edifice thus reared might not unaptly be compared to the gorgeous palace erected by Potemkin, that princely barbarian of Russia, to surprise and please his imperial mistress: huge blocks of ice were piled one upon another; Ionic pillars of chastest workmanship, in ice, formed a noble portico; and a dome of the same material, shone in the sun, which had just strength enough to gild, but not to melt it. It glittered afar, like a palace of crystals and diamonds; but there came one warm breeze from the south, and the stately building dissolved away, till none were able even to gather up the fragments. So with Law and his paper system. No sooner did the breath of popular mistrust blow steadily upon it, than it fell to ruins, and none could raise it up again.

The first slight alarm that was occasioned was early in 1720. The Prince de Conti, offended that Law should have denied him fresh shares in India stock, at his own price, sent to his bank to demand payment in specie of so enormous a quantity of notes, that three wagons were required for its transport. Law com-plained to the regent, and urged on his attention the mischief that would be done, if such an example found many imitators. The regent was but too well aware of it, and, sending for the Prince de Conti, ordered him, under penalty of his high displeasure, to refund to the bank two-thirds of the specie which he had withdrawn from it. The prince was forced to obey the despotic mandate. Happily for Law's credit, De Conti was an unpopular man: everybody condemned his meanness and cupidity, and agreed that Law had been hardly treated. It is strange, however, that so narrow an escape should not have made both Law and the regent more anxious to restrict their issues. Others were soon found who imitated from motives of distrust, the example which had been set by De Conti in revenge. The more acute stock jobbers imagined justly that prices could not continue to rise for ever. Bourdon and La Richardiere, renowned for their extensive operations in the funds, quietly and in small quantities at a time, converted their notes into specie, and sent it away to foreign countries. They also bought as much as they could conveniently carry of plate and expensive jewellery, and sent it secretly away to England or to Holland. Vermalet, a jobber, who sniffed the coming storm, procured gold and silver coin to the amount of nearly a million of livres, which he packed in a farmer's cart, and covered over with hay and cow-dung. He then disguised himself in the dirty smock-frock, or *blouse*, of a peasant, and drove his precious load in safety into Belgium. From thence he soon found means to transport it to Amsterdam.

Hitherto no difficulty had been experienced by any class in procuring specie for their wants. But this system could not long be carried on without causing a scarcity. The voice of complaint was heard on every side, and inquiries being instituted, the cause was soon discovered. The council debated long on the remedies to be taken, and Law, being called on for his advice, was of opinion, that an edict should be published, depreciating the value of coin five percent below that of paper. The edict was published accordingly; but failing of its intended effect, was followed by another, in which the depreciation was increased to ten per cent. The payments of the bank were at the same time restricted to one hundred livres in gold, and ten in silver. All these measures were nugatory to restore confidence in the paper, though the restriction of cash payments within limits so extremely narrow kept up the credit of the bank.

Notwithstanding every effort to the contrary, the precious metals continued to be conveyed to England and Holland. The little coin that was left in the country was carefully treasured, or hidden until the scarcity became so great, that the operations of trade could no longer be carried on. In this emergency, Law hazarded the bold experiment of forbidding the use of specie altogether. In February 1720 an edict was published, which, instead of restoring the credit of the paper, as was intended. destroyed it irrecoverably, and drove the country to the very brink of revolution. By this famous edict it was forbidden to any person whatever to have more than five hundred livres (20*l.*) of coin in his possession, under pain of a heavy fine, and confiscation of the sums found. It was also forbidden to buy up jewellery, plate, and precious stones, and informers were encouraged to make search for offenders, by the promise of one-half the amount they might discover. The whole country sent up a cry of distress at this unheard-of tyranny. The most odious persecution daily took place. The privacy of families was violated by the intrusion of informers and their agents. The most virtuous and honest were denounced for the crime of having been seen with a *louis d'or* in their possession. Servants betrayed their masters, one citizen became a spy upon his neighbor, and arrests and confiscations so multiplied, that the courts found a difficulty in getting through the immense increase of business thus occasioned. It was sufficient for an informer to say that he suspected any person of concealing money in his house, and immediately a search-warrant was granted. Lord Stair, the English ambassador, said, that it was now impossible to doubt of the sincerity of Law's conversion to the Catholic religion; he had established the inquisition, after having given abundant evidence of his faith in transubstantiation, by turning so much gold into paper.

Every epithet that popular hatred could suggest was showered upon the regent and the unhappy Law. Coin, to any amount above five hundred livres, was an illegal tender, and nobody would take paper if he could help it. No one knew today what his notes would be worth tomorrow. "Never," says Duclos, in his *Secret Memoirs of the Regency*, "was seen a more capricious government—never was a more frantic tyranny exercised by hands less firm. It is inconceivable to those who were witnesses of the horrors of those times, and who look back upon them now as on a dream, that a sudden revolution did not break out—that Law and the regent did not perish by a tragical death. They were both held in horror, but the people confined themselves to complaints; a sombre and timid despair, a stupid consternation, had seized upon all, and men's minds were too vile even to be capable of a courageous crime."

It would appear that, at one time, a movement of the people was organized. Seditious writings were posted up against the walls, and were sent, in handbills, to the houses of the most conspicuous people. One of them, given in the Memoires de la Regence, was to the following effect:—"Sir and madam,—

This is to give you notice that a St. Bartholomew's Day will be enacted again on Saturday and Sunday, if affairs do not alter. You are desired not to stir out, nor you, nor your servants. God preserve you from the flames! Give notice to your neighbors. Dated, Saturday, May 25th, 1720." The immense number of spies with which the city was infested rendered the people mistrustful of one another, and beyond some trifling disturbances made in the evening by an insignificant group, which was soon dispersed, the peace of the capital was not compromised.

The value of shares in the Louisiana, or Mississippi stock, had fallen very rapidly, and few indeed were found to believe the tales that had once been told of the immense wealth of that region. A last effort was therefore tried to restore the public confidence in the Mississippi project. For this purpose, a general conscription of all the poor wretches in Paris was made by order of government. Upwards of six thousand of the very refuse of the population were impressed, as if in time of war, and were provided with clothes and tools to be embarked for New Orleans, to work in the gold mines alleged to abound there. They were paraded day after day through the streets with their pikes and shovels, and then sent off in small detachments to the outports to be shipped for America. Two-thirds of them never reached their destination, but dispersed themselves over the country, sold their tools for what they could get, and returned to their old course of life. In less than three weeks afterwards, one-half of them were to be found again in Paris. The manceuvre, however, caused a trifling advance in Mississippi stock. Many persons of superabundant gullibility believed that operations had begun in earnest in the new Golconda, and that gold and silver ingots would again be found in France.

In a constitutional monarchy some surer means would have been found for the restoration of public credit. In England, at a subsequent period, when a similar delusion had brought on similar distress, how different were the measures taken to

*Duclos, Memoires Secrets de la Régence.

repair the evil! but in France, unfortunately, the remedy was left to the authors of the mischief. The arbitrary will of the regent, which endeavoured to extricate the country, only plunged it deeper into the mire. All payments were ordered to be made in paper, and between the 1st of February and the end of May, notes were fabricated to the amount of upwards of 1500 millions of livres, or 60,000,000*l* sterling. But the alarm once sounded, no art could make the people feel the slightest confidence in paper which was not exchangeable into metal. M. Lambert, the president of the parliament of Paris, told the regent to his face that he would rather have a hundred thousand livres in gold or silver than five millions in the notes of his bank. When such was the general feeling, the superabundant issues of paper but increased the evil, by rendering still more enormous the disparity between the amount of specie and notes in circulation. Coin, which it was the object of the regent to depreciate, rose in value on every fresh attempt to diminish it. In February, it was judged advisable that the Royal Bank should be incorporated with the Company of the Indies. An edict to that effect was published and registered by the parliament. The state remained the guarantee for the notes of the bank, and no more were to be issued without an order in council. All the profits of the bank, since the time it had been taken out of Law's hands and made a national institution, were given over by the regent to the Company of the Indies. This measure had the effect of raising for a short time the value of the Louisiana and other shares of the company, but it failed in placing public credit on any permanent basis.

A council of state was held in the beginning of May, at which Law, D'Argenson (his colleague in the administration of the finances), and all the ministers were present. It was then computed that the total amount of notes in circulation was 2600 millions of livres, while the coin in the country was not quite equal to half that amount. It was evident to the majority of the council that some plan must be adopted to equalize the currency. Some proposed that the notes should be reduced to the value of the specie, while others proposed that the nominal value of the specie should be raised till it was on an equality with the paper. Law is said to have opposed both these projects, but failing in suggesting any other, it was agreed that the notes should be depreciated one half. On the 21st of May, an edict was accordingly issued, by which it was decreed that the shares of the Company of the Indies, and the notes of the bank, should gradually diminish in value, till at the end of a year they should only pass current for one-half of their nominal worth. The parliament refused to register the edict— the greatest outcry was excited, and the state of the country became so alarming, that, as the only means of preserving tranquility, the council of the regency was obliged to stultify its own proceedings, by publishing within seven days another edict, restoring the notes to their original value.

On the same day (the 27th of May) the bank stopped payment in specie. Law and D'Argenson were both dismissed from the ministry. The weak, vacillating, and cowardly regent threw the blame of all the mischief upon Law, who, upon presenting himself at the Palais Royal, was refused admittance. At nightfall, however, he was sent for, and admitted into the palace by a secret door,* when the regent endeavoured to console him, and made all manner of excuses for the severity with which in public he had been compelled to treat him. So capricious was his conduct, that, two days afterwards, he took him publicly to the opera, where he sat in the royal box alongside of the regent, who treated him with marked consideration in face of all the people. But such was the hatred against Law that the experiment had well nigh proved fatal to him. The mob assailed his carriage with stones just as he was entering his own door; and if the coachman had not made a sudden jerk into the courtyard, and the domestics closed the gate immediately, he would, in all probability, have been dragged out and torn to pieces. On the following day, his wife and daughter were also assailed by the mob as they were returning in their carriage from the races. When the regent was informed of these occurrences he sent Law a strong detachment of Swiss guards, who were stationed night and day in the court of his residence. The public indignation at last increased so much, that Law, finding his own house, even with this guard, insecure, took refuge in the Palais Royal, in the apartments of the regent.

The Chancellor, D'Aguesseau, who had been dismissed in 1718 for his opposition to the projects of Law, was now recalled to aid in the restoration of credit. The regent acknowledged too late, that he had treated with unjustifiable harshness and mistrust one of the ablest, and perhaps the sole honest public man of that corrupt period. He had retired ever since his dis-grace to his country house at Fresnes, where, in the midst of severe but delightful philosophic studies, he had forgotten the intrigues of an unworthy court. Law himself, and the Chevalier de Conflans, a gentleman of the regent's household, were dispatched in a post-chaise with orders to bring the exchancellor to Paris along with them. D'Aguesseau consented to render what assistance he could, contrary to the advice of his friends, who did not approve that he should accept any recall to office of which Law was the bearer. On his arrival in Paris, five councillors of the parliament were admitted to confer with the Commissary of Finance; and on the 1st of June an order was published abolishing the law which made it criminal to amass coin to the amount of more than five hundred livres. Every one was permitted to have as much specie as he pleased. In order that the banknotes might be withdrawn, twenty-five millions of new notes were created, on the security of the revenues of the city of Paris, at two and a half percent. The banknotes withdrawn were publicly burned in front of the Hotel de Ville. The new notes were principally of the value of ten livres each; and on the 10th of June the bank was reopened, with a sufficiency of silver coin to give in change for them.

These measures were productive of considerable advantage. All the population of Paris hastened to the bank to get coin for their small notes; and silver becoming scarce, they were paid in copper. Very few complained that this was too heavy, although poor fellows might be continually seen toiling and sweating along the streets, laden with more than they could comfortably carry, in the shape of change for fifty livres. The crowds around the bank were so great that hardly a day passed that some one was not pressed to death. On the 9th of July, the multitude was so dense and clamorous that the guards stationed at the entrance of the Mazarin Gardens closed the gate and refused to admit any more. The crowd became incensed, and flung stones through the railings upon the soldiers. The latter, incensed in their turn, threatened to fire

> Aussitot que Lass arriva
>   Dans notre bonne ville,
>   Monsieur le Régent publia
>   Que Lass serait utile
>   Pour retablir la nation.
> *La faridondaine! la faridondon!*
>   Mais il nous a tous enrichi,
>   *Biribi!*
> *A la façon de Barbari,*
>   *Mon ami*
>   Ce parpaillot, pour attirer
>   Tout l'argent de la France,
>   Songea d'abord a s'assurer
>   De notre confiance.
>   Il fit son abjuration,
> *La faridondaine! la faridondon!*
>   Mais le fourbe s'est convert,
>   *Biribi!*
> *A la façon de Barbari,*
>   *Mon ami!*
>   Lass, le fils aine de Satan
>   Nous met tous a l'aumone,
>   Il nous a pris tout notre argent

Et n'en rend a personne.
Mais le Régent, humain et bon,
La faridondaine! la faridondon!
Nous rendra ce qu'on nous a pris,
Biribi!
A la façon de Barbari,
Mon ami!

The following epigram is of the same date:

Lundi, j'achetai des actions;
Mardi, je gagnai tes millions;
Mercredi, j'arrangeai mon ménage,
Jeudi, je pris un equipage,
Vendredi, je m'en fus au bal,
Et Samedi, a l'hôpital.

upon the people. At that instant one of them was hit by a stone, and, taking up his piece, he fired into the crowd. One man fell dead immediately, and another was severely wounded. It was every instant expected that a general attack would have been commenced upon the bank; but the gates of the Mazarin Gardens being opened to the crowd, who saw a whole troop of soldiers, with their bayonets fixed ready to receive them, they contented themselves by giving vent to their indignation in groans and hisses.

Eight days afterwards the concourse of people was so tremendous that fifteen persons were squeezed to death at the doors of the bank. The people were so indignant that they took three of the bodies on stretchers before them, and proceeded, to the number of seven or eight thousand, to the gardens of the Palais Royal, that they might show the regent the misfortunes that he and Law had brought upon the country. Law's coachman, who was sitting on the box of his master's carriage, in the courtyard of the palace, happened to have more zeal than discretion, and, not liking that the mob should abuse his master, he said, loud enough to be overheard by several persons, that they were all blackguards, and deserved to be hanged. The mob immediately set upon him, and thinking that Law was in the carriage, broke it to pieces. The imprudent coachman narrowly escaped with his life. No further mischief was done; a body of troops making their appearance, the crowd quietly dispersed, after an assurance had been given by the regent that the three bodies they had brought to shew him should be decently buried at his own expense. The parliament was sitting at the time of this uproar, and the president took upon himself to go out and see what was the matter. On his return he informed the councillors that Law's carriage had been broken by the mob. All the members rose simultaneously, and expressed their joy by a loud shout, while one man, more zealous in his hatred than the rest, exclaimed, *"And Law himself, is he torn to pieces?"*[*]

Much, undoubtedly, depended on the credit of the Company of the Indies, which was answerable for so great a sum to the nation. It was therefore suggested in the council of the ministry, that any privileges which could be granted to enable it to fulfill its engagements, would be productive of the best results. With this end in view, it was proposed that the exclusive privilege of all maritime commerce should be secured to it, and an edict to that effect was published. But it was unfortunately forgotten that by such a measure all the merchants of the country would be ruined. The idea of such an immense privilege was generally scouted by the nation, and petition on petition was presented to the parliament that they would refuse to register the decree. They refused accordingly, and the regent, remarking that they did nothing but fan the flame of sedition, exiled them to Blois. At the intercession of D'Aguesseau, the place of banishment was changed to Pontoise, and thither accordingly the councillors repaired, determined to set the regent at defiance. They made every arrangement for rendering their temporary exile as agreeable as possible.

* The Duchess of Orleans gives a different version of this story; but whichever be the true one, the manifestation of such feeling in a legislative assembly was not very creditable. She says that the president was so transported with joy, that he was seized with a rhyming fit, returning into the hall, exclaimed to the memebers:
    "Messieurs! Messieurs! bonne nouvelle!
    Le carosse de Lass est reduit en cannelle!"

The president gave the most elegant suppers, to which he invited all the gayest and wittiest company of Paris. Every night there was a concert and ball for the ladies. The usually grave and solemn judges and councillors joined in cards and other diversions, leading for several weeks a life of the most extravagant pleasure, for no other purpose than to show the regent of how little consequence they deemed their banishment, and that, when they willed it, they could make Pontoise a pleasanter residence than Paris.

Of all the nations in the world the French are the most renowned for singing over their grievances. Of that country it has been remarked with some truth, that its whole history may be traced in its songs. When Law, by the utter failure of his best-laid plans, rendered himself obnoxious, satire of course seized hold upon him; and while caricatures of his person appeared in all the shops, the streets resounded with songs, in which neither he nor the regent was spared. Many of these songs were far from decent; and one of them in particular counsel led the application of all his notes to the most ignoble use to which paper can be applied. But the following, preserved in the letters of the Duchess of Orleans, was the best and the most popular, and was to be heard for months in all the carrefours in Paris. The application of the chorus is happy enough.

Among the caricatures that were abundantly published, and that shewed as plainly as graver matters that the nation had preserved in the *Mémoires de la Régence*. It was thus described by its author: "The 'Goddess of Shares,' in her triumphal car, driven by the Goddess of Folly. Those who are drawing the car are impersonations of the Mississippi, with his wooden leg, the South Sea, the Bank of England, the Company of the West of Senegal, and of various assurances. Lest the car should not roll fast enough, the agents of these companies, known by their long fox-tails and their cunning looks, turn round the spokes of the wheels, upon which are marked the names of the several stocks and their value, sometimes high and sometimes low, according to the turns of the wheel. Upon

LAW IN A CAR DRAWN BY COCKS

the ground are the merchandise, day-books and ledgers of legitimate commerce, crushed under the chariot of Folly. Behind is an immense crowd of persons, of all ages, sexes, and conditions, clamoring after Fortune, and fighting with each other to get a portion of the shares which she distributes so bountifully among them. In the clouds sits a demon, blowing bubbles of soap, which are also the objects of the admiration and cupidity of the crowd, who jump upon one another's backs to reach them ere they burst. Right in the pathway of the car, and blocking up the passage, stands a large building, with three doors, through one of which it must pass, if it proceeds farther, and all the crowd along with it. Over the first door are the words, *'Hôpital des Foux,'* over the second, *'Hôspital des Malades,'* and over the third, *'Hôpital des Gueux."* Another caricature represented Law sitting in a large cauldron, boiling over the flames of popular madness, surrounded by an impetuous multitude, who were pouring all their gold and silver into it, and receiving gladly in exchange the bits of paper which he distributed among them by handfuls.

While this excitement lasted, Law took good care not to expose himself unguarded in the streets. Shut up in the apartments of the regent, he was secure from all attack; and whenever he ventured abroad, it was either incognito, or in one of the royal carriages, with a powerful escort. An amusing anecdote is recorded of the detestation in which he was held by the people, and the ill-treatment he would have met had he fallen into their hands. A gentleman of the name of Boursel was passing in his carriage down the Rue St. Antoine, when his farther progress was stayed by a hackney-coach that had blocked up the road. M. Boursel's servant called impatiently to the hackney-coachman to get out of the way, and, on his refusal, struck him a blow on the face. A crowd was soon drawn together by the disturbance, and M. Boursel got out of the carriage to restore order. The hackney-coachman, imagining that he had now another assailant, bethought him of an expedient to rid himself of both, and called out as loudly as he was able, "Help! help! murder! murder! Here are Law and his servant going to kill me! Help! help!" At this cry the people came out of their shops, armed with sticks and other weapons, while the mob gathered stones to inflict summary vengeance upon the supposed financier. Happily for M. Boursel and his servant, the door of the church of the Jesuits stood wide open, and, seeing the fearful odds against them, they rushed towards it with all speed. They reached the altar, pursued by the people, and would have been ill-treated even there if, finding the door open leading to the sacristy, they had not sprang through, and closed it after them. The mob were then persuaded to leave the church by the alarmed and indignant priests, and finding M. Boursel's carriage still in the streets, they vented their ill-will against it, and did it considerable damage.

The twenty-five millions secured on the municipal revenues of the city of Paris, bearing so low an interest as two and a half percent, were not very popular among the large holders of Mississippi stock. The conversion of the securities was, therefore, a work of considerable difficulty; for many preferred to retain the falling paper of Law's company, in the hope that a favourable turn might take place. On the 15th of August, with a view to hasten the conversion, an edict was passed, declaring that all notes for sums between one thousand and ten thousand livres should not pass current, except for the purchase of annuities and bank accounts, or for the payment of installments still due on the shares of the company.

In October following another edict was passed, depriving these notes of all value whatever after the month of November next ensuing. The management of the mint, the farming of the revenue, and all the other advantages and privileges of the India, or Mississippi Company, were taken from them, and they were reduced to a mere private company. This was the death-blow to the whole system, which had now got into the hands of its enemies. Law had lost all influence in the Council of Finance, and the company, being despoiled of its immunities, could no longer hold out the shadow of a prospect of being able to fulfil its engagements. All those suspected of illegal profits at the time the public delusion was at its height, were sought out and amerced in heavy fines. It was previously ordered that a list of the original proprietors should be made out, and that such persons as still retained their shares should place them in deposit with the company, and that those who had neglected to complete the shares for which they had put down their names should now purchase them of the company, at the rate of 13,500 livres for each share of 500 livres. Rather than submit to pay this enormous sum for stock which was actually at a discount, the shareholders packed up all their portable effects, and endeavoured to find a refuge in foreign countries. Orders were immediately issued to the authorities at the ports and frontiers, to apprehend all travellers who sought to leave the kingdom, and keep them in custody, until it was ascertained whether they had any plate or jewellery with them, or were concerned in the late stock-jobbing. Against such few as escaped, the punishment of death was recorded, while the most arbitrary proceedings were instituted against those who remained.

Law himself, in a moment of despair, determined to leave a country where his life was no longer secure. He at first only demanded permission to retire from Paris to one of his country-seats—a permission which the regent cheerfully granted. The latter was much affected at the unhappy turn affairs had taken, but his faith continued unmoved in the truth and efficacy of Law's financial system. His eyes were opened to his own errors; and during the few remaining years of his life he constantly longed for an opportunity of again establishing the system upon a securer basis. At Law's last interview with the prince, he is reported to have said,—"I confess that I have committed many faults. I committed them because I am a man, and all men are liable to error; but I declare to you most solemnly that none of them proceeded from wicked or dishonest motives, and that nothing of the kind will be found in the whole course of my conduct.'

Two or three days after his departure the regent sent him a very kind letter, permitting him to leave the kingdom whenever he pleased, and stating that he had ordered his passports to be made ready. He at the same time offered him any sum of money he might require. Law respectfully declined the money, and set out for Brussels in a post-chaise belonging to Madame de Prie, the mistress of the Duke of Bourbon, escorted by six horse-guards. From thence he proceeded to Venice, where he remained for some months, the object of the greatest curiosity to the people, who believed him to be the possessor of enormous wealth. No opinion, however, could be more erroneous. With more generosity than could have been expected from a man who during the greatest part of his life had been a professed gambler, he had refused to enrich himself at the expense of a ruined nation. During the height of the popular frenzy for Mississippi stock, he had never doubted of the final success of his projects in making France the richest and most powerful nation of Europe. He invested all his gains in the purchase of landed property in Francc a sure proof of his own belief in the stability of his schemes. He had hoarded no plate or jewellery, and sent no money, like the dishonest jobbers, to foreign countries. His all, with the exception of one diamond, worth about five or six thousand pounds sterling, was invested in the French soil; and when he left that country, he left it almost a beggar. This fact alone ought to rescue his memory from the charge of knavery, so often and so unjustly brought against him.

As soon as his departure was known, all his estates and his valuable library were confiscated. Among the rest, an annuity of 200,000 livres (8000*l.* sterling) on the lives of his wife and children, which had been purchased for five millions of livres, was forfeited, notwithstanding that a special edict, drawn up for the purpose in the days of his prosperity, had expressly declared that it should never be confiscated for any cause whatever. Great discontent existed among the people that Law had been suffered to escape. The mob and the parliament would have been pleased to have seen him hanged. The few who had not suffered by the commercial revolution rejoiced that the *quack* had left the country; but all those (and they were by far the most numerous class) whose fortunes were implicated regretted that his intimate knowledge of the distress of the country, and of the causes that had led to it, had not been rendered more available in discovering a remedy.

At a meeting of the Council of Finance and the General Council of the Regency, documents were laid upon the table, from which it appeared that the amount of notes in circulation was 2700 millions. The regent was called upon to explain how it happened that there was a discrepancy between the dates at which these issues were made and those of the edicts by which they were authorised. He might have safely taken the whole blame upon himself, but he preferred that an absent man should bear a share of it; and he therefore stated that Law, upon his own authority had issued 1200 millions of notes at different times, and that he (the regent), seeing that the thing had been irrevocably done, had screened Law by antedating the decrees of the council which authorized the augmentation. It would have been more to his credit if he had told the whole truth while he was about it, and acknowledged that it was mainly through his extravagance and impatience that Law had been induced to overstep the bounds of safe speculation. It was also ascertained that the national debt, on the 1st of January, 1721, amounted to upwards of 3100 millions of livres, or more than 124,000,000*l.* sterling, the interest upon which was 3,196,000*l.* A commission, or visa, was forthwith appointed to examine into all the securities of the state creditors, who were to be divided into five classes; the first four comprising those who had purchased their securities with real effects, and the latter comprising those who could give no proofs that the transactions they had entered into were real and bona fide. The securities of the latter were ordered to be destroyed, while those of the first four classes were subjected to a most rigid and jealous scrutiny. The result of the labors of the visa was a report, in which they counsel led the reduction of the interest upon these securities to fifty-six millions of livres. They justified this advice by a statement of the various acts of peculation and extortion which they had discovered; and an edict to that effect was accordingly published and duly registered by the parliaments of the kingdom.

Another tribunal was afterwards established under the title of the *Chambre de l'Arsenal*, which took cognizance of all the malversations committed in the financial departments of the government during the late unhappy period. A Master of Requests, named Falhonet, together with the Abbe Clement, and two clerks in their employ, had been concerned in divers acts of peculation to the amount of upwards of a million of livres. The first two were sentenced to be beheaded, and the latter to be hanged; but their punishment was afterwards commuted into imprisonment for life in the Bastille. Numerous other acts of dishonesty were discovered, and punished by fine and imprisonment.

D'Argenson shared with Law and the regent the unpopularity which had alighted upon all those concerned in the Mississippi madness. He was dismissed from his post of Chancellor to make room for D'Aguesseau; but he retained the title of Keeper of Seals, and was allowed to attend the councils whenever he pleased. He thought it better, however, to withdraw from Paris, and live for a time a life of seclusion at his country seat. But he was not formed for retirement; and becoming moody and discontented, he aggravated a disease under which he had long laboured, and died in less than a twelve-month. The populace of Paris so detested him, that they carried their hatred even to his grave. As his funeral procession passed to the church of St. Nicholas du Chardonneret, the burying-place of his family, it was beset by a riotous mob; and his two sons, who were following as chief mourners, were obliged to drive as fast as they were able down a by-street to escape personal violence.

As regards Law, he for some time entertained a hope that he should be recalled to France to aid in establishing its credit upon a firmer basis. The death of the regent in 1723, who expired suddenly as he was sitting by the fireside conversing with his mistress, the Duchess de Phalaris, deprived him of that hope, and he was reduced to lead his former life of gambling. He was more than once obliged to pawn his diamond, the sole remnant of his vast wealth, but successful play generally enabled him to redeem it. Being persecuted by his creditors at Rome, he proceeded to Copenhagen, where he received permission from the English ministry to reside in his native country, his pardon for the murder of Mr. Wilson having been sent over to him in 1719. He was brought over in the admiral's ship—a circumstance which gave occasion for a short debate in the House of Lords. Earl Coningsby complained that a man who had renounced both his country and his religion should have been treated with such honor, and expressed his belief that his presence in England, at a time when the people were so bewildered by the nefarious practices of the South-Sea directors, would be attended with no little danger. He gave notice of a motion on the subject; but it was allowed to drop, no other member of the House having the slightest participation in his lordship's fears. Law remained for about four years in England, and then proceeded to Venice, where he died in 1729, in very embarrassed circumstances. The following epitaph was written at the time:

"Ci gît cet Ecossais celébre,
Ce calculateur sans égal,
Qui, par les règles de l'algébre,
A mis la France a l'hôpital."

His brother, William Law, who had been concerned with him in the administration both of the bank and the Louisiana Company, was imprisoned in the Bastille for alleged malversation, but no guilt was ever proved against him. He was liberated after fifteen months, and became the founder of a family, which is still known in France under the title of Marquises of Lauriston.

In the next chapter will be found an account of the madness which infected the people of England at the same time, and under very similar circumstances, but which, thanks to the energies and good sense of a constitutional government, was attended with results far less disastrous than those which were seen in France.

THE SOUTH-SEA BUBBLE

At length corruption, like a general flood,
Did deluge all; and avarice creeping on,
Spread, like a low-born mist, and hid the sun.
Statesmen and patriots plied alike the stocks,
Peeress and butler shared alike the box;
And judges jobbed, and bishops bit the town.
And mighty dukes packed cards for half-a-crown:
Britain was sunk in lucre's sordid charms.—*Pope*.

THE South-Sea Company was originated by the celebrated Harley Earl of Oxford, in the year 1711, with the view of restoring public credit, which had suffered by the dismissal of the Whig ministry, and of providing for the discharge of the army and navy debentures, and other parts of the floating debt, amounting to nearly ten millions sterling. A company of merchants, at that time without a name, took this debt upon themselves, and the government agreed to secure them for a certain period the interest of six percent. To provide for this interest, amounting to 600,000*l*. per annum, the duties upon wines, vinegar, India goods, wrought silks, tobacco, whale-fins, and some other articles, were rendered permanent. The monopoly of the trade to the South Seas was granted, and the company, being incorporated by act of parliament, assumed the title by which it has ever since been known. The minister took great credit to himself for his share in this transaction, and the scheme was always called by his flatterers "the Earl of Oxford's masterpiece."

Even at this early period of its history the most visionary ideas were formed by the company and the public of the immense riches of the eastern coast of South America. Everybody had heard of the gold and silver mines of Peru and Mexico; every one believed them to be inexhaustible, and that it was only necessary to send the manufactures of England to the coast to be repaid a hundredfold in gold and silver ingots by the natives. A report industriously spread, that Spain was willing to concede four ports on the coasts of Chili and Peru for the purposes of traffic, increased the general confidence, and for many years the South-Sea Company's stock was in high favor.

Philip V. of Spain, however, never had any intention of admitting the English to a free trade in the ports of Spanish America. Negotiations were set on foot, but their only result was the *assiento* contract, or the privilege of supplying the colonies with negroes for thirty years, and of sending once a year a vessel, limited both as to tonnage and value of cargo, to trade with Mexico, Peru, or Chili. The latter permission was only granted upon the hard condition, that the King of Spain should enjoy one-fourth of the profits, and a tax of five percent on the remainder. This was a great disappointment to the Earl of Oxford and his party, who were reminded much oftener than they found agreeable of the

"*Parturiunt montes, nascitur ridiculus mus.*"

But the public confidence in the South-Sea Company was not shaken. The Earl of Oxford declared that Spain would permit two ships, in addition to the annual ship, to carry out merchandise during the first year; and a list was published, in which all the ports and harbors of these coasts were pompously set forth as open to the trade of Great Britain. The first voyage of the annual ship was not made till the year 1717, and in the following year the trade was suppressed by the rupture with Spain.

The king's speech, at the opening of the session of 1717, made pointed allusion to the state of public credit, and recommended that proper measures should be taken to reduce the national debt. The two great monetary corporations, the South-Sea Company and the Bank of England, made proposals to parliament on the 20th of May ensuing. The South-Sea Company prayed that their capital stock of ten millions might be increased to twelve, by subscription or otherwise, and offered to accept five per cent instead of six upon the whole amount. The bank made proposals equally advantageous. The house debated for some time, and finally three acts were passed, called the South-Sea Act, the Bank Act, and the General Fund Act. By the first, the proposals of the South-Sea Company were accepted, and that body held itself ready to advance the sum of two millions towards discharging the principal and interest of the debt due by the state for the four lottery funds of the ninth and tenth years of Queen Anne. By the second act, the bank received a lower rate of interest for the sum of 1,775,027L. 15s. due to it by the state, and agreed to deliver up to be cancelled as many exchequer bills as amounted to two millions sterling, and to accept of an annuity of one hundred thousand pounds, being after the rate of five per cent, the whole redeemable at one year's notice. They were further required to be ready to advance, in case of need, a sum not exceeding 2,500,000L. upon the same terms of five per cent interest, redeemable by parliament. The General Fund Act recited the various deficiencies, which were to be made good by the aids derived from the foregoing sources.

The name of the South-Sea Company was thus continually before the public. Though their trade with the South American States produced little or no augmentation of their revenues, they continued to flourish as a monetary corporation. Their stock was in high request, and the directors, buoyed up with success, began to think of new means for extending their influence. The Mississippi scheme of John Law, which so dazzled and captivated the French people, inspired them with an idea that they could carry on the same game in England. The anticipated failure of his plans did not divert them from their intention. Wise in their own conceit, they imagined they could avoid his faults, carry on their schemes for ever, and stretch the cord of credit to its extremist tension, without causing it to snap asunder.

It was while Law's plan was at its greatest height of popularity, while people were crowding in thousands to the Rue Quincampoix, and ruining themselves with frantic eagerness, that the South-Sea directors laid before parliament their famous plan for paying off the national debt. Visions of boundless wealth floated before the fascinated eyes of the people in the two most celebrated countries of Europe. The English commenced their career of extravagance somewhat later than the French; but as soon as the delirium seized them, they were determined not to be outdone. Upon the 22nd of January, 1720, the House of Commons resolved itself into a committee of the whole house, to take into consideration that part of the king's speech at the opening of the session which related to the public debts, and the proposal of the South-Sea Company towards the redemption and sinking of the same. The proposal set forth at great length, and under several heads, the debts of the state, amounting to 30,981-712*l*., which the company were anxious to take upon themselves, upon consideration of five percent per annum, secured to them until Midsummer 1727; after which time, the whole was to become redeemable at the pleasure of the legislature, and the interest to be reduced to four percent. The proposal was received with great favor; but the Bank of England had many friends in the House of Commons, who were desirous that that body should share in the advantages that were likely to accrue. On behalf of this corporation it was represented, that they had performed great and eminent services to the state in the most difficult times, and deserved, at least, that if any advantage was to be made by public bargains of this nature, they should be preferred before a company that had never done any thing for the nation. The further consideration of the matter was accordingly postponed for five days. In the mean time a plan was drawn up by the governors of the bank. The South-Sea Company, afraid that the bank might offer still more advantageous terms to the government than themselves, reconsidered their former proposal, and made some alterations in it, which they hoped would render it more acceptable. The principal change was a stipulation that the government might redeem these debts at the expiration of four years, instead of seven, as at first suggested. The bank resolved not to be outbidden in this singular auction, and the governors also reconsidered their first proposal, and sent in a new one.

Thus, each corporation having made two proposals, the house began to deliberate. Mr. Robert Walpole was the chief speaker in favor of the bank, and Mr. Aislabie, the Chancellor of the Exchequer, the principal advocate on behalf of the South-Sea Company. It was resolved on the second of February, that the proposals of the latter were most advantageous to the country. They were accordingly received and leave was given to bring in a bill to that effect.

Exchange Alley was in fervor of excitement. The company's stock which had been at one hundred and thirty the previous day gradually rose to three hundred, and continued to rise with the most astonishing rapidity during the whole time that the bill in its several stages was under discussion. Mr. Walpole was almost the only statesman in thee House who spoke out boldly against it. He warned them, ineloquent and solemn language, of the evils that would ensue. It sountenanced, he said, "the dangerous practice of stock-jobbing, and would divert the genius of the nation from trade and industry. It would hold out a dangerous lure to decoy the unwary to their ruin, by making them part with the earnings of their labor for a prospect of imaginary wealth. The great principle of the project was an evil of first-rate magnitude; it was to raise artificially the value of the stock, by exciting and keeping up a general infatuation, and by promising dividends out of funds which could never be adequate to the purpose." In a prophetic spirit he added, that if the plan succeeded, the directors would become masters of the government, form, a new and absolute aristocracy in the kingdom, and control the resolutions of the legislature. If it failed, which he was convinced it would, the result would bring general discontent and ruin upon the country. Such would be the delusion, that when the evil day came the people would start up, as from a dream, and ask themselves of these things could have been true. All his eloquence was in vain. He was looked upon as a false prophet, or compared to the hoarse raven, croaking omens of evil. His friends, however, compared him to Cassandra, predicting evils which would only be believed when they come home to men's hearths, and stared them in the face at their own boards. Although, in former times, the House had listened with the utmost attention to every word that fell from his lips, the benches became deserted when it was known that he would speak on the South-Sea question.

The bill was two months in its progress through the House of Commons. During this time every exertion was made by the directors and their friends, and more especially by the chairman, the noted Sir John Blunt, to raise the price of the stock. The most extravagant rumors were in circulation. Treaties between England and Spain were spoken of, whereby the latter was to grant a free trade to all her colonies; and the rich produce of the mines of Potosí-la-Paz was to be brought to England until silver should become almost as plentiful as iron. For cotton and woolen goods, with which we could supply them in abundance, the dwellers in Mexico were to empty their golden mines. The company of merchants trading to the South Seas would be the richest the world ever saw, and every hundred pounds invested in it would produce hundreds per annum to the stockholder. At last the stock was raised by these means to near four hundred; but, after fluctuating a good deal, settled at three hundred and thirty, at which price it remained when the bill passed the Commons by a majority of 172 against 55.

In the House of Lords the bill was hurried through all its stages with unexampled rapidity. On the 4th of April it was read a first time; on the 5th, it was read a second time; on the 6th, it was committed; and on the 7th, was read a third time and passed.

Several peers spoke warmly against the scheme; but their warnings fell upon dull, cold ears. A speculating frenzy had seized them as well as the plebeians. Lord North and Grey said the bill was unjust in its nature, and might prove fatal in its consequences, being calculated to enrich the few and impoverish the many.

The Duke of Wharton followed; but, as he only retailed at secondhand the arguments so eloquently stated by Walpole in the Lower House, he was not listened to with even the same attention that had been bestowed upon Lord North and Grey. Earl Cowper followed on the same side, and compared the bill to the famous horse of the siege of Troy. Like that, it was ushered in and received with great pomp and acclamations of joy, but bore within it treachery and destruction. The Earl of Sunderland endeavored to answer all objections; and on the question being put, there appeared only seventeen peers against, and eighty-three in favor of the project. The very same day on which it passed the Lords, it received the royal assent, and became the law of the land.

It seemed at that time as if the whole nation had turned stock-jobbers. Exchange Alley was every day blocked up by crowds, and Cornhill was impassable for the number of carriages. Every body came to purchase stock. "Every fool aspired to be a knave." In the words of a ballad published at the time, and sung about the streets,*

> "Then stars and garters did appear
> Among the meaner rabble;
> To buy and sell, to see and hear
> The Jews and Gentiles squabble.
>
> The greatest ladies thither came,
> And plied in chariots daily,
> Or pawned their jewels for a sum
> To venture in the Alley."

* A South-Sea Ballad; or, Merry Remarks upon Exchange-Alley Bubbles. To a new Tune called "The Grand Elixir; or, the Philosopher's Stone discovered."

The inordinate thirst of gain that had afflicted all ranks of society was not to be slaked even in the South Sea. Other schemes, of the most extravagant kind, were started. The share-lists were speedily filled up, and an enormous traffic carried on in shares, while, of course, every means were resorted to raise them to an artificial value in the market.

Contrary to all expectations, South-Sea stock fell when the bill received the royal assent. On the 7th of April the shares were quoted at three hundred and ten, and on the following day at two hundred and ninety. Already the directors had tasted the profits of their scheme, and it was not likely that they should quietly allow the stock to find its natural level without an effort to raise it. Immediately their busy emissaries were set to work. Every person interested in the success of the project endeavored to draw a knot of listeners around him, to whom he expatiated on the even live out that short span of existence. Every evening produced new schemes, and every morning new projects. The highest of the aristocracy were as eager in this hot pursuit of gain as the most plodding jobber in Cornhill. The Prince of Wales became governor of one company, and is said to have cleared 40,000*l.* by his speculations.* The Duke of Bridgewater started a scheme for the improvement of London and Westminster, and the Duke of Chandos another. There were nearly a hundred different projects, each more extravagant and deceptive than the other. To use the words of the Political State, they were "set on foot and promoted by crafty knaves, then pursued by multitudes of covetous fools, and at last appeared to be, in effect, what their vulgar appellation denoted them to be—bubbles and mere cheats." It was computed that near one million and a half sterling was won and lost by these unwarrantable practices, to the impoverishment of many a fool, and the enriching of many a rogue.

Some of these schemes were plausible enough, and, had they been undertaken at a time when the public mind was unexcited, might have been pursued with advantage to all

* *Coxe's Walpole*, Correspondence between Mr. Secretary Craggs and Earl Stanhope.

concerned. But they were established merely with the view of raising the shares in the market. The projectors took the first opportunity of a rise to sell out, and next morning the scheme was at an end. Maitland, in his *History of London,* gravely informs us, that one of the projects which received great encouragement, was for the establishment of a company "to make deal boards out of sawdust." This is no doubt intended as a joke; but there is abundance of evidence to shew that dozens of schemes, hardly a whit more reasonable, lived their little day, ruining hundreds ere they fell. One of them was for a wheel for perpetual motion—capital one million; another was "for encouraging the breed of horses in England, and improving of glebe and church lands, and repairing and rebuilding parsonage and vicarage houses." Why the clergy, who were so mainly interested in the latter clause, should have taken so much interest in the first, is only to be explained on the supposition that the scheme was projected by a knot of the fox-hunting parsons, once so common in England. The shares of this company were rapidly subscribed for. But the most absurd and preposterous of all, and which showed, more completely than any other, the utter madness of the people, was one started by an unknown adventurer, entitled, *"A company for carrying on an undertaking of great advantage, but nobody to know what it is."* Were not the fact stated by scores of credible witnesses, it would be impossible to believe that any person could have been duped by such a project. The man of genius who essayed this bold and successful inroad upon public credulity, merely stated in his prospectus that the required capital was half a million, in five thousand shares of 100*l.* each, deposit 2*l* per share. Each subscriber, paying his deposit, would be entitled to 100*l.* per annum per share. How this immense profit was to be obtained, he did not condescend to inform them at that time, but promised that in a month full particulars should be duly announced, and a call made for the remaining 98*l.* of the subscription. Next morning, at nine o'clock, this

> Lie waiting for the foundered skiffs,
> And strip the bodies of the dead."

Another fraud that was very successful was that of the "Globe Permits," as they were called. They were nothing more than square pieces of playing cards, on which was the impression of a seal, in wax, bearing the sign of the Globe Tavern, in the neighborhood of Exchange Alley, with the inscription of "Sail-Cloth Permits." The possessors enjoyed no other advantage from them than permission to subscribe at some future time to a new sailcloth manufactory, projected by one who was then known to be a man of fortune, but who was afterwards involved in the peculation and punishment of the South-Sea directors. These permits sold for as much as sixty guineas in the Alley.

Persons of distinction, of both sexes, were deeply engaged in all these bubbles; those of the male sex going to taverns and coffee-houses to meet their brokers, and the ladies resorting for the same purpose to the shops of millners and haberdashers. But it did not follow that all these people believed in the feasibility of the schemes to which they subscribed; it was enough for their purpose that their shares would, by stock-jobbing arts, be soon raides to a premium, when they got rid of them with all expedition to the really credulous. So great was the confusion of the crowd in the alley, that shares in the same bubble were known to have been sold at the same instant ten percent higher at one end of the alley than at the other. Sensible men beheld the extraordinary infatuation of the people with sorrow and alarm. There some both in and out of parliament who foresaw clearly the ruin that was impending. Mr. Walpole did not cease his gloomy forebodings. His fears were shared by all the thinking few, and impressed most forcibly upon the government. On the 11th of June, the day the parliament rose, the king published a proclamation, declaring that all these unlawful projects should be deemed public nuisances, and prosecuted accordingly, and forbidding any broker, under a penalty of five hundred pounds, from buying or selling any shares in them. Notwithstanding this proclamation, roguish speculators still carried them on, and the deluded people still encouraged them. On the 12th of July, an order of the Lords Justices assembled in privy council was published, dismissing all the petitions that had been presented for patents or charters, and dissolving all the bubble companies. The following copy of their lordship's order, containing a list of all these nefarious projects, will not be deemed uninteresting at the present time, when, at periodic intervals, there is but too much tendency in the public mind to indulge in similar practices:

great man opened an office in Cornhill. Crowds of people beset his door, and when he shut up at three o'clock, he found .."that no less than one thousand shares had been subscribed for, and the deposits paid. He was thus, in five hours, the winner of 2000*l*. He was philosopher enough to be contented with his venture, and set off the same evening for the Continent. He was never heard of again.

Well might Swift exclaim, comparing Change Alley to a gulf in the South Sea:

> "Subscribers here by thousands float,
> And jostle one another down,
> Each paddling in his leaky boat,
> And here they fish for gold and drown.
>
> Now buried in the depths below,
> Now mounted up to heaven again,
> They reel and stagger to and fro,
> At their wits' end, like drunken men.
> Meantime, secure on Garraway cliffs,
> A savage race, by shipwrecks fed,

"At the Council Chamber, Whitehall, the 12th day of July, 1720. Present, their Excellencies the Lords Justices in Council.

"Their Excellencies the Lords Justices, in council, taking into consideration the many inconveniences arising to the public from several projects set on foot for raising of joint-stock for various purposes, and that a great many of his majesty's subjects have been drawn in to part with their money on pretense of assurances that their petitions for patents and charters to enable them to carry on the same would be granted: to prevent such impositions, their excellencies this day ordered the said several petitions, together with such reports from the Board of Trade, and from his majesty's attorney and solicitor-general, as had been obtained thereon, to be laid before them; and after mature consideration thereof, were pleased, by advice of his majesty's privy council, to order that the said petitions be dismissed, which are as follow:

"1. Petition of several persons, praying letters patent for carrying on a fishing trade by the name of the Grand Fishery of Great Britain.

"2. Petition of the Company of the Royal Fishery of England, praying letters patent for such further powers as will effectually contribute to carry on the said fishery.

"3. Petition of George James, on behalf of himself and divers persons of distinction concerned in a national fishery, praying letters patent of incorporation, to enable them to carry on the same.

"4. Petition of several merchants, traders, and others, whose names are thereunto subscribed, praying to be incorporated for reviving and carrying on a whale fishery to Greenland and elsewhere.

"5. Petition of Sir John Lambert and others thereto subscribing, on behalf of themselves and a great number of merchants, praying to be incorporated for carrying on a Greenland trade, and particularly a whale fishery in Davis's Straits.

"6. Another petition for a Greenland trade.

"7. Petition of several merchants, gentlemen, and citizens, praying to be incorporated for buying and building of ships to let or freight.

"8. Petition of Samuel Antrim and others, praying for letters patent for sowing hemp and flax.

"9. Petition of several merchants, masters of ships, sail-makers, and manufacturers of sailcloth, praying a charter of incorporation, to enable them to carry on and promote the said manufactory by a joint-stock.

"10. Petition of Thomas Boyd and several hundred merchants, owners and masters of ships, sail-makers, weavers, and other traders, praying a charter of incorporation, empowering them to borrow money for purchasing lands, in order to the manufacturing sailcloth and fine holland.

"11. Petition on behalf of several persons interested in a patent granted by the late King William and Queen Mary for the making of linen and sailcloth, praying that no charter may be granted to any persons whatsoever for making sailcloth, but that the privilege now enjoyed by them may be confirmed, and likewise an additional power to carry on the cotton and cotton-silk manufactures.

"12. Petition of several citizens, merchants, and traders in London, and others, subscribers to a British stock for a general insurance from fire in any part of England, praying to be incorporated for carrying on the said undertaking.

"13. Petition of several of his majesty's loyal subjects of the city of London and other parts of Great Britain, praying to be incorporated for carrying on a general insurance from losses by fire within the kingdom of England.

"14. Petition of Thomas Burges and others his majesty's subjects thereto subscribing, in behalf of themselves and others, subscribers to a fund of 1,200,000*l.* for carrying on a trade to his majesty's German dominions, praying to be incorporated by the name of the Harburg Company.

"15. Petition of Edward Jones, a dealer in timber, on behalf of himself and others, praying to be incorporated for the importation of timber from Germany.

"16. Petition of several merchants of London, praying a charter of incorporation for carrying on a salt-work.

"17. Petition of Captain Macphedris of London,

merchant, on behalf of himself and several merchants, cloth-iers, hatters, dyers, and other traders, praying a charter of incorporation empowering them to raise a sufficient sum of money to purchase lands for planting and rearing a wood called madder, for the use of dyers.

"18. Petition of Joseph Galendo of London, snuff-maker, praying a patent for his invention to prepare and cure Virginia tobacco for snuff in Virginia, and making it into the same in all his majesty's dominions."

The following Bubble-Companies were by the same order declared to be illegal, and abolished accordingly:

1. For the importation of Swedish iron.

2. For supplying London with sea-coal. Capital, three millions.

3. For building and rebuilding houses throughout all England. Capital, three millions.

4. For making of muslin.

5. For carrying on and improving the British alum-works.

6. For effectually settling the island of Blanco and Sal Tartagus.

7. For supplying the town of Deal with fresh water.

8. For the importation of Flanders lace.

9. For improvement of lands in Great Britain. Capital, four millions.

10. For encouraging the breed of horses in England, and improving of glebe and church lands, and for repairing and rebuilding parsonage and vicarage houses.

11. For making of iron and steel in Great Britain.

12. For improving the land in the county of Flint. Capital, one million.

13. For purchasing lands to build on. Capital, two mullions.

14. For trading in hair.

15. For erecting saltworks in Holy Island. Capital, two millions.

16. For buying and selling estates, and lending money

on mortgage.

17. For carrying on an undertaking of great advantage; but nobody to know what it is.

18. For paving the streets of London. Capital, two mullions.

19. For furnishing funerals to any part of Great Britain.

20. For buying and selling lands and lending money at interest. Capital, five millions.

21. For carrying on the royal fishery of Great Britain. Capital, ten millions.

22. For assuring of seamen's wages.

23. For erecting loan-offices for the assistance and encouragement of the industrious. Capital, two millions.

24. For purchasing and improving leasable lands. Capital, four millions.

25. For importing pitch and tar, and other naval stores, from North Britain and America.

26. For the clothing, felt, and pantile trade.

27. For purchasing and improving a manor and royalty in Essex.

28. For insuring of horses. Capital, two millions.

29. For exporting the woolen manufacture, and importing copper, brass, and iron. Capital, four millions.

30. For a grand dispensary. Capital, three millions.

31. For erecting mills and purchasing lead mines. Capital, two millions.

32. For improving the art of making soap.

33. For a settlement on the island of Santa Cruz. 34. For sinking pits and smelting lead ore in Derbyshire.

35. For making glass bottles and other glass.

36. For a wheel for perpetual motion. Capital, one million.

37. For improving of gardens.

38. For insuring and increasing children's fortunes.

39. For entering and loading goods at the Custom-house, and for negotiating business for merchants.

40. For carrying on a woolen manufacture in the north

of England.

41. For importing walnut trees from Virginia. Capital, two millions.

42. For making Manchester stuffs of thread and cotton.

43. For making Joppa and Castile soap.

44. For improving the wrought-iron and steel manufactures of this kingdom. Capital, four millions.

45. For dealing in lace, hollands, cambrics, lawns, & c. Capital, two millions.

46. For trading in and improving certain commodities of the produce of this kingdom, & c. Capital, three millions.

47. For supplying the London markets with cattle.

48. For making looking-glasses, coach-glasses, & c. Capital, two millions.

49. For working the tin and lead mines in Cornwall and Derbyshire.

50. For making rape-oil.

51. For importing beaver fur. Capital, two millions.

52. For making pasteboard and packing-paper.

53. For importing of oils and other materials used in the woolen manufacture.

54. For improving and increasing the silk manufactures.

55. For lending money on stock, annuities, tallies, & c.

56. For paying pensions to widows and others, at a small discount. Capital, two millions.

57. For improving malt liquors. Capital, four millions.

58. For a grand American fishery.

59. For purchasing and improving the fenny lands in Lincolnshire. Capital, two millions.

60. For improving the paper manufacture of Great Britain.

61. The Bottomry Company.

62. For drying malt by hot air.

63. For carrying on a trade in the river Oronooko.

64. For the more effectual making of baize, in Colchester

TREE CARICATURE

and other parts of Great Britain.

65. For buying of naval stores, supplying the victualling, and paying the wages of the workmen.

66. For employing poor artificers, and furnishing merchants and others with watches.

67. For improvement of tillage and the breed of cattle.

68. Another for the improvement of our breed in horses.

69. Another for a horse-insurance.

70. For carrying on the corn trade of Great Britain.

71. For insuring to all masters and mistresses the losses they may sustain by servants. Capital, three millions.

72. For erecting houses or hospitals for taking in and maintaining illegitimate children. Capital, two millions.

73. For bleaching coarse sugars, without the use of fire or loss of substance.

74. For building turnpikes and wharfs in Great Britain.

75. For insuring from thefts and robberies.

76. For extracting silver from lead.

77. For making china and delft ware. Capital, one million.

78. For importing tobacco, and exporting it again to Sweden and the north of Europe. Capital, four millions.

79. For making iron with pit coal.

80. For furnishing the cities of London and Westminster with hay and straw. Capital, three millions.

81. For a sail and packing-cloth manufactory in Ireland.

82. For taking up ballast.

83. For buying and fitting out ships to suppress pirates.

84. For the importation of timber from Wales. Capital, two millions.

85. For rock-salt.

86. For the transmutation of quicksilver into a malleable fine metal.

Besides these bubbles, many others sprang up daily, in spite of the condemnation of the government and the ridicule of the still sane portion of the public. The printshops teemed with caricatures, and the newspapers with epigrams and satires, upon the prevalent folly. An ingenious cardmaker published a pack of South-Sea playing-cards, which are now extremely rare, each card containing, besides the usual figures of a very small size, in one corner, a caricature of a bubble company, with appropriate verses underneath. One of the most famous bubbles was "Puckle's Machine Company," for discharging round and square cannonballs and bullets, and making a total revolution in the art of war. Its pretensions to public favor were thus summed up on the eight of spades:

> "A rare invention to destroy the crowd
> Of fools at home instead of fools abroad.
> Fear not, my friends, this terrible machine,
> They're only wounded who have shares
> therein."

The nine of hearts was a caricature of the English Copper and Brass Company, with the following epigram:

> "The headlong fool that wants to be a swopper
> Of gold and silver coin for English copper,
> May, in Change Alley, prove himself an ass,
> And give rich metal for adultrate brass."

The eight of diamonds celebrated the company for the colonization of Acadia, with this doggerel:

> "He that is rich and wants to fool away
> A good round sum in North America.
> Let him subscribe himself a headlong sharer,
> And asses' ears shall honor him or bearer."

And in a similar style every card of the pack exposed some

knavish scheme, and ridiculed the persons who were its dupes. It was computed that the total amount of the sums proposed for carrying on these projects was upwards of three hundred millions sterling.

It is time, however, to return to the great South-Sea gulf, that swallowed the fortunes of so many thousands of the avaricious and the credulous. On the 29th of May, the stock had risen as high as five hundred, and about two-thirds of the government annuitants had exchanged the securities of the state for those of the South-Sea company. During the whole of the month of May the stock continued to rise, and on the 28th it was quoted at five hundred and fifty. In four days after this it took a prodigious leap, rising suddenly from five hundred and fifty to eight hundred and ninety. It was now the general opinion that the stock could rise no higher, and many persons took that opportunity of selling out, with a view of realizing their profits. Many noblemen and persons in the train of the king, and about to accompany him to Hanover, were also anxious to sell out. So many sellers, and so few buyers, appeared in the Alley on the 3rd of June, that the stock fell at once from eight hundred and ninety to six hundred and forty. The directors were alarmed, and gave their agents orders to buy. Their efforts succeeded. Towards evening, confidence was restored, and the stock advanced to seven hundred and fifty. It continued at this price, with some slight fluctuation, until the company closed their books on the 22nd of June.

It would be needless and uninteresting to detail the various arts employed by the directors to keep up the price of stock. It will be sufficient to state that it finally rose to one thousand per cent. It was quoted at this price in the commencement of August. The bubble was then full-blown, and began to quiver and shake preparatory to its bursting.

Many of the government annuitants expressed dissatisfaction against the directors. They accused them of partiality in making out the lists for shares in each subscription. Further uneasiness was occasioned by its being generally known that Sir John Blunt the chairman, and some others, had sold out.

During the whole of the month of August the stock fell, and on the 2nd of September it was quoted at seven hundred only.

The state of things now became alarming. To prevent, if possible, the utter extinction of public confidence in their proceedings, the directors summoned a general court of the whole corporation, to meet in Merchant Tailors' Hall on the 8th of September. By nine o'clock in the morning, the room was filled to suffocation; Cheapside was blocked up by a crowd unable to gain admittance, and the greatest excitement prevailed. The directors and their friends mustered in great numbers. Sir John Fellows, the sub-governor, was called to the chair. He acquainted the assembly with the cause of their meeting; read to them the several resolutions of the court of directors, and gave them an account of their proceedings; of the taking in the redeemable and unredeemable funds, and of the subscriptions in money. Mr. Secretary Craggs then made a short speech, wherein he commended the conduct of the directors, and urged that nothing could more effectually contribute to the bringing this scheme to perfection than union among themselves. He concluded with a motion for thanking the court of directors for their prudent and skilful management, and for desiring them to proceed in such manner as they should think most proper for the interest and advantage of the corporation. Mr. Hungerford, who had rendered himself very conspicuous in the House of Commons for his zeal in behalf of the South-Sea company, and who was shrewdly suspected to have been a considerable gainer by knowing the right time to sell out, was very magniloquent on this occasion. He said that he had seen the rise and fall, the decay and resurrection of many communities of this nature, but that, in his opinion, none had ever performed such wonderful things in so short a time as the South-Sea company. They had done more than the crown, the pulpit, or the bench could do. They had reconciled all parties in one common interest; they had laid asleep, if not wholly extinguished, all the domestic jars and animosities of the nation. By the rise of their stock, monied men had vastly increased their fortunes; country gentlemen had seen the value of their lands doubled and trebled in their hands. They had at the same time done good to the Church, not a few of the reverend clergy having got great sums by the project. In short, they had enriched the whole nation, and he hoped they had not forgotten themselves. There was some hissing at the latter part of this speech, which for the extravagance of its eulogy was not far removed from satire; but the directors and their friends, and all the winners in the room, applauded vehemently. The Duke of Portland spoke in a similar strain, and expressed his great wonder why any body should be dissatisfied; of course, he was a winner by his speculations, and in a condition similar to that of the fat alderman in Joe Miller's Jesus, who, whenever he had eaten a good dinner, folded his hands upon his paunch, and expressed his doubts whether there could be a hungry man in the world.

Several resolutions were passed at this meeting, but they had no effect upon the public. Upon the very same evening the stock fell to six hundred and forty, and on the morrow to five hundred and forty. Day after day it continued to fall, until it was as low as four hundred. In a letter dated September 13th, from Mr. Broderick, M.P., to Lord Chancellor Middleton, and published in Coxe's Walpole, the former says: "Various are the conjectures why the South-Sea directors have suffered the cloud to break so early. I made no doubt but they would do so when they found it to their advantage. They have stretched credit so far beyond what it would bear, that specie proves insufficient to support it. Their most considerable men have drawn out, securing themselves by the losses of the deluded, thoughtless numbers, whose understandings have been overruled by avarice and the hope of making mountains out of molehills. Thousands of families will be reduced to beggary. The consternation is inexpressible—the rage beyond description, and the case altogether so desperate, that I do not see any plan or scheme so much as thought of for averting the blow; so that I cannot pretend to guess what is next to be done." Ten days afterwards, the stock still falling, he writes: "The company have yet come to no determination, for they are in such a wood that they know not which way to turn. By several gentlemen lately come to town, I perceive the very name of a South-Sea-man grows abominable in every country. A great many goldsmiths are already run off, and more will daily. I question whether one-third, nay, one-fourth of them can stand it. From the very beginning, I founded my judgment of the whole affair upon the unquestionable maxim, that ten millions (which is more than our running cash) could not circulate two hundred millions beyond which our paper credit extended. That, therefore, whenever that should become doubtful, be the cause what it would, our noble state machine must inevitably fall to the ground."

On the 12th of September, at the earnest solicitation of Mr. Secretary Craggs, several conferences were held between the directors of the South Sea and the directors of the Bank. A report which was circulated, that the latter had agreed to circulate six millions of the South-Sea company's bonds, caused the stock to rise to six hundred and seventy; but in the afternoon, as soon as the report was known to be groundless, the stock fell again to five hundred and eighty; the next day to five hundred and seventy, and so gradually to four hundred.[*]

The ministry were seriously alarmed at the aspect of affairs. The directors could not appear in the streets without being insulted; dangerous riots were every moment apprehended. Dispatches were sent off to the king at Hanover, praying his immediate return. Mr. Walpole, who was staying at his country seat, was sent for, that he might employ his known influence with the directors of the Bank of England to induce them to accept the proposal made by the South-Sea company for circulating a number of their bonds.

---

[*] Gay (the poet), in that disastrous year, had a present from young Craggs of some South-Sea stock, and once supposed himself to be master of twenty thousand pounds. His friends persuaded him to sell his share, but he dreamed of dignity and splendour, and could not bear to obstruct his own fortune. He was then importuned to sell as much as would purchase a hundred a year for life, "which," says Fenton, "will make you sure of a clean shirt and a shoulder of mutton every day." This counsel was rejected; the profit and principal were lost, and Gay sunk under the calamity so low that his life became in danger.—Johnson's Lives of the Poets.

The Bank was very unwilling to mix itself up with the affairs of the company; it dreaded being involved in calamities which it could not relieve, and received all overtures with visible reluctance. But the universal voice of the nation called upon it to come to the rescue. Every person of note in commercial politics was called in to advise in the emergency. A rough draft of a contract drawn up by Mr. Walpole was ultimately adopted as the basis of further negotiations, and the public alarm abated a little.

On the following day, the 20th of September, a general court of the South-Sea company was held at Merchant Tailors' Hall, in which resolutions were carried, empowering the directors to agree with the Bank of England, or any other persons, to circulate the company's bonds, or make any other agreement with the Bank which they should think proper. One of the speakers, a Mr. Pulteney, said it was most surprising to see the extraordinary panic which had seized upon the people. Men were running to and fro in alarm and terror, their imaginations filled with some great calamity, the form and dimensions of which nobody knew:

> "Black it stood as night—
> Fierce as ten furies—terrible as hell."

At a general court of the Bank of England, held two days afterwards, the governor informed them of the several meetings that had been held on the affairs of the South-Sea company, adding that the directors had not yet thought fit to come to any decision upon the matter. A resolution was then proposed, and carried without a dissentient voice, empowering the directors to agree with those of the South-Sea to circulate their bonds, to what sum, and upon what terms, and for what time, they might think proper.

Thus both parties were at liberty to act as they might judge best for the public interest. Books were opened at the Bank for a subscription of three millions for the support of public credit, on the usual terms of 15*l.* percent deposit, 3*l.* percent premium, and 5*l*. percent interest. So great was the concourse of people in the early part of the morning, all eagerly bringing their money, that it was thought the subscription would be filled that day; but before noon the tide turned. In spite of all that could be done to prevent it, the South-Sea company's stock fell rapidly. Their bonds were in such discredit, that a run commenced upon the most eminent goldsmiths and bankers, some of whom, having lent out great sums upon South-Sea stock, were obliged to shut up their shops and abscond. The Swordblade company, who had hitherto been the chief cashiers of the South-Sea company, stopped payment. This being looked upon as but the beginning of evil, occasioned a great run upon the bank, who were now obliged to pay out money much faster than they had received it upon the subscription in the morning. The day succeeding was a holiday (the 29th of September), and the Bank had a little breathing time. They bore up against the storm; but their former rivals, the South-Sea company, were wrecked upon it. Their stock fell to one hundred and fifty, and gradually, after various fluctuations, to one hundred and thirty-five.

The Bank finding they were not able to restore public confidence, and stem the tide of ruin, without running the risk of being swept away with those they intended to save, declined to carry out the agreement into which they had partially entered. They were under no obligation whatever to continue; for the so-called Bank contract was nothing more than the rough draft of an agreement, in which blanks had been left for several important particulars, and which contained no penalty for their secession. "And thus," to use the words of the Parliamentary History, "were seen, in the space of eight months, the rise, progress, and fall of that mighty fabric, which, being wound up by mysterious springs to a wonderful height, had fixed the eyes and expectations of all Europe, but whose foundation, being fraud, illusion, credulity, and infatuation, fell to the ground as soon as the artful management of its directors was discovered."

In the heyday of its blood, during the progress of this

dangerous delusion, the manners of the nation became sensibly corrupted. The parliamentary inquiry, set on foot to discover the delinquents, disclosed scenes of infamy, disgraceful alike to the morals of the offenders and the intellects of the people among whom they had arisen. It is a deeply interesting study to investigate all the evils that were the result. Nations, like individuals, cannot become desperate gamblers with impunity. Punishment is sure to overtake them sooner or later. A celebrated writer* is quite wrong when he says "that such an era as this is the most unfavorable for a historian; that no reader of sentiment and imagination can be entertained or interested by a detail of transactions such as these, which admit of no warmth, no coloring, no embellishment; a detail of which only serves to exhibit an inanimate picture of tasteless vice and mean degeneracy." On the contrary,—and Smollett might have discovered it, if he had been in the humor,—the subject is capable of inspiring as much interest as even a novelist can desire. Is there no warmth in the despair of a plundered people?—No life and animation in the picture which might be drawn of the woes of hundreds of impoverished and ruined families? Of the wealthy of yesterday become the beggars of today? Of the powerful and influential changed into exiles and outcasts, and the voice of self-reproach and imprecation resounding from every corner of the land? Is it a dull or uninstructive picture to see a whole people shaking suddenly off the trammels of reason, and running wild after a golden vision, refusing obstinately to believe that it is not real, till, like a deluded hind running after an ignis fatuus, they are plunged into a quagmire? But in this false spirit has history too often been written. The intrigues of unworthy courtiers to gain the favor of still more unworthy kings, or the records of murderous battles and sieges, have been dilated on, and told over and over again, with all the eloquence of style and all the charms of fancy; while the circumstances which have most deeply affected the morals and welfare of the people have been passed over with but slight notice, as dry and dull, and

*Smollett

capable of neither warmth nor coloring.

During the progress of this famous bubble, England presented a singular spectacle. The public mind was in a state of unwholesome fermentation. Men were no longer satisfied with the slow but sure profits of cautious industry. The hope of boundless wealth for the morrow made them heedless and extravagant for today. A luxury, till then unheard of, was introduced, bringing in its train a corresponding laxity of morals. The overbearing insolence of ignorant men, who had arisen to sudden wealth by successful gambling, made men of true gentility of mind and manners blush that gold should have power to raise the unworthy in the scale of society. The haughtiness of some of these "ciphering cits," as they were termed by Sir Richard Steele, was remembered against them in the day of their adversity. In the parliamentary inquiry, many of the directors suffered more for their insolence than for their peculation. One of them, who, in the full-blown pride of an ignorant rich man, had said that he would feed his horse upon gold, was reduced almost to bread and water for himself; every haughty look, every overbearing speech, was set down, and repaid them a hundred fold in poverty and humiliation.

The state of matters all over the country was so alarming, that George I. shortened his intended stay in Hanover, and returned in all haste to England. He arrived on the 11th of November, and parliament was summoned to meet on the 8th of December. In the mean time, public meetings were held in every considerable town of the empire, at which petitions were adopted, praying the vengeance of the legislature upon the South-Sea directors, who, by their fraudulent practices, had brought the nation to the brink of ruin. Nobody seemed to imagine that the nation itself was as culpable as the South-Sea company. Nobody blamed the credulity and avarice of the people the degrading lust of gain, which had swallowed up every nobler quality in the national character, or the infatuation which had made the multitude run their heads with such frantic eagerness into the net held out for them by scheming projectors. These things were never mentioned. The people were a simple, honest, hard-working people, ruined by a gang of robbers, who were to be hanged, drawn, and quartered without mercy.

This was the almost unanimous feeling of the country. The two Houses of Parliament were not more reasonable. Before the guilt of the South-Sea directors was known, punishment was the only cry. The king, in his speech from the throne, expressed his hope that they would remember that all their prudence, temper, and resolution were necessary to find out and apply the proper remedy for their misfortunes. In the debate on the answer to the address, several speakers indulged in the most violent invectives against the directors of the South-Sea project. The Lord Molesworth was particularly vehement.

"It had been said by some, that there was no law to punish the directors of the South-Sea company, who were justly looked upon as the authors of the present misfortunes of the state. In his opinion, they ought upon this occasion to follow the example of the ancient Romans, who, having no law against parricide, because their legislators supposed no son could be so unnaturally wicked as to embrue his hands in his father's blood, made a law to punish this heinous crime as soon as it was committed. They adjudged the guilty wretch to be sewn in a sack, and thrown alive into the Tiber. He looked upon the contrivers and executors of the villanous South-Sea scheme as the parricides of their country, and should be satisfied to see them tied in like manner in sacks, and thrown into the Thames." Other members spoke with as much want of temper and discretion. Mr. Walpole was more moderate. He recommended that their first care should be to restore public credit. "If the city of London were on fire, all wise men would aid in extinguishing the flames, and preventing the spread of the conflagration, before they inquired after the incendiaries. Public credit had received a dangerous wound, and lay bleeding, and they ought to apply a speedy remedy to it. It was time enough to punish the assassin afterwards." On the 9th of December, an address, in answer to his majesty's speech, was agreed upon, after an amendment, which was carried without a division, that words should be added expressive of the determination of the House not only to seek a remedy for the national distresses, but to punish the authors of them.

The inquiry proceeded rapidly. The directors were ordered to lay before the House a full account of all their proceedings. Resolutions were passed to the effect that the calamity was mainly owing to the vile arts of stock-jobbers, and that nothing could tend more to the reestablishment of public credit than a law to prevent this infamous practice. Mr. Walpole then rose, and said, that "as he had previously hinted, he had spent some time upon a scheme for restoring public credit, but that the execution of it depending upon a position which had been laid down as fundamental, he thought it proper, before he opened out his scheme, to be informed whether he might rely upon that foundation. It was, whether the subscription of public debts and encumbrances, money subscriptions, and other contracts, made with the South-Sea company, should remain in the present state?" This question occasioned an animaled debate. It was finally agreed, by a majority of 259 against 117, that all these contracts should remain in their present state, unless altered for the relief of the proprietors by a general court of the South-Sea company, or set aside by due course of law. On the following day, Mr. Walpole laid before a committee of the whole house his scheme for the restoration of public credit, which was, in substance, to engraft nine millions of South-Sea Stock into the Bank of England, and the same sum into the East India company upon certain conditions. The plan was favorably received by the House. After some few objections, it was ordered that proposals should be received from the two great corporations. They were both unwilling to lend their aid, and the plan met with a warm but fruitless opposition at the general courts summoned for the purpose of deliberating upon it. They, however, ultimately agreed upon the terms on which they would consent to circulate the South-Sea bonds, and their report being presented to the committee, a bill was brought in under the superintendence of Mr. Walpole, and safely carried through both Houses of Parliament.

A bill was at the same time brought in for restraining the South-Sea directors, governor, sub-governor, treasurer, casnier, and clerks from leaving the kingdom for a twelvemonth, and for discovering their estates and effects, and preventing them from transporting or alienating the same. All the most influential members of the House supported the bill. Mr. Shippen, seeing Mr. Secretary Craggs in his place, and believing the injurious rumors that were afloat of that minister's conduct in the South-Sea business, determined to touch him to the quick. He said he was glad to see a British House of Commons resuming its pristine vigor and spirit, and acting with so much unanimity for the public good. It was necessary to secure the persons and estates of the South-Sea directors and their officers; "but," he added, looking fixedly at Mr. Craggs as he spoke, "there were other men in high station, whom, in time, he would not be afraid to name, who were no less guilty than the directors." Mr. Craggs arose in great wrath, and said, that if the innuendo were directed against him, he was ready to give satisfaction to any man who questioned him, either in the House or out of it. Loud cries of order immediately arose on every side. In the midst of the uproar, Lord Molesworth got up, and expressed his wonder at the boldness of Mr. Craggs in challenging the whole House of Commons. He, Lord Molesworth, though somewhat old, past sixty, would answer Mr. Craggs whatever he had to say in the House, and he trusted there were plenty of young men beside him, who would not be afraid to look Mr. Craggs in the face out of the House. The cries of order again resounded from every side; the members arose simultaneously; everybody seemed to be vociferating at once. The Speaker in vain called order. The confusion lasted several minutes, during which Lord Molesworth and Mr. Craggs were almost the only members who kept their seats. At last, the call for Mr. Craggs became so violent, that he thought proper to submit to the universal feeling of the House, and explain his unparliamentary expression. He said, that by giving satisfaction to the impugners of his conduct in that House, he did not mean that he would fight, but that he would explain his conduct. Here the matter ended, and the House proceeded to debate in what manner they should conduct their inquiry into the affairs of the South-Sea company, whether in a grand or a select committee. Ultimately, a secret committee of thirteen was appointed, with power to send for persons, papers, and records.

The Lords were as zealous and as hasty as the Commons. The Bishop of Rochester said the scheme had been like a pestilence. The Duke of Wharton said the House ought to shew no respect of persons; that, for his part, he would give up the dearest friend he had, if he had been engaged in the project. The nation had been plundered in a most shameful and flagrant manner, and he would go as far as anybody in the punishment of the offenders. Lord Stanhope said, that every farthing possessed by the criminals, whether directors or not directors, ought to be confiscated, to make good the public losses.

During all this time the public excitement was extreme. We learn from Coxe's Walpole, that the very name of a South-Sea director was thought to be synonymous with every species of fraud and villainy. Petitions from counties, cities, and boroughs, in all parts of the kingdom, were presented, crying for the justice due to an injured nation and the punishment of the villanous peculators. Those moderate men, who would not go to extreme lengths, even in the punishment of the guilty, were accused of being accomplices, were exposed to repeated insults and virulent invectives, and devoted, both in anonymous letters and public writings, to the speedy vengeance of an injured people. The accusations against Mr. Aislabie, Chancellor of the Exchequer, and Mr. Craggs, another member of the ministry, were so loud, that the House of Lords resolved to proceed at once into the investigation concerning them. It was ordered, on the 21st of January, that all brokers concerned in the South-Sea scheme should lay before the House an account of the stock or subscriptions bought or sold by them for any of the officers of the Treasury or Exchequer, or in trust for any of them, since Michaelmas 1719. When this account was delivered, it appeared that large quantities of stock had been transferred to the use of Mr. Aislabie. Five of the South-Sea directors, including Mr. Edward Gibbon, the grandfather of the celebrated historian, were ordered into the custody of the black rod. Upon a motion arrayed by Earl Stanhope, it was unanimously resolved, that the taking in or giving credit for stock without a valuable consideration actually paid or sufficiently secured; or the purchasing stock by any director or agent of the South-Sea company, for the use or benefit of any member of the administration, or any member of either House of Parliament, during such time as the South-Sea bill was yet pending in Parliament, was a notorious and dangerous corruption. Another resolution was passed a few days afterwards, to the effect that several of the directors and officers of the company having, in a clandestine manner, sold their own stock to the company, had been guilty of a notorious fraud and breach of trust, and had thereby mainly caused the unhappy turn of affairs that had so much affected public credit. Mr. Aislabie resigned his office as Chancellor of the Exchequer, and absented himself from parliament, until the formal inquiry into his individual guilt was brought under the consideration of the legislature.   In the mean time, Knight, the treasurer of the company, and who was entrusted with all the dangerous secrets of the dishonest directors, packed up his books and documents and made his escape from the country. He embarked in disguise, in a small boat on the river, and proceeding to a vessel hired for the purpose, was safely conveyed to Calais. The Committee of Secrecy informed the House of the circumstance, when it was resolved unanimously that two addresses should be presented to the king; the first praying that he would issue a proclamation offering a reward for the apprehension of Knight; and the second, that he would give immediate orders to stop the ports, and to take effectual care of the coasts, to prevent the said Knight, or any other officers of the South-Sea company, from escaping out of the kingdom. The ink was hardly dry upon these addresses before they were carried to the king by Mr. Methuen, deputed by the House for that purpose. The same evening a royal proclamation was issued, offering a reward of two thousand pounds for the apprehension of Knight. The Commons ordered the doors of the House to be locked, and the keys to be placed on the table. General Ross, one of the members of the Committee of Secrecy, acquainted them that they had already discovered a train of the deepest villainy and fraud that hell had ever contrived to ruin a nation, which in due time they would lay before the House. In the mean time, in order to a further discovery, the Committee thought it highly necessary to secure the persons of some of the directors and principal South-Sea officers, and to seize their papers. A motion to this effect having been made, was carried unanimously. Sir Robert Chaplin, Sir Theodore Janssen, Mr. Sawbridge, and Mr. F. Eyles, members of the House, and directors of the South-Sea company, were summoned to appear in their places, and answer for their corrupt practices. Sir Theodore Janssen and Mr. Sawbridge answered to their names, and endeavored to exculpate themselves. The House heard them patiently, and then ordered them to withdraw. A motion was then made, and carried *nemine contradicente*, that they had been guilty of a notorious breach of trust—had occasioned much loss to great numbers of his majesty's subjects, and had highly prejudiced the public credit. It was then ordered that, for their offence, they should be expelled the House, and taken into custody of the sergeant-at-arms. Sir Robert Chaplin and Mr. Eyles, attending in their places four days afterwards, were also expelled the House. It was resolved at the same time to address the king to give directions to his ministers at foreign courts to make application for Knight, that he might be delivered up to the English authorities, in case he took refuge in any of their dominions. The king at once agreed, and messengers were despatched to all parts of the continent the same night.

Among the directors taken into custody was Sir John Blunt, the man whom popular opinion has generally accused of having been the original author and father of the scheme. This man, we are informed by Pope, in his epistle to Allen Lord Bathurst, was a Dissenter, of a most religious deportment, and professed to be a great believer.* He constantly declaimed against the luxury and corruption of the age, the partiality of parliaments, and the misery of party-spirit. He was particularly eloquent against avarice in great and noble persons. He was originally a scrivener, and afterwards became not only a director, but the most active manager of the South-Sea company. Whether it was during his career in this capacity that he first began to declaim against the avarice of the great, we are not informed. He certainly must have seen enough of it to justify his severest anathema; but if the preacher had himself been free from the vice he condemned, his declamations would have had a better effect. He was brought up in custody to the bar of the House of Lords, and underwent a long examination. He refused to answer several important questions. He said he had been examined already by a committee of the House of Commons, and as he did not remember his answers, and might contradict himself, he refused to answer before another tribunal. This declaration, in itself an indirect proof of guilt, occasioned some commotion in the House. He was again asked peremptorily whether he had ever sold any portion of the stock to any member of the administration, or any member of either House of Parliament, to facilitate the passing of the bill. He again declined to answer. He was anxious, he said, to treat the House with all possible respect, but he thought it hard to be compelled to accuse himself. After several ineffectual attempts to refresh his memory, he was directed to withdraw. A violent discussion ensued between the friends and opponents of the ministry. It was asserted that the administration were no strangers to the convenient taciturnity of Sir John Blunt. The Duke of Wharton made a reflection upon the Earl Stanhope, which the latter warmly resented. He spoke under great excitement, and with such vehemence as to cause a

* "'God cannot love,' says Blunt, with tearless eyes 'The wretch he starves,' and piously denies... Much injur'd Blunt why bears he Britains hates. A wizard told him in these words our fate:' At length corruption, like a general flood So long by watchful ministers withstood Shall deluge all, and avarice, creeping on Spread like a low-worn mist, and blot the sun; Statesmen and patriot ply alike the stocks, Peeress and butler share alike the box And judges job, and bishops bite the town, And mighty dukes pack cards for half-a-crown: See Britain sunk in Lucre's sordid charms And France revenged on Anne's and Edward's arms.' 'Twas no court-badge great Scrivinir fir'd thy brain, Nor lordly luxury, nor city gain: No, 'twas the righteous end, asham'd to see Senates degen'rate, patriots disagree And nobly wishing party-rage to cease To buy both sides, and give thy country peace." Pope's Epistle to Allen Bonthurst.

sudden determination of blood to the head. He felt himself so ill that he was obliged to leave the House and retire to his chamber. He was cupped immediately, and also let blood on the following morning, but with slight relief. The fatal result was not anticipated. Towards evening he became drowsy, and turning himself on his face, expired. The sudden death of this statesman caused great grief to the nation. George I was exceedingly affected, and shut himself up for some hours in his closet, inconsolable for his loss.

Knight, the treasurer of the company, was apprehended at Tirlemont, near Liege, by one of the secretaries of Mr. Leathes, the British resident at Brussels, and lodged in the citadel of Antwerp. Repeated applications were made to the court of Austria to deliver him up, but in vain. Knight threw himself upon the protection of the states of Brabant, and demanded to be tried in that country. It was a privilege granted to the states of Brabant by one of the articles of the Joyeuse Entree, that every criminal apprehended in that country should be tried in that country. The states insisted on their privilege, and refused to deliver Knight to the British authorities. The latter did not cease their solicitations; but in the mean time, Knight escaped from the citadel.

On the 16th of February the Committee of Secrecy made their first report to the House. They stated that their inquiry had been attended with numerous difficulties and embarrassments; every one they had examined had endeavored, as far as in him lay, to defeat the ends of justice. In some of the books produced before them, false and fictitious entries had been made; in others, there were entries of money with blanks for the name of the stockholders. There were frequent erasures and alterations, and in some of the books leaves were torn out. They also found that some books of great importance had been destroyed altogether, and that some had been taken away or secreted. At the very entrance into their inquiry, they had observed that the matters referred to them were of great variety and extent. Many persons had been entrusted with various parts in the execution of the law, and under color thereof had acted in an unwarrantable manner, in disposing of the properties of many thousands of persons amounting to many millions of money. They discovered that, before the South-Sea Act was passed, there was an entry in the company's books of the sum of 1,259,325*l*., upon account of stock stated to have been sold to the amount of 574,500*l*. This stock was all fictitious, and had been disposed of with a view to promote the passing of the bill. It was noted as sold on various days, and at various prices, from 150 to 325 percent. Being surprised to see so large an account disposed of at a time when the company were not empowered to increase their capital, the Committee determined to investigate most carefully the whole transaction. The governor, sub-governor, and several directors were brought before them, and examined rigidly. They found that, at the time these entries were made, the company was not in possession of such a quantity of stock, having in their own right only a small quantity, not exceeding thirty thousand pounds at the utmost. Pursuing the inquiry, they found that this amount of stock was to be esteemed as taken in or holden by the company for the benefit of the pretended purchasers, although no mutual agreement was made for its delivery or acceptance at any certain time. No money was paid down, nor any deposit or security whatever given to the company by the supposed purchasers; so that if the stock had fallen, as might have been expected had the act not passed, they would have sustained no loss. If, on the contrary, the price of stock advanced (as it actually did by the success of the scheme), the difference by the advanced price was to be made good to them. Accordingly, after the passing of the act, the account of stock was made up and adjusted with Mr. Knight, and the pretended purchasers were paid the difference out of the company's cash. This fictitious stock, which had been chiefly at the disposal of Sir John Blunt, Mr. Gibbon, and Mr. Knight, was distributed among several members of the government and their connections, by way of bribe, to facilitate the passing of the bill. The Earl of Sunderland was assigned 50,000*l*. of this stock; to the Duchess of Kendal, 10,000*l*.; to the Countess of Platen, 10,000*l.*; to her two nieces, 10,000*l.*; to Mr. Secretary Craggs, 30,000*l.*; to Mr. Charles Stanhope (one of the secretaries of the Treasury), 10,000*l.*; to the Sword-blade company, 50,000*l.* It also appeared that Mr. Stanhope had received the enormous sum of 250,000*l.* as the difference in the price of some stock, through the hands of Turner, Caswall, and Co., but that his name had been partly erased from their books, and altered to Stangape. Aislabie, the Chancellor of the Exchequer, had made profits still more abominable. He had an account with the same firm, who were also South-Sea directors, to the amount of 794,451*l.* He had, besides, advised the company to make their second subscription one million and a half, instead of a million, by their own authority, and without any warrant. The third subscription had been conducted in a manner as disgraceful. Mr. Aislabie's name was down for 70,000*l.*; Mr. Craggs, senior, for 659,000*l.*; the Earl of Sunderland's for 160,000*l.*; and Mr. Stanhope for 47,000*l.* This report was succeeded by six others, less important. At the end of the last, the committee declared, that the absence of Knight, who had been principally entrusted, prevented them from carrying on their inquiries.

The first report was ordered to be printed, and taken into consideration on the next day but one succeeding. After a very angry and animated debate, a series of resolutions were agreed to, condemnatory of the conduct of the directors, of

---

* " 'God cannot love,' says Blunt, with tearless eyes
'The wretch he starves,' and piously denies....
Much-injur'd Blunt! why bears he Britain's hate?
A wizard told him in these words our fate:
'At length corruption, like a general flood
So long by watchful ministers withstood
Shall deluge all, and avarice, creeping on,
Spread like a low-born mist, and blot the sun;
Statesman and patriot ply alike the stocks,
Peeress and butler share alike the box,
And judges job, and bishops bite the town,
And mighty dukes pack cards for half-a-crown:
See Britain sunk in Lucre's sordid charms
And France revenge'd on Anne's and Edward's arms!'
'Twas no court-badge, great Scrivener! fir'd thy brain,
Nor lordly luxury, nor city gain:
No, 'twas thy righteous end, asham'd to see
Senates degen'rate, patriots disagree,
And nobly wishing party-rage to cease,
To buy both sides, and give thy country peace."
Pope's Epistle to Allen Lord Bathurst.

the members of the parliament and of the administration concerned with them; and declaring that they ought, each and all, to make satisfaction out of their own estates for the injury they had done the public. Their practices were declared to be corrupt, infamous, and dangerous; and a bill was ordered to be brought in for the relief of the unhappy sufferers.

Mr. Charles Stanhope was the first person brought to account for his share in these transactions. He urged in his defence that, for some years past, he had lodged all the money he was possessed of in Mr. Knight's hands, and whatever stock Mr. Knight had taken in for him, he had paid a valuable consideration for it. As for the stock that had been bought for him by Turner, Caswall, and Co., he knew nothing about it. Whatever had been done in that matter was done without his authority, and he could not be responsible for it. Turner and Co. took the latter charge upon themselves; but it was notorious to every unbiased and unprejudiced person that Mr. Stanhope was a gainer of the 250,000l. which lay in the hands of that firm to his credit. He was, however, acquitted by a majority of three only. The greatest exertions were made to screen him. Lord Stanhope, the son of the Earl of Chesterfield, went round to the wavering members, using all the eloquence he was possessed of to induce them either to vote for the acquittal, or to absent themselves from the House. Many weak-headed country gentlemen were led astray by his persuasions, and the result was as already stated. The acquittal caused the greatest discontent throughout the country. Mobs of a menacing character assembled in different parts of London; fears of riots were generally entertained, especially as the examination of a still greater delinquent was expected by many to have a similar termination. Mr. Aislabie, whose high office and deep responsibilities should have kept him honest, even had native principle been insufficient, was very justly regarded as perhaps the greatest criminal of all. His case was entered into on the day succeeding the acquittal of Mr. Stanhope. Great excitement prevailed, and the lobbies and avenues of the House were beset by crowds impatient to know the result. The debate lasted the whole day. Mr. Aislabie found few friends: his guilt was so apparent and so heinous that nobody had courage to stand up in his favor. It was finally resolved, without a dissentient voice, that Mr. Aislabie had encouraged and promoted the destructive execution of the South-Sea scheme with a view to his own exorbitant profit, and had combined with the directors in their pernicious practices, to the ruin of the public trade and credit of the kingdom: that he should for his offences be ignominiously expelled from the House of Commons, and committed a close prisoner to the Tower of London; that he should be restrained from going out of the kingdom for a whole year, or till the end of the next session of parliament; and that he should make out a correct account of all his estate, in order that it might be applied to the relief of those who had suffered by his malpractices.

This verdict caused the greatest joy. Though it was delivered at half-past twelve at night, it soon spread over the city. Several persons illuminated their houses in token of their joy. On the following day, when Mr. Aislabie was conveyed to the Tower, the mob assembled on Tower-hill with the intention of hooting and pelting him. Not succeeding in this, they kindled a large bonfire, and danced around it in the exuberance of their delight. Several bonfires were made in other places; London presented the appearance of a holiday, and people congratulated one another as if they had just escaped from some great calamity. The rage upon the acquittal of Mr. Stanhope had grown to such a height, that none could tell where it would have ended, had Mr. Aislabie met with the like indulgence.

To increase the public satisfaction, Sir George Caswall, of the firm of Turner, Caswall, and Co., was expelled from the House on the following day, committed to the Tower, and ordered to refund the sum of 250,000L.

That part of the report of the Committee of Secrecy which related to the Earl of Sunderland was next taken into consideration. Every effort was made to clear his lordship from the imputation. As the case against him rested chiefly on the evidence extorted from Sir John Blunt, great pains were taken to make it appear that Sir John's word was not to be believed, especially in a matter affecting the honor of a peer and privy councillor. All the friends of the ministry rallied around the earl, it being generally reported that a verdict of guilty against him would bring a Tory ministry into power. He was eventually acquitted by a majority of 233 against 172; but the country was convinced of his guilt. The greatest indignation was everywhere expressed, and menacing mobs again assembled in London. Happily no disturbance took place.

This was the day on which Mr. Craggs the elder expired. The morrow had been appointed for the consideration of his case. It was very generally believed that he had poisoned himself. It appeared, however, that grief for the loss of his son, one of the secretaries of the Treasury, who had died five weeks previously of the smallpox, preyed much on his mind. For this son, dearly beloved, he had been amassing vast heaps of riches: he had been getting money, but not honestly; and he for whose sake he had bartered his honor and sullied his fame was now no more. The dread of further exposure increased his trouble of mind, and ultimately brought on an apoplectic fit, in which he expired. He left a fortune of a million and a half, which was afterwards confiscated for the benefit of the sufferers by the unhappy delusion he had been so mainly instrumental in raising.

One by one the case of every director of the company was taken into consideration. A sum amounting to two millions and fourteen thousand pounds was confiscated from their estates towards repairing the mischief they had done, each man being allowed a certain residue in proportion to his conduct and circumstances, with which he might begin the world anew. Sir John Blunt was only allowed 5000L. out of his fortune of upwards of 13,000L.; Sir John Fellows was allowed l0,000L. out of 243,000L.; Sir Theodore Janssen, 50,000L. out of 243,000L.; Mr. Edward Gibbon, l0,000L. out of 106,000L.; Sir John Lambert, 5000L. out of 7,000L. Others, less deeply involved, were treated with greater liberality. Gibbon, the historian, whose grandfather was the Mr. Edward Gibbon so severely mulcted, has given, in the *Memoirs of his Life and Writings*, an interesting account of the proceedings in parliament at this time. He owns that he is not an unprejudiced witness; but, as all the writers from which it is possible to extract any notice of the proceedings of these disastrous years were prejudiced on the other side, the statements of the great historian become of additional value. If only on the principle of *audi alteram partem*, his opinion is entitled to consideration. "In the year 1716," he says, "my grandfather was elected one of the directors of the South-Sea company, and his books exhibited the proof that before his acceptance of that fatal office, he had acquired an independent fortune of 60,000L. But his fortune was overwhelmed in the shipwreck of the year 1720, and the labors of thirty years were blasted in a single day. Of the use or abuse of the South-Sea scheme, of the guilt or innocence of my grandfather and his brother directors, I am neither a competent nor a disinterested judge. Yet the equity of modern times must condemn the violent and arbitrary proceedings, which would have disgraced the cause of justice, and rendered injustice still more odious. No sooner had the nation awakened from its golden dream, than a popular and even a parliamentary clamor demanded its victims; but it was acknowledged on all sides, that the directors, however guilty, could not be touched by any known laws of the land. The intemperate notions of Lord Molesworth were not literally acted on; but a bill of pains and penalties was introduced—a retroactive statute, to punish the offences which did not exist at the time they were committed. The legislature restrained the persons of the directors, imposed an exorbitant security for their appearance, and marked their character with a previous note of ignominy. They were compelled to deliver, upon oath, the strict value of their estates, and were disabled from making any transfer or alienation of any part of their property. Against a bill of pains and penalties, it is the common right of every subject to be heard by his counsel at the bar. They prayed to be heard. Their prayer was refused, and their oppressors, who required no evidence, would listen to no defence. It had been at first proposed, that one-eighth of their respective estates should be allowed for the future support of the directors; but it was especially urged that, in the various shades of opulence and guilt, such a proportion would be too light for many, and for some might possibly be too heavy. The character and conduct of each man were separately weighed; but, instead of the calm solemnity of a judicial inquiry, the fortune and honor of thirty-three Englishmen were made the topics of hasty conversation, the sport of a lawless majority; and the basest member of the committee, by a malicious word or a silent vote, might indulge his general spleen or personal animosity. Injury was aggravated by insult, and insult was embittered by pleasantry. Allowances of 20*l.* or 1*s.* were facetiously moved. A vague report that a director had formerly been concerned in another project, by which some unknown persons had lost their money, was admitted as a proof of his actual guilt. One man was ruined because he had dropped a foolish speech, that his horses should feed upon gold; another, because he was grown so proud, that one day, at the Treasury, he had refused a civil answer to persons much above him. All were condemned, absent and unheard, in arbitrary fines and forfeitures, which swept away the greatest part of their substance. Such bold oppression can scarcely be shielded by the omnipotence of parliament. My grandfather could not expect to be treated with more lenity than his companions. His Tory principles and connections rendered him obnoxious to the ruling powers. His name was reported in a suspicious secret. His well-known abilities could not plead the excuse of ignorance or error. In the first proceedings against the South-Sea directors, Mr. Gibbon was one of the first taken into custody, and in the final sentence the measure of his fine proclaimed him eminently guilty. The total estimate, which he delivered on oath to the House of Commons, amounted to 106,543*L.* 5*s.* 6*d.*, exclusive of antecedent settlements. Two different allowances of 15,000*L.* and of 10,000*L.* were moved for Mr. Gibbon; but on the question being put, it was carried without a division for the smaller sum. On these ruins, with the skill and credit of which parliament had not been able to despoil him, my grandfather, at a mature age, erected the edifice of a new fortune. The labors of sixteen years were amply rewarded; and I have reason to believe that the second structure was not much inferior to the first."

The next consideration of the legislature, after the punishment of the directors, was to restore public credit. The scheme of Walpole had been found insufficient, and had fallen into disrepute. A computation was made of the whole capital stock of the South-Sea company at the end of the year 1720. It was found to amount to thirty-seven millions eight hundred thousand pounds, of which the stock allotted to all the proprietors only amounted to twenty-four millions five hundred thousand pounds. The remainder of thirteen millions three hundred thousand pounds belonged to the company in their corporate capacity, and was the profit they had made by the national delusion. Upwards of eight millions of this were taken from the company, and divided among the proprietors and subscribers generally, making a dividend of about 33*l*. 6*s*. 8*d*. percent. This was a great relief. It was further ordered, that such persons as had borrowed money from the South-Sea company upon stock actually transferred and pledged at the time of borrowing to or for the use of the company, should be free from all demands, upon payment of ten percent of the sums so borrowed. They had lent about eleven millions in this manner, at a time when prices were unnaturally raised; and they now received back one million one hundred thousand, when prices had sunk to their ordinary level.

But it was a long time before public credit was thoroughly restored. Enterprise, like Icarus, had soared too high, and melted the wax of her wings; like Icarus, she had fallen into a sea, and learned, while floundering in its waves, that her proper element was the solid ground. She has never since attempted so high a flight.

In times of great commercial prosperity there has been a

tendency to over-speculation on several occasions since then. The success of one project generally produces others of a similar kind. Popular imitativeness will always, in a trading nation, seize hold of such successes, and drag a community too anxious for profits into an abyss from which extrication is difficult. Bubble companies, of a kind similar to those engendered by the South-Sea project, lived their little day in the famous year of the panic, 1825. On that occasion, as in 1720, knavery gathered a rich harvest from cupidity, but both suffered when the day of reckoning came. The schemes of the year 1836 threatened, at one time, results as disastrous; but they were happily averted before it was too late.*

* The South-Sea project remained until 1845 the greatest example in British history of the infatuation of the people for commercial gambling. The first edition of these volumes was published some time before the outbreak of the Great Railway Mania of that and the following year.

THE TULIPOMANIA

Quis furor, o cĩves!—Luçan.

THE tulip—so named, it is said, from a Turkish word, signifying a turban—was introduced into western Europe about the middle of the sixteenth century. Conrad Gesner, who claims the merit of having brought it into repute,—little dreaming of the commotion it was shortly afterwards to make in the world,—says that he first saw it in the year 1559, in a garden at Augsburg, belonging to the learned Counsellor Herwart, a man very famous in his day for his collection of rare exotics. The bulbs were sent to this gentleman by a friend at Constantinople, where the flower had long been a favorite. In the course of ten or eleven years after this period, tulips were much sought after by the wealthy, especially in Holland and Germany. Rich people at Amsterdam sent for the bulbs direct to Constantinople, and paid the most extravagant prices for them. The first roots planted in England were brought from Vienna in 1600. Until the year 1634 the tulip annually increased in reputation, until it was deemed a proof of bad taste in any man of fortune to be without a collection of them. Many learned men, including Pompeius de Angelis, and the celebrated Lipsius of Leyden, the author of the treatise "De Constantia," were passionately fond of tulips. The rage for possessing them soon caught the middle classes of society, and merchants and shopkeepers, even of moderate means, began to vie with each other in the rarity of these flowers and the preposterous prices they paid for them. A trader at

Harlaem was known to pay one-half of his fortune for a single root, not with the design of selling it again at a profit, but to keep in his own conservatory for the admiration of his acquaintance.

One would suppose that there must have been some great virtue in this flower to have made it so valuable in the eyes of so prudent a people as the Dutch; but it has neither the beauty nor the perfume of the rose hardly the beauty of the "sweet, sweet-pea;" neither is it as enduring as either. Cowley, it is true, is loud in its praise. He says—

> "The tulip next appeared, all over gay,But wanton,
> full of pride, and full of play;
> The world can't show a dye but here has place;
> Nay, by new mixtures, she can change her face;
> Purple and gold are both beneath her care,
> The richest needlework she loves to wear;
> Her only study is to please the eye,
> And to outshine the rest in finery."

This, though not very poetical, is the description of a poet. Beck Mann, in his History of Inventions, paints it with more fidelity, and in prose more pleasing than Cowley's poetry. He says, "There are few plants which acquire, through accident, weakness, or disease, so many variegations as the tulip. When uncultivated, and in its natural state, it is almost of one color, has large leaves, and an extraordinarily long stem. When it has been weakened by cultivation, it becomes more agreeable in the eyes of the florist. The petals are then paler, smaller, and more diversified in hue; and the leaves acquire a softer green colour. Thus this masterpiece of culture, the more beautiful it turns, grows so much the weaker, so that, with the greatest skill and most careful attention, it can scarcely be transplanted, or even kept alive."

Many persons grow insensibly attached to that which gives them a great deal of trouble, as a mother often loves her sick and ever-ailing child better than her more healthy offspring. Upon the same principle we must account for the unmerited encomia lavished upon these fragile blossoms. In 1634, the rage among the Dutch to possess them was so great that the ordinary industry of the country was neglected, and the population, even to its lowest dregs, embarked in the tulip trade.

As the mania increased, prices augmented, until, in the year 1635, many persons were known to invest a fortune of 100,000 florins in the purchase of forty roots. It then became necessary to sell them by their weight in perits, a small weight lessthan a grain. A tulip of the species called Admiral Liefken,weighing 400 perits, was worth 4400 florins; an Admiral Vander Eyck, weighing 446 perits, was worth 1260 florins; a Childer of 106 perits was worth 1615 florins; a Viceroy of 400 perits, 3000 florins; and, most precious of all, a Semper Augustus, weighing 200 perits, was thought to be very cheap at 5500 florins. The latter was much sought after, and even an inferior bulb might command a price of 2000 florins.

It is related that, at one time, early in 1636, there were only two roots of this description to be had in all Holland, and those not of the best. One was in the possession of a dealer in Amsterdam, and the other in Harlaem. So anxious were the speculators to obtain them, that one person offered the fee-simple of twelve acres of building-ground for the Harlaem tulip. That of Amsterdam was bought for 4600 florins, a new carriage, two gray horses, and a complete set of harness.

Munting, an industrious author of that day, who wrote a folio volume of one thousand pages upon the tulipomania, has preserved the following list of the various articles, and their value, which were delivered for one single root of the rare species called the Viceroy:

Two lasts of wheat	448
Four lasts of rye	558
Four fat oxen	480
Eight fat swine	240
Twelve fat sheep	120
Two Hogsheads of wine	70
Four tuna of beer	32
Two tuna of butter	192
	2500
One thousand lbs. of cheese	120
A complete bed	100
A suit of clothes	80
A silver drinking-cup	60

People who had been absent from Holland, and whose chance it was to return when this folly was at its maximum, were sometimes led into awkward dilemmas by their ignorance. There is an amusing instance of the kind related in Blainville's Travels. A wealthy merchant, who prided himself not a little on his rare tulips, received upon one occasion a very valuable consignment of merchandise from the Levant. Intelligence of its arrival was brought him by a sailor, who presented himself for that purpose at the counting-house, among bales of goods of every description. The merchant, to reward him for his news, munificently made him a present of a fine red herring for his breakfast. The sailor had, it appears, a great partiality for onions, and seeing a bulb very like an onion lying upon the counter of this liberal trader, and thinking it, no doubt, very much out of its place among silks and velvets, he silly seized an opportunity and slipped it into his pocket, as a relish for his herring. He got clear off with his prize, and proceeded to the quay to eat his breakfast. Hardly was his back turned when the merchant missed his valuable Semper Augustus, worth three thousand florins, or about 280l. sterling. The whole establishment was instantly in an uproar; search was everywhere made for the precious root, but it was not to be found. Great was the merchant's distress of mind. The search was renewed, but again without success. At last some one thought of the sailor.

The unhappy merchant sprang into the street at the bare suggestion. His alarmed household followed him. The sailor, simple soul! had not thought of concealment. He was found quietly sitting on a coil of ropes, masticating the last morsel of his "onion." Little did he dream that he had been eating a breakfast whose cost might have regaled a whole ship's crew for a twelvemonth; or, as the plundered merchant himself expressed it, "might have sumptuously feasted the Prince of Orange and the whole court of the Stadtholder." Anthony caused pearls to be dissolved in wine to drink the health of Cleopatra; Sir Richard Whittington was as foolishly magnificent in an entertainment to King Henry V.; and Sir Thomas Gresham drank a diamond dissolved in wine to the health of Queen Elizabeth, when she opened the Royal Exchange; but the breakfast of this roguish Dutchman was as splendid aseither. He had an advantage, too, over his wasteful predecessors: their gems did not improve the taste or the wholesomeness of their wine, while his tulip was quite delicious with his red herring. The most unfortunate part of the business for him was, that he remained in prison for some months on a charge of felony preferred against him by the merchant.

Another story is told of an English traveler, which is scarcely less ludicrous. This gentleman, an amateur botanist, happened to see a tulip-root lying in the conservatory of a wealthy Dutchman. Being ignorant of its quality, he took out his penknife, and peeled off its coats, with the view of making experiments upon it. When it was by this means reduced to half its size, he cut it into two equal sections, making all the time many learned remarks on the singular appearances of the unknown bulb. Suddenly the owner pounced upon him, and, with fury in his eyes, asked him if he knew what he had been doing? "Peeling a most extraordinary onion," replied the philosopher. "Hundert tausend duyvel!"said the Dutchman; "it's an Admiral Van der Eyck." "Thank you," replied the traveller, taking out his notebook to make a memorandum of the same; "are these admirals common in your country?" "Death and the Devil!" said the Dutchman, seizing the astonished man of science by the collar; "come before the syndic, and you shall see." In spite of his remonstrances, the traveller was led through the streets followed by a mob of persons. When brought into the presence of the magistrate, he learned, to his consternation, that the root upon which he had been experimentalizing was worth four thousand florins; and, notwithstanding all he could urge in extenuation, he was lodged in prison until he found securities for the payment of this sum.

The demand for tulips of a rare species increased so much in the year 1636, that regular marts for their sale were established on the Stock Exchange of Amsterdam, in Rotterdam,

Harlaem, Leyden, Alkmar, Hoorn, and other towns. Symptoms of gambling now became, for the first time, apparent. The stock-jobbers, ever on the alert for a new speculation, dealt largely in tulips, making use of all the means they so well knew how to employ to cause fluctuations in prices. At first, as in all these gambling mania, confidence was at its height, and every body gained. The tulip-jobbers speculated in the rise and fall of the tulip stocks, and made large profits by buying when prices fell, and selling out when they rose. Many individuals grew suddenly rich. A golden bait hung temptingly out before the people, and one after the other, they rushed to the tulip-marts, like flies around a honey-pot. Every one imagined that the passion for tulips would last for ever, and that the wealthy from every part of the world would send to Holland, and pay whatever prices were asked for them. The riches of Europe would be concentrated on the shores of the Zuyder Zee, and poverty banished from the favour Ed clime of Holland. Nobles, citizens, farmers, mechanics, seamen, footmen, maid-servants, even chimney-sweeps and old clothes women, dabbled in tulips. People of all grades converted their property into cash, and invested it in flowers. Houses and lands were offered for sale at ruinously low prices, or assigned in payment of bargains made at the tulip-mart. Foreigners became smitten with the same frenzy, and money poured into Holland from all directions. The prices of the necessaries of life rose again by degrees: houses and lands, horses and carriages, and luxuries of every sort, rose in value with them, and for some months Holland seemed the very antechamber of Plutus. The operations of the trade became so extensive and so intricate, that it was found necessary to draw up a code of laws for the guidance of the dealers. Notaries and clerks were also appointed, who devoted themselves exclusively to the interests of the trade. The designation of public notary was hardly known in some towns, that of tulip-notary usurping its place. In the smaller towns, where there was no exchange, the principal tavern was usually selected as the "show-place," where high and low traded in tulips, and confirmed their bargains over sumptuous entertainments. These dinners were sometimes attended by two or three hundred persons, and large vases of tulips, in full bloom, were placed at regular intervals upon the tables and sideboards for their gratification during the repast.

At last, however, the more prudent began to see that this folly could not last for ever. Rich people no longer bought the flowers to keep them in their gardens, but to sell them again at cent per cent profit. It was seen that somebody must lose fearfully in the end. As this conviction spread, prices fell, and never rose again. Confidence was destroyed, and a universal panic seized upon the dealers. A had agreed to purchase ten Semper Augustines~from B, at four thousand florins each, at six weeks after the signing of the contract. B was ready with the flowers at the appointed time; but the price had fallen to three or four hundred florins, and A refused either to pay the difference or receive the tulips. Defaulters were announced day after day in all the towns of Holland. Hundreds who, a few months previously, had begun to doubt that there was such a thing as poverty in the land suddenly found themselves the possessors of a few bulbs, which nobody would buy, even though they offered them at one quarter of the sums they had paid for them. The cry of distress resounded every where, and each man accused his neighbor.

The few who had contrived to enrich themselves hid their wealth from the knowledge of their fellow-citizens, and invested it in the English or other funds. Many who, for a brief season, had emerged from the humbler walks of life, were cast back into their original obscurity. Substantial merchants were reduced almost to beggary, and many a representative of a noble line saw the fortunes of his house ruined beyond redemption.

When the first alarm subsided, the tulip-holders in the several towns held public meetings to devise what measures were best to be taken to restore public credit. It was generally agreed that deputies should be sent from all parts to Amsterdam, to consult with the government upon some remedy for the evil.

The government at first refused to interfere, but advised the tulip-holders to agree to some plan among themselves. Several meetings were held for this purpose; but no measure could be devised likely to give satisfaction to the deluded people, or repair even a slight portion of the mischief that had been done. The language of complaint and reproach was in every body's mouth, and all the meetings were of the most stormy character. At last, however, after much bickering and ill-will, it was agreed, at Amsterdam, by the assembled deputies, that all contracts made in the height of the mania, or prior to the month of November, 1636, should be declared null and void, and that, in those made after that date, purchasers should be freed from their engagements, on paying ten percent to the vendor. This decision gave no satisfaction. The vendors who had their tulips on hand were, of course, discontented, and those who had pledged themselves to purchase, thought themselves hardly treated. Tulips which had, at one time, been worth six thousand florins, were now to be procured for five hundred; so that the composition of ten percent was one hundred florins more than the actual value. Actions for breach of contract were threatened in all the courts of the country; but the latter refused to take cognizance of gambling transactions.

The matter was finally referred to the Provincial Council at the Hague, and it was confidently expected that the wisdom of this body would invent some measure by which credit should be restored. Expectation was on the stretch for its decision, but it never came. The members continued to deliberate week after week, and at last, after thinking about it for three months, declared that they could offer no final decision until they had more information. They advised, however, that, in the meantime, every vendor should, in the presence of witnesses, offer the tulips in natura to the purchaser for the sums agreed upon. If the latter refused to take them, they might be put up for sale by public auction, and the original contractor held responsible for the difference between the actual and the stipulated price. This was exactly the plan recommended by the deputies, and which was already shown to be of no avail. There was no court in Holland which would enforce payment. The question was raised in Amsterdam, but the judges unanimously refused to interfere, on the ground that debts contracted in gambling were no debts in law.

Thus the matter rested. To find a remedy was beyond the power of the government. Those who were unlucky enough to have had stores of tulips on hand at the time of the sudden reaction were left to bear their ruin 25 philosophically as they could; those who had made profits were allowed to keep them; but the commerce of the country suffered a severe shock, from which it was many years ere it recovered.

The example of the Dutch was imitated to some extent in England. In the year 1636 tulips were publicly sold in the Exchange of London, and the jobbers exerted themselves to the utmost to raise them to the fictitious value they had acquired in Amsterdam. In Paris also the jobbers strove to create a tulipomania. In both cities they only partially succeeded. However, the force of example brought the flowers into great favour, and amongst a certain class of people tulips have ever since been prized more highly than any other flowers of the field. The Dutch are still notorious for their partiality to them, and continue to pay higher prices for them than any other people. As the rich Englishman boasts of his fine race-horses or his old pictures, so does the wealthy Dutchman vaunt him of his tulips.

In England, in our day, strange as it may appear, a tulip will produce more money than an oak. If one could be found, rara in terns, and black as the black swan of Juvenal, its price would equal that of a dozen acres of standing corn. In Scotland, towards the close of the seventeenth century, the highest price for tulips, according to the authority of a writer in the supplement to the third edition of the Encyclopedia Britannica, was ten guineas. Their value appears to have diminished from that time till the year 1769, when the two most valuable species in England were the Don Quevedo and the Valentinier, the former of which was worth two guineas and the latter two guineas and a half. These prices appear to have been the minimum. In the year 1800, a common price was fifteen guineas for a single bulb. In 1835, a bulb of the species called the Miss Fanny Kemble was sold by public auction in London for seventy-five pounds. Still more remarkable was the price of a tulip in the possession of a gardener in the King's Road, Chelsea;—in his catalogues it was label led at two hundred guineas.

TRADERS PRESS ™
INCORPORATED
P.O. BOX 6206
GREENVILLE, S.C. 29606

BOOKS AND GIFTS
FOR INVESTORS
AND TRADERS

TRADERS PRESS stocks and distributes hundreds of items of interest to investors and traders. Other items may be special ordered upon request. To receive a current TRADERS CATALOG, which describes all items in stock, write, call or fax your request today.

800-927-8222
803-298-0222
FAX 803-298-0221